The Next Draft

WRITERS ON WRITING
Jay Parini, Series Editor

A good writer is first a good reader. Looking at craft from the inside, with an intimate knowledge of its range and possibilities, writers also make some of our most insightful critics. With this series we will bring together the work of some of our finest writers on the subject they know best, discussing their own work and that of others, as well as concentrating on craft and other aspects of the writer's world.

Poet, novelist, biographer, and critic, Jay Parini is the author of numerous books, including *The Apprentice Lover* and *One Matchless Time: A Life of William Faulkner*. Currently he is D. E. Axinn Professor of English & Creative Writing at Middlebury College.

The Next Draft

Inspiring Craft Talks from the
Rainier Writing Workshop

Edited by Brenda Miller

University of Michigan Press

Ann Arbor

For questions or permissions, please contact um.press.perms@umich.edu
Individual authors retain copyright to their work.

Published in the United States of America by the
University of Michigan Press
Manufactured in the United States of America
Printed on acid-free paper
First published March 2024

A CIP catalog record for this book is available from the British Library.

Library of Congress Cataloging-in-Publication data has been applied for.

ISBN 978-0-472-07646-8 (hardcover : alk. paper)
ISBN 978-0-472-05646-0 (paper : alk. paper)
ISBN 978-0-472-22136-3 (e-book)

Contents

—⚏—

Foreword

—␊—

In 2024, the Rainier Writing Workshop will observe its twentieth anniversary as the low-residency MFA program in creative writing at Pacific Lutheran University in Tacoma, Washington. *The Next Draft* is, then, a culmination and a celebration.

Founded by the writers Judith Kitchen and Stan Sanvel Rubin, the Rainier Writing Workshop, more fondly referred to as RWW, had its first residency on the PLU campus in the summer of 2004. Since then, aside from two residencies held on Zoom due to the COVID pandemic, the program's ten-day residencies have taken place in Tacoma with a characteristic abundance of strong conversation and transformative learning. Each day of the residency begins with a talk by a faculty member and ends with readings by the faculty; in between are workshops, craft classes, and other activities that galvanize for the residency a kind of nerdy communal joy. Gathered at Xavier Hall, the students and faculty of RWW experience each morning's lecture as a common text—a text that often sets the terms for the day's discussions about the intricacies of craft and genre, the obsessions of writers, and the role of artists during times of disorienting richness and precarity, which is our own time.

I have had the delight of directing RWW for the past ten years. In the decade before that, the program was passionately led by Judith and Stan, who gave the program its DNA of intellectual rigor and fierce camaraderie. A student in the program attends four summer residencies and has three yearlong mentorships, with each mentorship customized toward the student's projects and goals. A graduate of RWW joins several hundred other graduates of the program who are not only producing good literary work but are also engaged in doing good works in their various communities. A graduate recently served as her state's poet laureate, while another founded a program focused on environmental writing and wilderness exploration at the high school where he teaches. Still another recent graduate codirects an organization that supports emerging Latinx writers in her region.

For RWW graduates, the work of advocacy and citizenship is coupled, of course, with the writer's work of imagination, language making, and witness. One recent graduate's thesis was a memoir about her early life in apartheid-era South Africa. Another student's fiction drew on his family's history as African American sharecroppers in North Carolina. And still another student's poetry described the opioid epidemic raging through his region of Appalachia. These stories matter, and they speak to the storytelling that is at the heart of a program like RWW. Empowering its students with voice, as well as with historical and technical knowledge about literature and its making, RWW is grounded in an ethos of intent care for the self, community, and creation. In giving students the means to see the truths of their experiences, the program adds to the quotient of complex stories being told—and to the empathy and nuanced understanding that these stories generate.

By the time an RWW student graduates into what Judith Kitchen called their "fourth year," which is to say the rest of their writing life, that student will have gained a resourcefulness gleaned from every expected and unexpected part of their time at RWW—the late-night conversation with friends on the cool summertime grass, the writing exercise from an afternoon craft class, the nervous sharing of new work at the open mic, and, as shown in *The Next Draft*, the talks that bring us together each summer morning, wake us up, and change us.

—*Rick Barot, 2023*

Introduction

—⁓—

Picture this: For ten days every summer, the Pacific Lutheran University campus wakes up for another day packed with talks, workshops, classes, and readings. Students young and old can be seen wandering toward Xavier Hall, coffee cups in hand, eyes bleary from the late night before. But they're also excited, because they are about to experience a "Morning Talk" by one of the illustrious faculty at the Rainier Writing Workshop, the low-residency MFA program at PLU.

These Morning Talks have become legendary among students and faculty alike. Each speaker sets the bar higher, and those of us still in the lineup instantly begin revising our own talks in our heads to make them better. Though attendance at these events is not required for faculty members, we wouldn't miss them for the world, no matter how quickly we must bolt down our breakfast to get there in time. These talks show innovative approaches to craft and literature across genres, and they often become the touchstone for our conversations throughout the residency. We emerge from Xavier Hall excited about how to read literature differently and how to bring our own writing to a new level.

As I edited this representative collection, I saw (or rather *heard*) how, just as during the residencies, these talks immediately began resonating with one another, echoing particular themes, approaching aspects of craft and the writing life from various angles while also cohering through a passionate commitment to making our work matter. You'll hear, for example, how Kent Meyers interrogates the "gap between imagination and creativity," while Fleda Brown expresses her desire for "language to mirror what I think is out there. What *seems* to be there. Yet, what's there but what I've created?" The driving force to write butting up against the real work it takes to get words on paper; the wellspring of words we have at our disposal while those words shy away from the vision in our minds: this is what we do always, a labor that often tests our commitment. Our title, *The Next Draft*, comes from Kent's talk; note that it is not the *final* draft we're after here, as there is no real finality in the writing process, just the next and the next and the next . . . until we have to be done. As Kevin Clark puts it: "How can writers find the path to the ending without worrying about getting there? How can we open the doors to the imagination without concerning ourselves with the finished product? Which means what we all know: in order to write well, every day we must risk utter failure."

You'll hear a lot more here about risk in the writing process—risks we must take in order to evolve, and how we can learn about taking risks from writers we admire. Renee Simms explores how, in the wildly inventive book *Zong!*, M. NourbeSe Philip "took great risks: she risked meaning, narrative, grammar, syntax." Scott Nadelson asks us to risk disorientation, to surrender to "a narrative that at times seems to spin out of the writer's control." At the same time, Jennifer Foerster reminds us that "[t]o sing of the turning world without becoming disoriented is, perhaps, a fundamental work of the poet. We must become architects, makers of spaces through which the songs echo, screens upon which our memories may surface and pass beyond the vanishing point."

We're also reminded that we can risk our writerly identities by pushing against the limits of genre and expectations. Sequoia Nagamatsu unpacks the genre debate and asks us to reconsider how we categorize our own work and the work of others. "I say open the doors and wander the halls," he encourages. "Please do find your kindred spirits, those people who will always understand you, your cafeteria table. But be kind, be open and maybe, just maybe, join that weird table in the back of the room and ask what gets them excited." Oliver de la Paz, in exploring documentary poetics, tells us, "I am very much interested in work that interrogates lines and limitations . . . the ways that they break down borders of genre, serve as conduits for meaning, and ultimately carry new ideas and ways of thinking about their subjects."

Throughout the talks, we hear about both reading and writing as fundamental practices that require patience and sustained attention. Wendy Call, while delving into the artistic, ancient sources of writing, tells us that she is "drawn to the idea of artifying. This concept makes my writing into a practice—which is something more compelling and less intimidating to me. Reading and writing are both difficult for us—they are possible *only* with practice." Jenny Johnson encourages us to build our stamina through developing our observational skills, and through this practice transform both the seer and the seen: "If you attend long enough, subjectivities can change, patterns can form and reform, temporalities can open, and new intimacies can arise. And you, the writer—though it may seem as if you're doing so little, just by picturing, just by blinking, just by holding still—you are part of the scene, you're shifting, too."

And we need not rely only on our limited experiences and subjectivities. "Consider the range of subjects that come to light if we think of our subjects not so much as invented as *discovered* through an act of close attention to an existing text," Marjorie Sandor tells us, "be it sacred scroll, famous legend, historical incident, official document, memory, rumor, shred of family gossip—essentially, any document that shows a capacity for interpretation reveals to us that it is not in fact a closed case, but a story waiting for us to discover what else it holds."

Discovery, surprise, delight: you'll hear these themes recur as these writers urge us to quiet all the noise that surrounds us. Lia Purpura urges us to slow down and rediscover enchantment in the ordinary world, a practice that may infuse our writing with transcendence. She writes: "The most recognizable drives of my writing life have been a belief in hard-to-pin states of being and perceptions and the search for language and form that bodies them forth, as well as faith in the conversational possibilities between objects, creatures, us." Barrie Jean Borich encourages us to see our world, and our work, as constantly evolving. Writing well means being in a symbiotic relationship with our material; it changes us as we shape the work, and ideally we'll be as surprised as the reader by what we discover. "As writers, and as humans, how do we keep thinking about ourselves and our environments in new ways?" she asks. "When I suggest that the art of essaying requires an embrace of surprise I am suggesting that the essay is always, in some way, about change."

And, of course, these talks often reflect and interrogate the times in which we live. Speaking from within the depths of the COVID-19 pandemic, Rebecca McClanahan gives us the pep talk we all need to continue writing in the face of not only the world's incessant distractions, but our own self-sabotaging tendencies. She commiserates: "Even in times that pass as normal, when external forces are not waging battle against our writing life, internal forces intervene to keep us from our work—distraction, doubt, fear, envy, despair, perfectionism, inertia, shame—all those forces living inside us just waiting to interrupt the time and space reserved for writing." Suzanne Berne investigates how both reading and writing novels can be an antidote to the fast-information lanes in which we travel these days. She writes: "I believe in the *capacity* of the novel, in its formal demonstration of the possibility for greater insight and compassion over time. . . . Especially now, when so much information is continually coming at us, so fast, from all directions, it's hard to know what to pay attention to, what to trust—and anyway, who has time to decide? Something else is always trending."

I still remember, quite vividly, the standing ovation Ann Pancake received after her Morning Talk that brought home to us the necessity of telling both our own stories and the stories of our communities. She reminded us that "throughout human history, the mythmakers, the culture creators, those who dream forward for their communities, have been the artists." She encouraged us to think of writing as a form of collective activism.

This collection is bookended by two meditations by Geffrey Davis—the first from a panel on contemporary pedagogical practices, and the second from his toast to the 2022 graduates as they prepared to embark on their writing lives from the cocoon of the MFA program. He tells us "the wind has a voice, and it's saying your name . . ." May we all hear his words—and the words of all the other writers/teachers in this collection—as affirmations for our writing lives.

We're so glad you've joined us here in this convivial and vibrant space. Now go forth and write your next drafts!

—Brenda Miller, 2023

Breaking the Silence

Geffrey Davis

—〰—

A Story

In a car of chatty arts-organization volunteers headed across Arkansas, a young aspiring storyteller sitting beside me asked our driver, Kathy McGregor, for some beginner's guidance. Kathy, the project director for the Prison Story Project and a nationally recognized storyteller with more than thirty years of experience performing at various festivals, said something like this:

> This is a story:
> HAHA;
> AHA;
> AHH;
> AMEN.

After being stunned by what immediately (if only impressionistically) seemed true to us, the car asked her to, you know, say more. And so she talked about how reading a room can sometimes tell a storyteller how far to move an audience along that psychic scale of story. If you have very little context or very little permission or very little time, you might only move a room to laughter (*HAHA*) or from laughter to recognition (*AHA*). If you have more overlap or more permission or more time, you might move that room from understanding or satisfaction (*AHH*) to rapture (*AMEN*). She was also suggesting that pushing people further along that scale than they were prepared or willing to go is to risk losing—if not hurting—a room.

While preparing for the Rainier Writing Workshop's panel "Breaking the Silence: New Pedagogies for the Workshop," I began wondering about a scale of psychic intensity as experienced by writers in the workshop setting. How many writers arrive wanting to approach their most rapturous relationship to their art? I tend to ground my approach to workshops with challenging pieces, such as Sean Thomas Dougherty's poem addressing a writer friend who has stopped writing, called "Why Bother?":

> Because right now, there is   someone
>
> out there with
> a wound   in the exact shape
>   of your words.

But how many writers have I silenced by assuming all want to or would grow by approaching or knowing that intensity? Year after year, in conscious and unconscious ways, my relation to academia alters some, and I lose more and more experiential traction on how each new cohort of writers feels about the workshop's ability to care for them through such intense artistic stakes. What quality of context or permission or time do workshops need to cultivate safe and ethical artistic growth? What new structures of care can the workshop allow or invent?

Because the MFA workshop is set within an institution, and because institutions have poor track records with caring for individuated personhoods, and because (despite my own discomforts and resistances) I am an agent of the institution, I tend to open workshops by inviting writers to cultivate a healthy irreverence toward the endeavor and toward myself: "Do NOT lay your voice at the feet of this institution," I beg them. "You might not recognize what you need to say as you leave." I also warn them about the urge to conflate their achievement of admission with their validity and/or identity as an artist, if only because I want them to claim and honor a literary wondering and wandering that they started before and should continue after their workshop experience—but also because they need to know that a writer's most liberatory developments may not necessarily happen in the workshop setting.

• • •

A Home

Cofounded in 1996 as a remedy for the underrepresentation and isolation of Black poets in the literary landscape, Cave Canem has imagined itself into a "home" for Black poetry. Through intensive summer writing retreats for Black poets, Cave Canem has been building and expanding (and sometimes renovating) a belonging where Black writers can cultivate their artistic and professional growth.

I became a member of that home in 2012, the summer after completing my own MFA program, and I can tell you with veritable certainty that there is a distinct *before* and *after* Cave Canem for me, not only to my sense of self as a writer but also to my approach as a teacher of writing. In no small part, that pedagogical development was the result of getting to experience several new and diversly stunning writers who each led workshops in their own distinct ways. (The math here is that I jumped from having experienced six different workshop styles from just two institutions to over twenty different workshop styles from dozens of institutions.) One major, if obvious, takeaway: the greater diversity of workshop models that you witness, the richer your pool of instincts and imagination for writing and workshop possibilities. This is one of the treasures of RWW's residency and mentorship model.

But I have a conviction that I was especially moved and changed as a writer and a teacher by experiencing what happens when a literary institution chooses (without necessity) to commit itself to building the stakes and structures of *home* around artists.

In addition to the shared identifier of writer or artist (which can and does mean a distinct thing to each individual), it would be too easy (and maybe even dead-ass wrong) to suggest that what Cave Canem cracked was how artists will thrive if you add just one more common identity denominator, that of Blackness (which also can and does mean a distinct thing to each individual). I would suggest that what it's added is *belonging*. If only because in the MFA's predominantly white space with all the cultural messaging and trappings that would seem to bend toward an assumption of their core values and institutional needs, I've witnessed countless white writers suffer from questions of *belonging*, from an absence of *home*.

If like me, however, you've witnessed the disruption or dismantling of a home—the veiling myth of its predetermined safety turned sour by economic instability and/or violence and/or changes in leadership—you know homes that go unmaintained can become dangerous for those who have built their belonging there. Can an MFA become and then stay a home? Can a workshop? Should it? My own line of questioning feels ripe for both doubt and inspiration, fatigue, and hope.

But I can't shake what I witnessed through Cave Canem and experienced myself—the kind of personal fulfillment and artistic transformation that can occur within an institutional context that risks calling itself *home*—the communal possibility of such growth for all involved seems worth risking its failure.

—2022

The Ram in the Thicket

Midrash and the Contemporary Creative Writer

Marjorie Sandor

—꿈—

Darash: a verb as rich in lost stories as the ancient landscape from which it emerged. A primitive Hebrew root, its definitions gather around the verb "to seek into, to inquire" and, intriguingly, "to tread a place." If the word sounds dimly familiar, maybe it's because it dwells in the marrow of the venerable art of making midrash: the practice of close reading, asking questions, and filling in gaps in the Hebrew bible, or Torah. But quite beyond its literary-biblical context, the process of darashing a given text—be it myth, historical document, or mysterious road sign—offers the contemporary writer a secret entrance into the cave of making, a portal rich with subversive possibilities.

Did I say, "gaps"? And did I use the word *subversive* in connection with a venerable form of spiritual commentary?

• • •

Midrash is a concept with multiple meanings and a rich history. It refers to the collections of these interpretive pieces—in the plural, *midrashim*—created by scholars and rabbis between the second and eleventh centuries, and also to the results of a single exploration of a biblical moment that snagged a rabbi's attention and suggested something missing, repressed, or obscured. The practice of making midrash has continued to evolve into the contemporary moment, spilling out of its scholarly confines to provide a place for literary and visual artists, musicians, filmmakers, and dancers to play.

In its original form, the process might have gone like this: a midrashist, reading along in the Torah, would find himself caught on a word or phrase—a sticky spot, if you will—that invited questioning. Picture an extremely alert close reader of a complex modern novel. She's not just reading for plot. She's listening for resonances and repetitions that signal buried stories in the language itself: a nuanced elevation of diction here, a sharp juxtaposition between images there, foreshadowing and echoes that connect even the farthest-flung episodes.

From these signals, the midrashist would locate a *gap*, an entrance point, and dive down, expanding the episode from within, giving voice to the submerged characters and complexities brimming beneath the unforthcoming surface of a biblical episode. No wonder some midrashim read like short stories, complete with dialogue and scene. No wonder they tend to bring to center stage marginal figures barely mentioned in the biblical narrative.

At the heart of this exercise in interpretation, in its original incarnation, was the desire to deepen the connections between the ancient biblical text and the urgent concerns of the midrashist's own historical moment. These early close readers did not see themselves as making anything up or changing the sacred text. For them, Torah was a living thing, a gift of teachings as rich in the unspoken as the spoken. They saw themselves as participating in that gift by making these interpretations, by filling in the gaps for themselves and their congregations.

It's this notion of participation through time that has kept the process alive and evolving, connecting generations of imaginative thinkers across time. If we consider the work of darashing as a creative practice apart from its biblical application, where might it take us? Consider the range of subjects that come to light if we think of our subjects not so much as invented as *discovered* through an act of close attention to an existing text, be it sacred scroll, famous legend, historical incident, official document, memory, rumor, shred of family gossip—essentially, any document that shows a capacity for interpretation, revealing to us that it is not, in fact, a closed case, but a story waiting for us to discover what else it holds.

Something to *darash*. To tread, as if it were as much place as text.

• • •

To tread a place: the phrase allows us to think of reading as a physical act, to picture the gap between two words as a cave entrance leading to an unsuspected world beneath: a neglected or silenced habitat in which we might, as readers, pause a moment and take a look around. What's that old photo there on the wall? And whose voice do I hear, in the far corner, quietly weeping while the grand heroic action proceeds on stage? Maybe if I look around long enough, I'll discover something that was here all along, hidden in plain sight.

Could this image help the harried twenty-first-century writer to slow down as the world rushes madly on?

• • •

Recall, for example, the biblical story of Abraham commanded by God to take his son Isaac to a certain mountaintop, bind him, and offer him up as a sacrifice. At the climax of the test, an angel calls Abraham's name and stays his hand, pointing out a substitute: a ram caught by its horns in a thicket.

There is more than one midrash exploring the ambiguities of this terrifying sequence, probably because of its very ambiguity. In the words of Avivah Gottlieb Zornberg, who has written extensively about midrash, "the terror of the narrative is the plainest thing about it and the most mysterious." She goes on to quote the Danish philosopher Søren Kierkegaard: "There were countless generations who knew the story of Abraham by heart, word for word, but how many did it render sleepless?"

Knowing the story blocks the heart, says Zornberg; "only in the sleepless dark can one engage with its paradoxes."

Of the many midrashim exploring Abraham and Isaac on the mountain, one is particularly surprising, for it recognizes the absence of, and lifts into prominence, a female figure who does not appear during the journey, but would have been deeply affected by its terror: the potential victim's mother, Sarah. It's worth pausing to see how and where the ninth-century midrashist, Rabbi Tanhuma, burrowed his way into the text and cracked it open.

We have to go back to the end of the original episode in Genesis to see what caught his eye in the first place: after the ram is sacrificed, the angel speaks again, offering a few triumphant concluding lines, telling Abraham what the future holds. A new section begins, sans transition. Abruptly, we learn that Abraham's wife Sarah has died:

> *And the lifetime of Sarah was a hundred and twenty-seven years; (these) were the years of the life of Sarah.*
> *And Sarah died in Kiryath-arba, the same in Hebron in the land of Canaan; and Abraham came to mourn for Sarah, and to weep for her.*

This abrupt shift, and the close textual proximity of the mention of Sarah's death to her son's near slaughter by her husband, was a sticky spot for Rabbi Tanhuma. The mention of Abraham, who "came to mourn," raised yet another question: where did Abraham *come from* to mourn her?

Rabbi Tanhuma's midrash on Sarah's death begins by expanding the brief telling of Abraham's near sacrifice of his son. Isaac, bound and lying on the altar under the upheld knife, even manages to speak: "Father, bind my hands and legs, for the soul is impudent, and when I see the knife I may be frightened and the sacrifice will be no good because my trembling will cause you to make a blemish." And a moment later, "Father, do not tell my mother when she is by the well, or when she is standing on the roof, lest she fall and die . . ." Tanhuma imagines Abraham actually opening a gash on his son's cheek, and even gets Satan into the picture, before the angel of God famously stays Abraham's hand and points out the ram in the thicket as a substitute sacrifice.

Suspense! Human interaction! And then it gets weirder: Satan slips away, only to reappear miles away, disguised as her son, before the still-living Sarah. Standing there as Isaac, he tells the terrifying tale of his near death at his father's hand, with such rising tension that before he could finish, "Sarah's soul fled from her." The midrash ends thus: "'And Abraham *came* to mourn for Sarah and to weep for her.' Where did he come from? From Mount Moriah [where the binding of Isaac took place]."

It's a heartbreaking human story now: a mother so devastated by what she's heard—let alone the *sight* of her son with blood on his cheek—that she dies, midsentence, from the shock of the news.

This midrash connects Sarah to this powerful central story in the tradition—and undoes the perfect closure of the story of Isaac's binding: *not so fast*, says the midrashist, and he keeps the whole story alive for later generations.

• • •

The midrashic method proceeds by holding still long enough to notice something odd, ask a question, probe, then dream its way into repressed or otherwise blocked emotional material in a text. It's this aspect of the process that suggests its potential for students and teachers of literary craft, as we try to help each other find a path into difficult or silenced territory or material that feels out of reach, intimidating, or heavily explored by others before us. What stories from long ago render us sleepless? How might we keep ourselves from thinking we already know the story, from having our hearts blocked?

What might each of us find in the act of darashing small fractures in the wall of history, given the urgencies of our own time and place and experience? How might this practice help us enter the improvisatory groove of writing? How might we learn to identify potentially "darashy" moments in a given text? And let's expand the idea of "text" to include whatever you see, hear, and otherwise sense in any given moment.

A rough guide to contemporary darashing might look something like this:

1. A particular text (interpret that word as broadly as you like) seems ambiguous to you, even if it is widely accepted, canonical. Despite this status, you feel, as you read/observe/listen, a hole or gap lurking between phrases or sentences . .
2. You pick up on words/images/even rhythms in the text that create a hint of something unsaid—a repressed potential story in the seam between two sentences, between two "adjacent" moments. Moments where you want to say, "wait." Let me *tread* here a bit longer.
3. You spot a moment in a given text or story that invites a question: What happened to Unknown X while Famous Y was in the limelight?

Earlier, I suggested that the midrashic method holds subversive possibilities. Consider Anna Akhmatova's famous 1924 poem "Lot's Wife," part of a short cycle titled *Biblical Verses*. It opens up a silenced place in a famous biblical moment, while also performing a powerful modern function: the poet expresses "through allusion to history and myth what she cannot herself say openly" in the new, repressive Soviet state.

Akhmatova's poem, like a traditional midrash, incorporates details from a biblical story. In this case the text is from Genesis 19. An angel warns Lot of coming devastation and directs him to flee, with his family, to a certain mountain. In the biblical verse, we know nothing about Lot's wife until the moment of her single act of trespass—that of looking back at her home city—for which she is turned to a pillar of salt.

One sentence. One action. Obliterating consequence. A woman barely seen is suddenly gone. But if you read the biblical passage, you might notice something else: there's no interpretation or comment on her action. It's simply an action. Which, strictly speaking, suggests a gap, a place for story.

Akhmatova's poem cracks open the sealed story around Lot's wife. It opens:

And the just man trailed God's shining agent,
Over a black mountain, in his giant track,
While a restless voice kept harrying his woman:
"It's not too late, you can still look back . . ."

That voice follows her with tender images of her native city, the intimate spaces of home now lost to her. This "restless" voice's motive is mysterious: Is it the ancient voice of temptation (perhaps the one that whispered in Sarah's ear of the near slaughter of her son)? Or is it the woman's own inner voice, resisting the foretold, the narrative fetters of the angel's warning? In its aching, free-floating anonymity, its unknowable source, it is unsettling—and profoundly modern. What is the nature of the test? And who knows what will make us pause and turn to look behind us?

The poem's concluding verse brings us fully into the speaker's own historical moment: "Who will grieve for this woman? Does she not seem/ Too insignificant for our concern?"

This is the question at the heart of the poem. By asking it, the speaker brings this marginal figure to center, where she becomes a monument to all the silenced victims of history, their "swift legs rooted to the ground." And nearly 100 years after its writing, we can, ourselves, look back and darash Akhmatova's own midrash for the repressed—and future—losses it foretells. Choosing to turn, to look *behind*. Choosing to bear witness. In Akhmatova's case, to keep writing, at terrible cost.

> *Who will grieve for this woman? Does she not seem*
> *Too insignificant for our concern?*
> *Yet in my heart I will never deny her,*
> *Who suffered death because she chose to turn.*

• • •

How, in our own historical moment, might we expand the possibilities of darashing beyond the biblical? How might the act of "inquiring" or "treading a place" help us locate the gaps in other kinds of texts? The drive to darash is as individual as a fingerprint. Each of us will notice gaps in different places, and each of us will ask different sorts of questions.

Consider a poem by Jennifer Richter from her 2016 collection, *No Acute Distress,* "Demeter Accounts for This Year's Indian Summer." Demeter, Greek Goddess of the earth, has lost her only daughter, Persephone, to Hades, king of the underworld. Demeter's grief brings a withering drought and famine to the earth. Negotiations ensue, and Hades is persuaded to release his new queen, Persephone, from the land of the dead: but first he makes her eat a pomegranate seed in his garden, ensuring that she will return to him for part of the year. It is her annual departure that creates our winter.

According to Richter, the poem was sparked by the desire to "enter the myth in places where either the given narrative doesn't ring true to my own lived experience (as mother or daughter) or the narrative doesn't address what feels to me like essential details or scenes (there are trouble-some gaps in the story)." She continues:

> I was sparked by the impulse to make the narrative more emotion-ally, humanly accurate and timely. In *No Acute Distress*, the poem "Demeter Accounts for This Year's Indian Summer" is thinking about the cyclical nature of that myth, a story which offers the same explanation for the turning of the seasons every year. But moth-ers learn early on to roll with days/weeks/years that don't go as planned. I was thinking about how mothers' lives can get sidetracked and consumed when a child is sick. What happens when Persephone gets sick in the Underworld and needs her mom? The myth doesn't account for variations like that, so: there's the poem. In the varia-tion. In the unspoken. What happens? Demeter drops everything to care for her daughter. And because she's grateful to have Persephone (temporarily) back and needing her in a way she often doesn't any-more, Demeter's (temporarily) happy, so the typical seasonal cycle is disrupted: the earth resumes its bloom post-frost (hence the Indian Summer of the title).

> Here is the poem itself:

> *She'd gone; I'd answered with a killing frost.*
> *Crops languished. Then she sweet-talked him to leave.*
> *Fevered, she hurried home. Her steps melted*
> *A clear path back. Even queens need mothers:*
> *Flushed as the sunset undersides of clouds,*
> *She sank into my lap. Stayed there for days.*
> *To think I often prayed for that: my kid*
> *Napping. To think I always watched her then.*
> *One bite buried her.*

Richter uses the familiar parameters of the myth, especially its relation-ship to our seasons, to locate an unexplored variant. Down she dives, giv-ing the immortal mother of the earth a yearning every mortal will recog-nize: Remember when I used to hold her? The three-time repetition of "to think" brings the yearning, the act of looking back, to a pitch. We fall that much further with the final line, itself an act of imagination and interpre-tation to a moment Demeter—like Sarah, miles away from the unimag-inable mountaintop—wasn't allowed to witness, the moment of her daughter's greatest vulnerability: "One bite buried her."

Like Ahkmatova, Richter probes a mother's own surprise at her maternal hunger, the difficulty of letting go. In their landscapes of confrontation, these mothers are transfigured by the act of pausing, of turning to regard the human tragedy looming both behind and ahead.

Both poets demonstrate the essence of darashing: slowing down to turn and look back at our own "ram in the thicket." Notice the kinds of stories you are drawn to: What happens in them? A little self-darashing here and there might help us locate—without trampling on—the subjects waiting for release in our own underworlds.

• • •

Alice Munro's 1988 short story "Meneseteung" takes, as its text, neither biblical story nor Greek myth, but a fictional Victorian-era book of poems gathering dust on a library shelf in a provincial Canadian town. Munro, in a 1994 *Paris Review* interview, discussed her own harvesting process:

> I never have a problem with finding material. I wait for it to turn up, and it always turns up. It's dealing with the material I'm inundated with that poses the problem. For the historical pieces I have had to search out a lot of facts. I knew for years that I wanted to write a story about one of the Victorian lady writers, one of the authoresses of this area. Only I couldn't find quite the verse I wanted: all of it was so bad that it was ludicrous. I wanted to have it a little better than that. So *I* wrote it. When I was writing that story I looked in a lot of old newspapers, the kind of stuff my husband has around—he does historical research about Huron County, our part of Ontario . . . I got very strong images of the town . . . I got very strong images from newspaper clippings . . .

The story opens with a bit of verse as an epigraph. Its first lines are documentary in tone: "Offerings, the book is called. Gold lettering on a dull blue cover." Someone—we never know who—is gathering fragments in search of a lost figure whom the local newspaper, *The Vidette*, calls "our poetess," and whose daguerreotype in the front of the book seems, like her verses, to suggest a perfectly impenetrable surface of Victorian propriety.

Seems. Or. Probably. Might. Perhaps. These unprepossessing words crackle the story's cool, firm surface. *Seems* operates here as a kind of undoing, a light pressure tapping away on resistant material. Hairline fractures appear: the first suggestions of a narrator's questions about the perfect picture being presented. Gradually, these words begin to dislodge the certainties around "our poetess," Almeda Joynt Roth. Here's an early gesture that creates a passageway:

> It's the untrimmed, shapeless hat, something like a soft beret, that makes me see artistic intentions, or at least a shy and stubborn eccentricity, in this young woman, whose long neck and forward-inclining head indicate as well that she is tall and slender and somewhat awkward. From the waist up, she looks like a young nobleman of another century. But perhaps it was the fashion.

The story will continue to mine this vein of tension: between private eccentricity and public propriety, between the secret, feverish persistence of the imaginative life and the ease with which it might be denied by social conventions. "But perhaps it was the fashion." This last line strikes me as particularly subversive: by participating in the refutation, it *appears* to apologize for or undercut the narrator's tentative speculations. But by acknowledging a presumed reader's skepticism to such a fancy, it disarms the skeptic, just enough to go forward, ultimately kicking all such barriers over and dropping, by degrees, into Almeda's own point of view and consciousness, constructing a shockingly visceral portrait of a woman's life in that time and place; a life, finally, that offers an alternate view of "our poetess" and her work.

It only takes a small gesture to aid the darasher's descent. Following that first fissure of an opening, the "untrimmed shapeless hat . . . that makes me see artistic intentions," the narrator quotes from Almeda's brief autobiographical preface, then recites a catalogue of her poems' titles and topics, which do not suggest an eccentric, yet lay a crucial groundwork by bringing Almeda's own voice into the narrative that has, till now, been claimed by the local newspaper.

A new section begins with another fragment of verse and a brief scene setting in past tense: "In 1879 Almeda Roth was still living in the house at the corner of Pearl and Dufferin." Then this: "The house is there today; the manager of the liquor stores lives in it." This tiny toggle to present tense blurs the boundaries between present and past. A photograph, taken in the 1880s, allows the narrator further license to immerse herself in a present tense unfolding of a past scene: one that is static for a few sentences, before coming cinematically to life through images and sounds of the street. "I read about that life in the *Vidette*," the narrator tells us.

A brief coming up for air.

Then down the narrator drops again, animating the past life of the town, holding us there with present tense and wringing sensory details from the dry facts offered by *The Vidette*, until those details lead, inevitably, to the town's disreputable back alleys and wild swampland, and to a nighttime incident—the sounds of a violent altercation in the alley, and Almeda's own trembling discovery, the next morning, of something shocking. As an extraordinary sequence is set in motion, our narrator/ researcher will burrow deeper into Almeda's world and point of view until our vision—and Almeda's—is fully transformed. By the time the story is over, even the innocuous domestic act of making grape jelly will have been transformed.

Who knew that something as small as a well-prepared tense shift could allow a story's tone, perspective, and dramatic structure to alter so completely?

And how, you might ask, will this fictive researcher rise back out of the depths she's been exploring? How else, but by the artifact she introduced so cannily in the story's opening.

The Vidette.

• • •

For practitioners of creative nonfiction, darashing has particularly rich and surprising possibilities, as in the opening of Lia Purpura's essay "Jump," from her 2011 collection *Rough Likeness.* "Jump" takes as its originating document an artifact even more humble—even more apparently resistant to investigation—than a book of Victorian verse.

That artifact is a sign on a bridge. A red-and-white metal sign containing nine words and a date.

> It's a small thing that holds me.
> On the sign that reads Last Death from Jumping or Diving from Bridge, June 15, 1995, it's the *or* I can't shake. Why fuss with ambivalence when real mystery abides: here stood intolerable grief or failure. Sheerest abandon, joy in a long summer evening. A dare. Need for adventure/a history of. Why work at precision when, hitched as they are to Death in this fragment, both Jump and Dive convey a misjudging of depth, of current, ignorance of rocks below the dark water, and, with "June" added, an insistent sun peaking the river with camouflage ripples. And isn't it Death that I, passerby, secret entertainer of edges and precipices, should instead linger over— approaching, riding, then putting behind me the impulse as I cross the bridge, daily this winter?

"It's the *or* I can't shake," Purpura writes. Dwelling on "the *or*" invites her to take into account not only the word's possibilities, but its intersection with her own position in time and space: mid-February, Iowa—the place where she *treads*. The literal signpost is only the first of several markers she'll identify in the course of the essay, markers that suggest the outline of possible depths, possible inquiries. The signpost itself begins the darashing process, perhaps because it displays the same peculiar combination of plainspokenness and "gappiness" Avivah Zornberg observes in the story of Abraham and Isaac on the mountain, when she notes that "the terror of the narrative is the plainest thing about it, and the most mysterious."

Purpura writes:

> . . . the sign is so sketchy, it feels, instead, like attention dropped off and interest waned. And in that way, the jumper/diver, the subject of one particular moment—a moment en route to being taleworthy—passed out of mind.
>
> But it hasn't passed out of mind. Not for me. The moment, the story, the last death has been nagging.
>
> It's June now.

Like Munro's "Meneseteung," "Jump" will toggle between past tense and present, hauling into its net different geographies, too, creating, in just a few pages, a breathtaking sense of scope. A small gesture, a tense released, and whole worlds and attitudes we never imagined come into being. "[E]mpty space isn't empty at all . . . The land is seeded with incident, marked imperfectly but even in imperfect signs, stories go on vibrating."

"Jump" makes one more turn: it *darashes* itself. Purpura not only imagines several possibilities of event and character within the sign's invisible origin story, but she turns the exercise on herself, noticing the attitudes, or "stances," she finds herself taking as she explores. She catalogues her sketches of possible jumpers or divers until the list reveals something about her own character and habits. It's a moment not unlike the one in which the angel of God instructs Abraham to turn and look *behind*, away from what appears to be a frightening wall of inevitability, *behind*, where a ram in a thicket awaits—a narrative surprise that lies just out of view, but within range. You have to make some kind of turn, a move you didn't plan, to see it.

Like Abraham, we all find ourselves trapped in tight places, in writing as well as life. It happens at every age and stage of the pursuit of art. In his essay "The Habit of Writing," the late Andre Dubus II describes a moment, at midcareer, when he recognized that he felt distant from his characters.

He was having trouble with a character named Anna. He told friends, "as far as I know, I don't know anyone who's committed armed robbery."

The next morning, as he sat down at his desk, he decided:

I would not leave a sentence until I knew precisely what Anna was feeling. I told myself that even if I wrote only fifty words, I would stay with this . . . I held my pen and hunched my shoulders and leaned my head down, physically trying to look more deeply into the page of the notebook. I did this for only a moment before writing, as a batter takes practice swings while he waits in the on-deck circle. In that moment I began what I call vertical writing, rather than horizontal. I had never before thought in these terms . . . I did become her, through her senses. You must know what a glass of beer feels like in her hand, I told myself; you must know everything . . . I had not written very many words, and suddenly I knew that this was a story about two people who loved each other. It was not a story of betrayal. Walls fell down and everything was open: I knew nothing of what would happen next, and that was frightening—though simple to solve—but it was wonderful, it was elating, I was both lost and free.

• • •

Lost and free. The writer must court, must invite insomnia, sensitivity, openness to the terror and mystery of the night on the mountain of Abraham, a night on which he no longer recognized the voice of his beloved God. Think of Lot's wife, too, as Akhmatova revived her, that unnamed woman who risked everything for a single look back at a place—a time— about to be lost forever, to more than just herself.

Is this what the writer must do each time she sits down? Dive from the bridge—or jump? Enter a small, dark Victorian kitchen and listen to the "leisurely, censorious" *plop-plup* of grape jelly straining overnight, until it starts to sound like something else? Stay there, listen, hear what it has to say. What is the thing in yourself that needs darashing? Dive deep. Stay down there as long as you can.

—*2017*

DaVinci's Helicopter, Michelangelo's Marble

Imagination and Creativity

Kent Meyers

—⚏—

Several years ago, at a writing conference, a young man approached me for advice. He had attempted to write several novels. Each time, he had a clear idea of the plot and wrote with great energy for several weeks, but at about fifty pages, everything ground to a halt. Frustrated by five such attempts, he was desperate and thought there might be something personally wrong with him.

I doubted that there was. Creative troubles like this arise, in my experience, out of the gap between imagination and creativity. Though we often think of these two words as synonyms, imagination lies solely in the mind, whereas creativity also involves the body and the material world, and its ultimate end is a physical product independent of the mind that originated it. Anyone building even a simple thing like a bookshelf will find that the material world introduces both problems and possibilities that weren't imagined beforehand. When we consider how intricate literature is and the thousands of connotations caught by the individual words and magnified by their resonance with other words, we can sense how large the gulf is between what we imagine and what we create.

A long-running debate within writing circles pits "the muse" against "craft." The debate can be followed in the English tradition through Coleridge and Carlyle and into the twentieth century and the recurring discussions about whether MFA programs overemphasize craft to the detriment of originality. Philosophically this might be an interesting question, but as a practical matter, it seems hardly worth worrying about. To craft something is to make it material, and what writer hasn't been inspired, and made major changes to a piece, because a just-right word or metaphor appeared on the page? Did inspiration produce the word, or did the word, as a material object in the world, inspire the recognition? And if the word was produced because the writer had learned some element of craft, how do we separate craft from inspiration or muse?

The Greek Muses are children of Zeus, god of intellect, and Mnemosyne, Titaness of memory and daughter of Gaia. It is a telling genealogy: intellect inseminates memory, which, itself daughter of the material world, reflects upon that world to birth possibilities. When we remember and think about what we have experienced in the material world, we can creatively conceive. In turn, to muse upon our work is to remember its problems and revelations. Creativity is this essential interplay between attempting to make what we imagined, discovering the material world's resistance and revelations, and then returning to our making.

Leonardo DaVinci brilliantly imagined how air had substance that a helicopter could rise into, but he couldn't imagine the paradoxical tons of metal required to make his vision real, nor that the earth could produce fuel so volatile it would explode within steel cylinders so precisely made they would convert that brute violence into a rotary force that would lift his concept, made implausibly massive, into air. In fact, none of these things could be imagined without a parallel attempt to make them, inspiration and craft ratcheting each other along.

• • •

For many years, the IQ test was a standard for intelligence, measuring what researchers now call *convergent thinking*—the ability to converge upon a single correct answer. In response to the inability of such tests to predict success, however, tests of *divergent thinking* were developed: *Name twenty uses for a brick*, for instance. A person with a talent for divergent thinking might rattle off dozens of uses, beginning with "to build a wall" but diverging into such things as "a substitute for a truncheon," or "to anchor a boat," or "to crush into a powder and use as makeup."

Divergent thinking is essentially imagination, and while it is good to have it recognized as a valid intellectual ability, these tests show how small a part of full creativity it is. These answers require no investment or effort or perseverance or discipline or patience, or skill in tool use, or knowledge of a tradition. Consider how far from creative realization my examples of divergent thinking are: now that we've imagined makeup from brick powder, let's mix some up and use it when we attend our next elegant party, or let's take a brick with us instead of our trusty truncheon to our next gang fight. Between the conceived ideas and their birth into the real world, much labor must occur.

When we try to make our imagined ideas real, the material world insists on convergence to a solution that actually works, or to what Mihaly Csikszentmihalyi calls the expectations of the "domain." Brick powder and grease might work for Halloween makeup, but "fine makeup" is a more refined domain. A literary work likewise lies within a domain, and a writer must work to understand what the domain demands. Domains themselves, of course, are creative, and their expectations diverge and reconverge, so that free verse became part of poetry's domain, jazz part of music's. Such innovations, however, were possible not because the innovators ignored their domains but because they understood them so well they could play with and expand them.

Csikszentmihalyi's concept of domains lets us see that it is possible to do fulfilling creative work in almost limitless ways. A person could write and play music for family members and enrich their lives with it. He has chosen to work within a worthwhile, if less demanding, domain than that defined by Carnegie Hall. Nevertheless, his chosen domain has expectations. If he refuses the convergence of being on key, his family will avoid his efforts to enrich them, just as they will if he refuses divergence by writing a single tune and singing it over and over.

Henri Poincaré, writing about mathematical discovery, puts it this way: "The true work of the inventor consists in choosing among those combinations so as to eliminate the useless ones or rather avoid the trouble of making them." In other words, the divergent thinking that produced the various "combinations" (of possible equations) has to be constrained at some point by the "choosing," convergent-thinking mind, because Poincaré is very aware of the "trouble" of attempting to make the imagined thing. He suggests a three-step process: think divergently, think convergently to eliminate most of your ideas, and, finally, attempt to make.

In the bodily act of making, dozens of intelligences and abilities, involving space and sequence and perception and sensitivity to the revealed, play their parts. The interaction among these ways of thinking, the body, and the material world—the hand making, the eye seeing, the mind rejudging and reconceiving, the hand re-remaking until a beautiful or workable real-world thing emerges—is creativity.

• • •

Creativity often aligns in interesting ways with spirituality, and creative wisdom can be found in many religious stories. Seen as a story about creativity, the parable of the prodigal son of the Christian New Testament sheds light on the issue of muse and craft, imagination and work (Luke 15:11–32). The prodigal son models a divergent thinker who believes only in the muse. He wants his full inheritance right now, without having to develop or commit to it, and he dissipates his energies in fancy and conjecture, coming up with ideas but never settling down to the effort of realizing them.[1] Imagination by itself is not grown up. It flits prodigally off down the road when effort and discipline are called for. Thus it is impoverished, and it produces nothing useful or enriching.

The prodigal son's stay-at-home older brother, on the other hand, never has any fun. He just keeps working. He believes creativity involves duty and the "right way." He would be the writer who believes how-to books can give him the secret to inspiration and thinks it is largely a matter of willpower. He gets upset when he's told there is no "correct" way to write a story or poem, and he wonders, in a surly way, why the teacher thinks she has anything to teach if she doesn't, by god, have anything to *teach*. He can't figure out why there is dance music coming into the darkness through an open window, or even what people *do* with such music.

In creative terms, the younger and older brothers are the same person, and the parable suggests that only when we learn to integrate their different powers do we achieve our full creative inheritance and become both players and workers in the creative kingdom.

• • •

For me, as for many writers I know, imagination exists largely within the act of writing. I can't remember a story I have written where I knew the ending when I began, or even one where I knew the beginning, since my beginnings change from one draft to another. I never know the structure, seldom know all the characters, often don't know what voice should tell the story. Because I know my imagination works through the act of writing, I'm sanguine in the face of these seeming difficulties. I have no particular destination in mind, so a detour isn't a detour, but an opportunity to discover a destination I didn't know about. Writing isn't a trip, but a journey.

If my imagination were strong enough to hold more of a story in my mind, I might become more frustrated by the real world's intransigency. It would be like road rage, which erupts because freeways are built on the assumption that the only reason to get into a car is to reach your destination. Thus if someone cuts in front of you, she shatters your whole purpose in that moment. Road rage doesn't occur on gravel roads, much less on walking paths or hiking trails. The more the reason for

---

1. At a young age, this son asks his father for his full inheritance, then leaves the estate, dissipates the wealth, and eats pig food to survive until he finally returns and is welcomed home by his father. The dutiful older brother, working in the fields, hears the celebration, finds out what has happened, and becomes envious.

moving partakes of "getting there," the more frustration will erupt when obstacles arise.

People who use hand tools or work with stubborn materials have an almost transcendent patience. It is apparent even in YouTube videos—the deliberate movements, the care with which the smallest action is performed. I have a Japanese pull saw with a kerf so thin it cuts precisely the width of a pencil line. When I saw down that line and then put a straight-edge to the board and see no light between straightedge and board, I'm pleased in a way a power saw with a fence will not produce. This suggests a link between creativity and another religious tradition, the Buddhist idea of doing things the hard way. The hard way is the *Way* rather than the means to *Get There*, and no time or effort can be wasted when you take it because the whole Way, not merely the arrival, is worthwhile. The Way involves both doing and achieving.

This enigmatic transcendence of the world of bulk and mass through a total engagement with it is a different pathway to transcendence than that of asceticism or meditation. It is a transcendence built from letting oneself completely engage the obstinacy of matter until it leads you by its strange and Musean grace along, and you become lifted from its difficulties because you are inside them, no longer resisting.

• • •

All of this suggests that one of the most important questions any writer can ask is where her natural beginning lies on the continuum from divergent, imaginative thinking to convergent, how-to thinking. In what virtual location does she tend to conceive ideas? Is she an imaginative younger sister, forming notions in her head and wanting them to be real *right now*—and inclined therefore to the impoverishment of never completing anything, feeding off the scraps of creative production but wishing always for the substance of the real meal? If a writer recognizes this tendency in herself, she may have to consciously nurture patience with the physical work of material formation and even learn to enjoy it, learn to accept advice with hope, and try to develop a sensitivity to the revelations that emerge during the act of writing.

If instead a person inclines toward being a dutiful older brother doing the work as he thinks he should but finding that it doesn't dance, he may want to ease up and space out more, get weirder, conform less to what seems correct, quit asking for permission, use language not to reach a practical end but to distract himself from it, dig crooked rows rather than straight, plant seeds he doesn't recognize but that might, if he tends them, produce flowers rather than vegetables. This writer wants to nurture what-if-ness and a sensitivity to the things occurring in his language at the edges of his focused attention.

• • •

With all this said, I can return to the frustrated young novelist. As he described his failed novels to me, I was impressed with his imagination but also heard extended summaries in which he pushed characters from one plot point to another. This is easy to do in the imagination, where characters are without mass. Moved into material creativity, however, they take on substance and coalesce, as if under the force of actual gravity, into galaxies of relationship. This makes them much harder to push around. It's a writer's version of DaVinci's helicopter problem—an actual helicopter has to be really, really heavy. It is easy for writers to forget that the written or spoken word is a physical thing. Produced, it imbues the made thing with mass and weight, obduracy and inertia.

A plot can be summarized in a few words—*Anna Karenina*, for instance: *a rich woman has an affair, goes crazy, and loses everything.* But plots are fulfilled by characters in relationships, and when you add these, complications abound. *Anna Karenina* again: *a rich woman, bored with her patient husband...* With the simple addition of "bored" and "patient," character and relationship bloom, and this second description, though incomplete, is weightier than the first.

The movement from imagination into creativity is a movement into a whole new order of existence. Thus it is easy to misdiagnose our problems in negotiating it. The young man who approached me assumed that his problems with finishing his novels were located between pages 1 and 50 of his attempts. Convinced he had written some wrong thing that led him to dead ends but unable to find the problem, he began new novels, but the problem cropped up again. Five attempts later, he was ready to blame a defect in his psyche.

This shows how confused we can become if we don't keep clear the difference between imagination and creativity. I didn't believe he had any such defect, and I also didn't believe he had made an egregious, hidden writing error. He had, after all, begun a novel. There is no better way to attempt to write a novel. But if the problem didn't lie in either his mind or what he had written, where did it lie? His mistake lay in thinking he'd made a mistake. As a result, he kept returning to imagination—new beginnings, full-fledged but insubstantial—rather than converging to a single idea to wrestle into materiality.

An early step in any creative process is gathering and preparing raw material. Painters bring paints and canvas together. Sculptors find a chunk of stone. Writers, though, can fall under the illusion that we require no raw material. We have to bear in mind that words, made physical by the act of writing, are those raw materials. Until a writer has produced them in the physical world, she can't begin working with them. It would be like a sculptor chiseling air as he imagines the stone.

• • •

A famous but probably apocryphal story about Michelangelo says that when asked how he conceived his sculptures, the artist answered that when he looked at a block of marble he could see the sculpture waiting to emerge, and all he did was remove the excess. Such a story fosters the notion of the artist as see-er or seer who finds nature's hidden meanings through a vision inaccessible to others. It's a story that makes craft a mere servant to the kingly Muse. It is understandable that people are drawn to this idea about great artists, since the arts often do seem to be a pathway into mysterious realms that cannot be approached through other means.

Nevertheless, it is an inhibitory concept. If we accept the idea of artist as seer, the artistic act lies not in the work—of, say, sculpting or writing—but in this mysterious "seeing" that occurs in an instant cut off from bodily activity. It is a younger-brother mentality that discourages actual labor and is injurious to apprentice creators. It encourages them to worry about "finding their muse," or their "subject," or their "true artistic self," as if a person finds such things by fretting about them rather than by developing a sensitivity to the world and to one's chosen artistic medium by the bodily act of sculpting or writing or painting until that work reveals something formidable and worthwhile.

It was obvious that the young man who spoke to me had absorbed this notion. His novels weren't coming into being as he "saw" them, so rather than concluding that he hadn't worked hard enough, he thought he was inadequate to the act of creation. That led him to chase inspiration rather than work, constantly starting new novels, staying close to imagination, which he found easy, rather than journeying into the material world and its resistant prodding.

Unfortunately, artists and writers themselves often promote the idea that inspiration is a seer-like thing. Elizabeth Gilbert's *Big Magic: Creative Living Beyond Fear* is a recent example. Creativity isn't just magic, but *Big* magic. At first glance it seems appealing, until you realize it implies that creative powers can't be developed but instead somehow magically happen. Most of us can't even perform little magic. Why would we attempt to write if it requires big magic? Gilbert claims that ideas exist in the world free-form, floating around, looking for minds to attach themselves to.

Again, that might seem charming, but what if ideas aren't as attracted to your mind as they apparently are to Gilbert's? She disparages MFA programs and implies that writing cannot be learned, noting that no Pulitzer-prize winner has come through an MFA. Even if we accept the premise that the Pulitzer represents the best in American writing, Gilbert confuses correlation and cause. Would anyone argue that college basketball programs obviously don't develop players, because some of the greatest players in the game skipped college? Such thinking is a formula for giving up. The idea of creator as seer turns us into worshippers of someone else's genius rather than seekers after our own.

• • •

Even if the story about Michelangelo is true, it is patently incomplete. By the time Michelangelo saw a block of marble, an artisan's highly skilled eyes had examined the striations in a quarry wall and seen a pattern indicating an interesting block. Accidents had happened in its removal and new structures were revealed, leading the artisans to follow different grain patterns. By the time the block was freed, it had been creatively shaped by numerous minds and eyes and hands. In this gathering of raw material, imagination had already crossed the boundary into physical creation.

What Michelangelo saw—if, in fact, he "saw"—was not some pure sculpture suggested by nature or spirit, but one influenced by other human beings' preceding creative processes, as well as by the convergences imposed by his culture. Why, after all, were all those Christian images trapped inside that Carrara marble all those millennia? Weren't there any animals—aurochs or bison—crunched in there waiting for release? If Michelangelo had procured his own marble, this story about his process could not have been so facile. The story more likely would be that Michelangelo's ideas came as he worked on removing the block. They came through the blows of the hammer; in the spewing chips; in the shadows of birds against the quarry walls changing, in flittering instants, the way the light played upon the stone; in the feel of the chisel probing a particular grain; in the gritty sweat he wiped from his eyes, remembering as he did, perhaps, a lit corner in a church and his fascination as a boy with the idea of killing giants. Through his memory and work, the physical world would be admitted as elements of inspiration.

Michelangelo borrowed the sweat and work. He borrowed the hammer blows. He borrowed the eyes of the quarriers. That's fine. He's still a great artist. But let's not let a story about him obscure the process for the rest of us and make it mystically out of our reach.

• • •

Though every creative effort borrows raw materials, writing may be as independent of others' pre-creation as an art can be. Writing instruments are made by others, but the raw material of the work itself consists of some image or tension the writer draws from the world or memory and turns into the rough-hewn block of words that is the first draft. When this block of raw material is fully quarried—freed from the writer's mind and a separate object in the world—she may "see" what resides within it, but while she is doing the drafting, she is probably less like Michelangelo than a sweaty and dusty artisan on a quarry wall.

Poincaré suggests that creative processes involve imaginative/divergent thinking, reason/convergent thinking, and work/production. In every creative domain I know, this last step is itself divided into amassing/accreting and sculpting/deleting. The story about Michelangelo can make him appear mystical because it gives him the luxury of borrowing those first chaotic steps and going straight to sculpting. Not only that, the story allows him to never experience failure, which is a crippling model for any creator to believe in. Surely he rejected some blocks of marble because they weren't adequate to great art. Such rejection would seem brilliant— nothing to "see" there—but only because the story lets him impose that failure on the artisans. If he had spent a year confidently hammering away at that block only to find it unworthy, he would have to own the failure.

Of course, I am criticizing not Michelangelo, but rather the myths we invent about creativity and the ways those myths inhibit us. The most humbling reality of creative work is that we will fail at it. My first and third and sixth novels are all unpublished, chunks of prose I have amassed and chiseled, now mere files in my computer's memory. If they were marble, they would fill a warehouse. I thought they might work, but after (sometimes) years of trying, I had to admit they were failed visions. I rejected the marble I myself had spent so much time quarrying. This was an emotional hurdle I struggled with in spite of my Michelangelo-like brilliance in rejecting what wasn't workable. The story about Michelangelo allows him the triumphal wisdom of rejection without the crushing humility that comes when the thing one rejects represents one's own work and belief.

Editing is my favorite part of writing. I love its clarifying power, the way it lets me find what I'd been looking for all along. It can seem as if the true story appears like a mystical apparition out of the obscuring fog of excess words. During this stage of writing, I can feel like a seer, having only to cut out the words that hide my vision. But I know the feeling is a false one, because I've been that sweaty artisan clinging to the quarry wall, and I know that when I was quarrying I was no more brilliant than anyone else mucking around in the mess of drafting. Drafting has its pleasures, but thinking you're a mystic is not one of them.

Sean Kane writes about the preternatural "sixth sense" of hunter-gatherers, who will feel prey or predator near without knowing why they feel it. Kane thinks this sixth sense is a subconscious response to slight changes in the entire forest's sensory output—shifts in the tonal quality of birdsong or the faintest changes in the sound of animals moving. Through long and intimate contact with their surroundings, these people have learned to detect an entire sensorium of data that they interpret at a sub-consciousness level, so that the hunter says he *feels* a jaguar in the vicinity. It seems like a mystical union with the forest.

I would love to believe that these hunter-gatherers commune with their environment and the earth in esoteric and uncanny ways, but I sus-pect that Kane is right: they do the work of hunting until it changes them. Perhaps artists develop similar connective capabilities, their engagement with their culture and with the world so intimate and deeply involved that they feel sadness in the architecture, misery in the lancing light, and unfulfilled yearning in the glances of strangers, and they find ways to express these feelings in a physical medium. If Kane is right, and you want to develop that sixth sense that tells you when the jaguar or the poem is near, you have to go with an elder into the forest, engage the danger, study tracks, listen to birdsong—how it changes, quavers, goes barely flat, opens a silence in which you can almost hear great lungs moving air.

• • •

I advised the frustrated writer to forget about starting a new novel and conduct an experiment with an old one—rewrite it, but treat it as a new one. Rather than word process, retype. Plagiarize from himself anything useful, but stay sensitive to potential new developments and follow them. Abandon the old material for new whenever the new is more interesting. Retyping, I told him, would re-engage him in physical creation and incline his mind toward originality and freshness, while keeping him in closer contact with his language and characters. It would create a radical equality between what he had already written and what he could write, an equality we have to work at because we tend to give the already written more authority than it can possibly deserve.

If he did this, I suggested, using what he had written only as raw mate-rial to be reshaped, added to, built upon, and thrown out, he would auto-matically write a fuller story. It might be messy, but it would be more developed. Without even knowing how or why, he would write past fifty pages, because every single period put to a sentence would open a new door to possibility. He would deliberately be journeying away from the safety of his original vision and into the thornier material world, but new potential would emerge, and the novel he didn't know was possible might reveal itself. He couldn't force that creative discovery, but it would probably come if he just worked at his chosen trade rather than depending so much on pure imagination.

Perhaps I should have been more sensitive to how much creative enigmas can sound like mumbo jumbo, but the young man so clearly wanted help that I thought he would be willing to conduct the experiment. As I talked, however, a look of irritation grew on his face, and when I finished he burst out in a tone that verged on accusation: "But doesn't that bother you? I'll just waste those fifty pages. All that work—I'll just be throwing it away."

• • •

It's ironic that this young writer didn't equate five unfinished novels with wasted work, but the deeper irony lies in his notion of work as something we don't like to do. This returns us to notions of play and engagement, and another creative enigma becomes clear: if we don't try to bring a material product to fruition, we're working not creatively but only imaginatively; but if we don't work just because we enjoy it—in other words, if our work isn't play—we can't allow ourselves the necessary excess and abandonment that creativity requires.

Another New Testament parable is useful in understanding this enigma (Matthew 20:1–16). A vineyard owner goes in the morning to the square where workers wait to be hired and hires every worker available for an agreed-upon daily wage. A few hours later he returns and hires more workers. He does this several times, hiring the last group only a few hours before sunset. When dark falls, he first pays those he hired last, giving them a full day's wages. The ones hired in the morning observe this and anticipate a bonus, but he pays them what they agreed to. When they complain, the owner reminds them that they thought the wages were fair that morning. "Are you envious because I am so generous?" he asks.

This parable is usually interpreted to mean that a person having a deathbed conversion is as worthy of salvation as one who has lived his entire life by faith. Maybe so, but the story is far more interesting as a literal description of creative work. The complaining vineyard workers think about vineyards the way Henry Ford thought about factories or the way the frustrated young writer thought about writing novels—that work's sole purpose is to arrive at a product, so there has to be a consistent ratio between time and value: one hour equals one peck of grapes or installed transmission or finished page.

Creative work doesn't *work* this way. Sometimes when I sit down to write, nothing is worth keeping. Other mornings, my mind brims with insights that flow onto the page, and in fifteen minutes I write what might have taken me four hours the day before. In the creative vineyard, there is no identifiable relationship between effort and result. Work is absolutely necessary, but the product doesn't pile up into some guaranteed amount of creative stuff.

Is it fair that Coleridge could wake from a drug-induced sleep and pop out "Kubla Khan," or that Picasso could finish a painting in the time it takes another artist to set up her easel? The concept of fairness doesn't apply. Admiration of another's work is a generous response that turns a creative worker back with renewed dedication to her own efforts, but envy keeps a person focused on someone else's rewards, which, precisely because they are creative rewards, can never be anyone else's, nor would we want them to be.

Doesn't that bother you? Well, no. Sometimes everything a creative worker picks in the vineyard is bird pecked or shriveled, but he picks it anyway. Other times, the grapes are all luscious, and he moves through the vines with his bucket held out, and the grapes drop themselves into it. And sometimes the grapes he thought were shriveled and useless turn out to have the best flavor, and the grapes that came easily had too much rain and too little sugar for fine wine. We can't know these things unless we fill the bucket.

All we can do is show up and work. The vineyard owner realizes in her generosity that all the labor is worthy and necessary, and her deepest generosity lies in her refusal to define her workers by a quota. The vineyard owner represents our own best creative selves. Be generous to yourself, the parable says. As a creative (or, okay, spiritual) being, you cannot be reduced to so many buckets of product. If the Muse does speak to us, this is its true voice—a voice not opposed to craft but that, when we withdraw to write, holds the world's assigned meanings at bay and insists that the work we do comes from and leads back to a value beyond quantifiable measurement. This is creativity's greatest generosity and the voice that inhabits everything we craft.

—2019

Inside the Conch Shell

Fleda Brown

—॰॰॰—

"Originality," Jane Hirshfield reminds me, "requires the aptitude for exile." I sure enough have the aptitude, yet here I am, on my way to visit my father. It takes me six, maybe eight minutes to walk from our large brick condo building at Grand Traverse Commons down the path, over the little wooden bridge, and across the lawn to his place at Willow Cottage Assisted Living. We moved him from Missouri to Michigan a year ago, in May. He calls me or I call him, or visit him, almost every day.

When I left home, I basically wanted the hell out of there—physically and psychologically—away from my brain-damaged brother and his constant seizures, from my whole family, but mostly from my father. Now look.

• • •

"When are you going to quit writing about your family?" This was Gerald Stern. He'd just picked my second book of poems as winner of a contest, and he'd stopped in Delaware on his way home to New Jersey to help me with revision. As I drove him back to the train station, that's what he said.

That was twenty years ago. Haven't I grown up yet? Haven't I had enough of this? This rehashing, this perpetual dusk of childhood. I'm tired of it, really I am. Haven't I exhausted the subject?

I submit to you James Baldwin, who insists that "the responsibility of a writer is to excavate the experience of the people who produced him." Excavate. Not your own experience, but that of those who produced you. What produced William Blake? Heaven is his mother, Hell his father, or vice versa. What produced Emily Dickinson? She can hardly bear to look. Donald Hall, when asked what he wrote about, blurted out, "Love, death, and New Hampshire." It seems as if a core requirement for this work is an obsession with solving the great mystery of our existence by filling in enough background with our words so that we become visible. Even our fictions, maybe especially our fictions, are filling in what might have been there—what *is* there in the alternate world that's able to illuminate this one.

Rilke writes to the young writer Baladine Klossowska that "in order for a Thing to speak to you, you must regard it for a certain time as *the only one that exists,* as the one and only phenomenon which, through your laborious and exclusive love, is now placed at the center of the universe."

So, there he is, my father, his stentorian voice cutting through all attempt at conversation. Day after day he passionately struggles with his books, with his mind, to prove Einstein wrong. All my life. Not for any reason except the rule of reason, which my father supposedly maintains. He was an economist, about as close as you can get to a full-blooded scientist without being one. He once said he didn't know why people talk except to convince someone or to learn something that might change their minds.

To him, words themselves have no power. He says this in the middle of an argument: "If you call me an idiot and a liar, what's it to me? Those are only words. And what's 'emotional trauma'? What's metaphor, what's religion, what's God? If you can't touch it, if you can't prove it . . ." And here he gets his little-boy snide smile that says the foolishness at this point is beyond words.

Already I am falling back into the pit here, attempting to explain this to you again, all the way to the bottom. There is no bottom. The blackness down there is my confusion. Why am I confused? I know how he is—a person with functional autism, full of old poems and dates and names and other things I am not full of. I cannot recite my own poems; he can recite all of Alfred Noyes's "The Highwayman," plus dozens of others. He's 98.

Within a couple of months of my father's arrival, he was on the printed weekly activities program at Willow—Wednesdays, he reads poems to the other residents. He loves this, spending hours picking through the books we've brought him plus his God-knows-how-old *101 Favorite Poems.* He wheels up to the third floor where tea and cake are being served, skips the tea and cake because he was told he was spilling it all over himself trying to read at the same time. He doesn't notice such things. His clothes get filthy in one day.

• • •

What can be done? My mother cried and folded clothes. Isn't the creative life about folding clothes while crying? Organizing through it all—not *because of* but *through.* Our gesture.

Yet the subject has spoken to me so loudly that all my experience compacts subtly inside its shape. I resent his crowding out. I have resented it all my life. Crowd out my mother, crowd out my sisters, crowd out me. You could call my poems small hidden rebellions. He might be in them, but he can't figure them out. They aren't rational. Longfellow is rational. Robert W. Service. Poe. Tennyson. At least by my father's lights. It isn't that he refuses to see beyond. He *cannot* see beyond. So, I let my attention merge, meander, emerge, locate itself both here and in the beyond where he can't pester me.

• • •

He wanted to read two of my poems to the group. He's puzzled, can't get why something's a poem that doesn't rhyme and doesn't have a clear story. In some way he's proud of me, but not sure whether what I do merits it. I have all these books, but that makes no sense to him. I'd rather he didn't read my poems, I think. Well, I'm pleased, but . . . This is what I mean by wanting to locate myself where his rationality can't hurt me. He won't make fun of my work, but he won't like it. I'm surprised by how much this matters to me.

Yet, I need you to see how interesting he is, with his one leg, wheeling around his tiny assisted-living room after another book! Or fixing his three clocks, one of which he has turned on its side to make it keep the right time. This is the windup clock, the one we bought him because he said he wanted an alarm clock.

He wanted an alarm clock because his days are full, so he'd better get at it. The young women come to help him walk with his prosthesis. He will never master this. He is 98—I told you that. He can walk a short way down the hall with a walker, but that's all. The attention is what he wants. And the challenge. In his eighties, he won three 100-mile medals from his bike club. He was their patron saint. But as did everything else, that activity fell away with no regrets, no looking back. Now it's this.

• • •

Does he even think about my mother? He's settled into his story that he didn't mean to marry her. He just asked in a letter (he was in the army, in the Philippines at the time) what she would *say if* he asked her to marry him, and, he says, the next thing he knew, she sent him the engagement notice from the newspaper. Maybe, maybe not. I dug through the heaps of photos and papers when we cleaned out the house. I found both the engagement announcement and, among his letters, a poem he wrote her while he was overseas. It's full of poetic cliché and forced rhyme, but if he wasn't in love with my mother, he was certainly in love with love, and with language. Here's an excerpt:

The fog is closing in. I sit alone
And watch the blinking lights across the bay
Or 'neath the haloed moon with its soft play
Of silver light upon the pebbled strand
I hear the tinkling wavelets on the sand . . .
Yet as I sit and gaze upon the scene
So unsurpassed in beauty and serene
As peace itself, within my breast
There is a quiet but deep unrest,
A secret longing not akin to pain,
A yearning to come back to you again . . .

Now, in his room, we look at old photos. There's one he took of another young woman back then. He says, "I would've married her [the other one] in a minute, but I didn't think I could support a family." My mother was beautiful, I have to say. She tried all her life to please him. At least that's how it looked to me. But she grew to hate him, too, because he couldn't, just couldn't, have any real, normal feelings toward her. His attitude was clinical. She might have been anyone, was how it seemed. Any woman who isn't mean is as good as any other, he'd intimate frequently, although it's highly preferable to have an attractive one.

Flannery O'Connor says, "At its best our age is an age of searchers and discoverers, and at its worst, an age that has domesticated despair and learned to live with it happily." I was watching. I was entranced by the tangle. I thought the—yes, maybe happy—purpose of my life was to try to sort things out. Not to fix them, which I deemed impossible, but to understand. Her tears were easy to understand. But him? Entrancingly funny, as handsome as they come, remarkably skilled mechanically, and smart. Yet stupid, unable to see, strangely unaware of his own self, and unable to think abstractly at all (unless we're talking about physics, and even then, on a mechanical level). Through the years, he has remained determined to get to the root of the time-space problem and to demonstrate that Einstein was simply nuts—literally and theoretically—to claim that a person can travel into space and come back younger.

Here I am again, telling you a story. The "ferocious appetite" of sequential structure, as Ellen Bryant Voigt calls it, that keeps eating itself up, playing against the presumption of its stability. The lyric, on the other hand, Voigt calls "perception." Stopping, holding still. The points on a graph. Connect them and you have the narrative. There I was, a child, suffering because I was invisible, and because the world was scary, holding myself still and safe inside my thoughts. Look at me, all serious, thinking of God and of trees, making little forts in the woods. Making tiny bowls out of acorns. Staying small, thinking myself into smallness.

What is the relationship between seeing and feeling? We write words and they box us in. At the same time, they're our only tool to point toward the lump in the throat, the deep interior wound we call *parent*.

• • •

When I visit, he is working on time-space again. I sit, at the age of seventy-one myself, in the one chair in his room. I could be ten, or twenty, or any age. I am a fixture he can talk at.

Not that he doesn't value me: "I sure hope your cancer doesn't come back," he says frequently—his sledgehammer way of saying he cares. I know he worries that if I die, his finances might not be so well taken care of, but that's not fair of me to say, because I know he loves me as he can. Hard to sort these things out. Hard to remember what's now and what I've lugged along from the past.

Pills plus extreme old age have rendered him very sweet. There is a moment when neither of us can think what to say next. He smiles at me. This feels wonderful and terrifying, the lens scrubbed clean; *Here it is*, I'm thinking, *what was pushed away, driven away, covered over with fierce anger. The love, the hurt, the anguish. Me, looking into my own eyes. Me, writing to me.*

• • •

No wonder I resist writing these words. I am in over my head. But what other words are there? What is the reason for writing anything? To *amuse, inspire, inform*—I learned that once. There is a reader out there—a *you.* "See," I say, "*you* have to see. He is too interesting to pass up."

When I was a child, I kept one eye always on the familial weather vane. Will he see that Mother spent money on Kleenex brand instead of generic and take off on a rant? Will this simple rift in the fabric unleash the Furies? Or will he start whistling in the garden and make all the angels sing? There is this unique being, this unique moment in time. They are on the move. I am born to trace their trajectory. My tracings will save my soul. And if I can bring you along, maybe I can shine a small light into our mutual great dark.

• • •

He was living in Missouri when we got the call that he'd been taken to the hospital with leg pain. By the time my sister and I got there, the aneurysm behind his knee had been unsuccessfully repaired. The surgeon wanted to amputate his leg right away. But then the second surgeon said, when pressed, "I don't know. Maybe I wouldn't. Maybe he's better off just dying. The leg is beginning to rot; he'll go into a coma. Maybe letting him go is better than trying to put him through another surgery which could likely kill him anyway."

I kind of agreed with the second surgeon. My father was weak and tired, he'd said over and over that he didn't want to live any longer, and he hurt a lot. I laid out the blunt choices for him, but I was pretty sure what he'd say: I knew my father didn't want to die. I suppose it would take a pretty strong or hopeless or depressed person to say *Yes, okay, I'll die now.* He said, of course, "Let's amputate."

Another surgeon was called in to do the operation, after hours on a Saturday evening. My sister and I did yoga stretches in the waiting room, expecting the worst. The surgeon came out. "Strong as an ox," he said. "His heart is fine. He'll be fine." And on rounds the next morning he asked, "How are you this morning, Mr. Brown?"

"Well, one leg's shorter than the other," said my father with a bemused smile.

• • •

I am mourning the gap, the loss of his leg—well, all my losses—but my father is living in the present. My mind begins pouring its stored images and feelings into the gap. Sensations act as if they were still in the leg. Blank space refuses to remain blank. One thing follows another; before long, a string of thoughts and feelings coheres into a narrative. The horses' heads are turned toward eternity, Emily Dickinson surmised; we just start in and we go.

I did not want to get caught up in the narrative because that's not where my heart lies. My heart is a rip current, moving away from shore, cutting through the lines of breaking waves—a countervalent language, a language weaving shakily on one leg. I want somehow to leave Point A and get someplace that isn't Point B, but it's so hard, so much against. So uncertain is the goal, so uncertain the gait, that the traveling itself becomes the point.

• • •

My father gets down the short hallway and has to take a break. The aide pushes his wheelchair behind him so he can sit. He works hard at this. Language works hard lugging the image across the perceived gap between then and now, and between the feeling of this and the way it appears.

I wheel him up to the third floor, where there is cake and tea. The residents are gathered around the table. He opens his *101 Poems* with its pink stickers to mark the pages. I sit across from him on the piano bench, where he can see me but I'm not interfering. He asks if he can read a little prose first. The audience isn't capable of much response: smiles and occasional clapping gestures—except for Bill, who smiles at almost everything. He likes my father. And there's frizzy-haired Nancy, who sits next to my father, pats him on the hand, and seems proud to sit there. He reads a passage from "My Last Walk with the Schoolmistress," by Oliver Wendell Holmes, a sentimental piece about the moment the speaker realizes he has his heart's desire, the love of the schoolmistress. They will never part again.

Here is what's baffling. My father is moved by this. And he is moved by a painfully sentimental poem called "My Mother's Hands." This is a man who says people love other people primarily because they want or need things. We do what we do because of our genetic predisposition. There is no free will. Love is explained by our desire to reproduce so that our genes will survive. Here I am on the piano bench, watching his chin tremble.

• • •

Who am I? Who is this person who left home, who made a life unrelated to her father, who thought of home as a place not to be from? I know nothing. Growing up I did not know who he was, and I do not now know. He reads the poem and the words take him under some surface. What lives there he knows not, but his chin is trembling. He is as mysterious as my own mind. He *is* my mind, what I made up. I was not wrong, I was not right.

It's a mess. Leads and tangles. You follow until the trail goes cold. You do this over and over. When there are no more leads, you stand there, hands at your sides, and watch the sunset. What accumulates when there is no clear point is *wonder*. The trembling, the rhythms of the substructure begin to be felt. Meaning does not accumulate in the retelling—awe does.

• • •

I want language to mirror what I think is out there. What *seems* to be there. Yet, what's there but what I've created? My words themselves create a solitude, a rounding down of my mind as if I'm in a conch shell. I start at the outer edge and curve inward until I can't see any farther. Father. I can't see any father. There is killing in the streets, there is war, there is ISIS, there is betrayal, there is child abuse. Not out there—not *just* out there. They're deep in here. When I keep looking, there's a point where they eventually must touch each other. Where they must be seen and touched with silence. With the countervalent force of silence.

• • •

He goes on about the speed of light. Supposedly, the speed of light in a vacuum is the same no matter what. How can that hold equally true, he asks, if you're moving toward it or away from it? He says *redshift*, he says *Doppler effect*, he says *flashlights*, he says *stars*. The light of stars is the only thing we can see, not stars themselves. Unless they're close, like our sun. Then they're the real deal.

What is the real deal made of, but light? Waves of electromagnetic radiation that arrive bundled into little packets called photons. Just energy in lumps, everything we see. These bundles of letters called words, these bundles of words called meaning. These bundles of metaphor, all of them, curling down inside themselves, hard little shells to contain the vastness, to hold off the vastness.

• • •

Didn't I want to write poems because of their solitariness? Because of their curling, because their meaning reflects like nacre on the inside of a shell. Like a mirror. A classic Zen poem, "Song of the Jewel Mirror Samadhi," says:

> The meaning is not in the words,
> yet it responds to the inquiring impulse.
> Move and you are trapped;
> miss and you fall into doubt and vacillation.

My stories are held in suspension by the silence. To tell them, I have to press them against the membrane of words. I have to wrap my father in his scarf, his heavy coat, his knit cap, and push his wheelchair over to our place. The one leg rest catches on the concrete, so I take it off to raise it a bit. I can't. I can't get the metal nub to slide up to the next hole. "Let me see if I can do it," he says, and he fixes it. So simple when you see the exact motion necessary.

• • •

I wanted to get his attention. I wanted him to be proud of me. His attention has been on Einstein. Inside Einstein is a kingdom where people come back younger than when they left. Maybe they could live their lives again, try all this some other way. But if time and space are inseparable, if there is only space-time, there is no "some other way" and no "again." I have to get it right this time.

Once upon a time there was my father. The word *once*, that creates time: *time*, that busily concocts a narrative. There was *father*: that perception of separation, that gap between him and my understanding, between him and my need for love, for recognition. When my poem turned the corner at the end of the line, there was a satisfying feeling of being held back, held in, and also the grief of not being let in on a secret. But still, the poem was an oxygen mask that allowed for breathing, when otherwise . . .

• • •

The day looks promising for sailing, a good wind. My father is a skillful sailor and finds the gusts to travel on. Our lake is gusty. When we are beyond seeing, down by Recreation Point, the wind dies. I am twelve, seeing a little beyond my childhood but still ruled by it. We will not hear the dinner bell. They can't see us from around the point. He catches every slight breeze; we take turns with the one canoe paddle. I am full of despair and single-mindedness. I am full of joy.

Nothing has changed in the six intervening decades. I am in constant despair, constant joy. The connection called family is almost broken, but of course not really. "There is one story and one story only," Robert Graves wrote in a poem. My family may be at the end of the dock right now, looking for me.

The lines of a poem walk out to the end, and then what? They stop, weighing all possibilities. They are mathematical in their attempt to weigh, although that might not be visible on the surface. The mind lurches, trying to get traction.

"Pythagorean," by Linda Gregerson, is a good way to map this attempt:

> Square of the square of the
> > root
> that holds it all together, maybe the geometricians
>
> were right. Or maybe
> > it's music after all,
> > the numbers in their other incarnation, makes

the planets make us what we are,
           which means
       in turn . . .

"Maybe the geometricians // were right." I am left hanging, with the word "geometricians" poised there for a couple of beats—letting it soak in on its own, without giving it value yet.

The poem is spoken by someone who has given up eating meat after seeing an ox slaughtered for food. "How strange," it says, "we need these turnings-against / / before we're allowed to see." The poem ends this way: "I don't know // what I will be or what I should call the thing / I am, / but I know what I used to be."

The poem halts and restarts. It is, as Wallace Stevens's "Of Modern Poetry" begins, "The poem of the mind in the act of finding / what will suffice." The mind stumbling along, not knowing what comes next. Gregerson's is a poem of a modern sensibility, a shared recognition of the conjunction of interior and exterior uncertainty. It cannot depend upon "what was in the script," as Stevens says; "It has to be living." Caught in the act of living. It is—and this is Stevens again—"a poem of the act of the mind."

It is a father and daughter on a becalmed sailboat, paddling a little, tacking to catch any suggestion of wind. How do we get home? Little by little as the sun goes down, the air cools more quickly than the water. Off-shore breezes pick up. We watch for evidence in the rippling and point our sails to catch what we can. I am dangling my feet over the side, making little kicking motions as if I could hurry us along. I am frustrated, anxious, and angry. (He did this again! Took us too far away to get back easily.) I am delighted by the motion of my foot. I am glad to have this time alone with my father, the one I love and hate.

He broke my heart. He broke my mother's heart. He looked straight at me and couldn't see that I was only a child. His child. I was a sounding board. He lectured to me on economics, science, as if I were his colleague. I couldn't get it. I had to get it so he would want to bother with me. I loved him. I could not love him because he was dangerous. His dissatisfaction, his anger, flew everywhere. You could imagine anything. Murder—or worse, leaving. He was, as I said, strong, funny, and more. Oh lord, so much to pull a person in, only to be lost. Not an oscillation but a tension, unto breaking.

• • •

Lines break. And deeper inside the conch shell of a poem, the mind hears a more fundamental resistance, the stutter of consonants against the glide of vowels. Gerard Manley Hopkins, for example: listen to him taking resistance to the most exquisite extremes—the most private language, breaking itself against itself, barely able to be spoken.

> Not, I'll not, carrion comfort, Despair, not feast on thee;
> Not untwist—slack they may be—these last strands of man
> In me, or, most weary, cry *I can no more*. I can;
> Can something, hope, wish day come, not choose not to be.

Hopkins's rhythms are full of surprises. He *said* he was reviving the rhythms of common speech he heard in folk songs and early poems. Each line could contain any number of feet. He allowed for between one and four syllables per foot, while the feet in accentual poetry (iambic, trochaic, anapestic, dactylic) normally contain only two or three. Hopkins also stressed the first syllable in each foot, so you get this breathlessness, this pushing forward—in some ways like Emily Dickinson's, but more tortured, more broken. You might think of him as bridging between the prescribed patterns of accentual verse and free verse, which follows no prescribed pattern.

Hopkins is struggling with his small canoe paddle in the middle of a great lake, looking for home. Have I left my own suffering, my loneliness, to hide inside Hopkins? Very well, I am large, now. I contain multitudes.

• • •

The poems my father likes have no stutters, no gaps. They tell their tender and tragic stories in splendid language. They do not make mistakes in meter to disrupt the forward movement. They do not disrupt, and in this lack of disruption they are public rather than private. They are incantation, recitation in and/or for a collective ear. They are to be recited around the table at Willow Cottage. They are for me, sitting across from him, watching his face while he reads aloud. I do love this poem. It says what it says:

> The wind was a torrent of darkness among the gusty trees.
> The moon was a ghostly galleon tossed upon cloudy seas.
> The road was a ribbon of moonlight over the purple moor,
> And the highwayman came riding—
> Riding—riding—
> The highwayman came riding, up to the old inn-door.

Nonetheless, even while the heart is sure of its own meter, the mind lurches. Gusts drive it in all directions. It takes skill—both practice and art—to handle the lines and rudder. Here is my father. I am stuck with him in the boat forever. When he dies I will still be stuck with him. He is the iconic presence that drives me down into myself. He is the emblem of eternal mystery, and I am a fool who will never understand.

I say to myself the end of the "Song of the Jewel Mirror Samadhi":

Practice secretly, working within,
like a fool, like an idiot.
Just to continue in this way
is called the host within the host

I say the last stanza of James Wright's "Wherever Home Is":

Goodbye to Leonardo, good riddance
To decaying madmen who cannot keep alive
The wanderers among trees,
I am going home with the lizard,
Wherever home is,
And lie beside him unguarded
In the clear sunlight.
We will lift our faces even if it rains.
We will both turn green.

I say to myself, by way of warning, that any writer who goes home—wherever home is—has to accept the consequence of going home, which is effacement of ego in the service of what's there, what's green. What has not turned to stone.

—*2019*

Writing and/as Art

The Long/Wide View

Wendy Call

——◦◦——

Is writing art? For a long time, I did not think of myself as an "artist" by any stretch, even as I received grants and attended residencies that were supposedly "for artists." As I've come to learn more about that troublesome word—*ART*—my thinking about what I'm doing, about what all creators are doing, has changed. In English, *art* is not a verb, but *write* is. We tend to think of art as the product, but the process—how art comes into being—is far more interesting to me. Can we write art, as well as make art? *Art* is a highly contested term, so much so that some scholars of art refuse to use the term at all. What a relief to know that I am not alone in my discomfort!

Let's start at the beginning, with the oldest-known art in the world. Cupules are rounded pockmarks beaten into rock. They compose our longest-surviving art, though *not* the world's first art. Like figurative rock art and pyramids—both of which came *much* later than cupules—we are lucky enough to be able to see cupules today only because they were created on such durable surfaces. Of course, it's extremely unlikely that early humans would have chosen some of the world's hardest rocks as their very *first* artistic canvases, so we will probably never know the world's oldest visual art, which was likely marks on the human body.

Cupules are collections of "cups" pounded or ground into rock. They occasionally appear singly, but more often they appear in small or very large groupings, sometimes in obvious designs. The oldest cupules that we have found, in what is now Syria, are at least 1.8 million years old. That is a dazzlingly long time ago: before *Homo sapiens* had evolved, before our forebears had learned to use fire or make arrowheads, perhaps even before they developed complex language.

Early humans and our prehuman ancestors pounded or ground out cupules all over the world. In South Africa's Kalahari Desert, large cupules were pounded into stone a few hundred thousand years ago. In a rockshelter in Arizona, 700 cupules decorate the bedrock floor. Bedrock! In

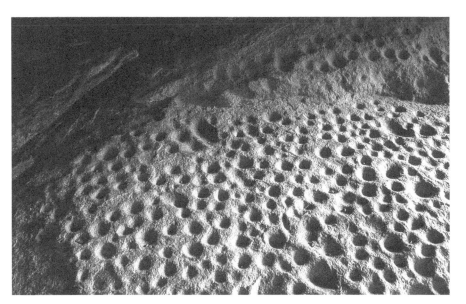

Fig. 5.1. Cupules in a large grouping; photo: Ekkehart Malotki, from *Early Rock Art of the American West: The Geometric Enigma* by E. Malotki and E. Dissanayake

northwestern Australia, where the first humans are thought to have arrived on that continent, nearly 7,000 cupules were pecked into vertical rock walls. Seven thousand! These cupules on vertical walls disprove the hypothesis that cupules were not art, but rather utilitarian vessels. Across the peaks of the Pyrenees and the Alps, cupules are scattered abundantly on mica schist and granite. Early humans, Neanderthals, and our prehuman ancestors pounded cupules on rock floors, walls, and even ceilings; they placed cupule-decorated rocks on altars and at burial sites. Three hundred thousand years ago, humans and our cousins were making cupules in groupings that were clearly intentional and seem to have been decorative, even symbolic. So, yes, visual art is 300 eons old.

Cupules are still being created. For example, in the 1940s, a community in Australia pounded cupules as a fertility ritual for pink cockatoos, an important food source. Because the tradition continues, we know quite a bit about how they were likely made long ago. Their creators pound or grind tools called hammerstones onto the rock surface for a long time—many hours, over days or weeks. Some individual cupules require 30,000 blows to be created. In a sense, creating these cupules was a performance before it was a permanent art installation. Some cupules are an artifact of a group of people creating a collective rhythm, drumming stone on earth. Whether they worked alone or in groups, the cupule creators eventually covered entire rock faces or walls with evidence of their drumming. A collection of cupules was a process before it was a product.

• • •

The oldest-known writing—Sumerian cuneiform—is only 5,400 years old. Humans have been mark making (creating visual art) for sixty times longer than they have been writing. If our entire history of mark making were one calendar year, we would have started writing six days ago.

• • •

In 1995, I encountered the oldest writing in the Americas—about half as old as Sumerian cuneiform—at Monte Albán in Oaxaca, Mexico. I stared at the beautiful stone stelae and took pictures of them, but I had no idea that I was observing the first American writing. I learned that six years later, when I visited Monte Albán again with a local historian, Juan de Dios Gómez. As far as we know—and we don't know very much—the Zapotec stelae I saw at Monte Albán commemorate the dates of kings coming to power. A translation of the glyphs on one stela: "In the year 4 Lightning a man named 8 Water, a firstborn son, was seated in office." On a flat stone, burnished by many hands, many centuries, and many storms, fat dots balance on lines and anvil shapes; thick circles enclose water-carrying pots and birds and monsters. It is no accident that the same word is used for "draw" and "write" in Zapotec—and in the language of the Maya, who borrowed the idea of writing from the Zapotecs. Stelae 12 and 13 at Monte Albán were once among many written recordings of Zapotec history; few have survived.

Sometime around 600 BCE, the Zapotecs started carving glyphs onto stone pillars. As far as we know, Mayan society got the idea of writing from the Zapotecs. These Zapotec glyphs are a stunning act of original thinking. They represent the *only* time in the history of the Western Hemisphere that the idea of writing was invented, rather than adopted from another culture. They are probably one of only four or perhaps five times in world history that writing was independently invented. (Scientists are confident that writing was invented in Mesopotamia between 5,300 and 5,400 years ago, but they aren't sure whether the Egyptians and Chinese came up with the idea of writing on their own, as well, or adopted it from others.)

We humans are far better mimics than we are inventors. And so, dear writers and creators, take heart: there is nothing new under the sun. You need not strive to be original.

To build Monte Albán, ancient Oaxacans razed the top of a moun-

Fig. 5.2. Zapotec stela at Mount Albán; photo: Wendy Call

tain, flattening an enormous site that overlooks a large valley. The stones of the pyramids and stelae were carried—without beasts of burden—up the steep mountainside. I was struck more by the beauty, elegance, and sheer improbability of the stelae than I was by the fact that I was looking at one of the hemisphere's oldest manifestations of my trade. Only later did I really consider that latter fact. In some ways, my personal experience mimicked our fundamental, human experience with reading. Most young children are curious about letters and words long before they can decode them.

• • •

I would like to invite you to pause for a moment and consider the follow-ing: What was your earliest aesthetic experience? The first time you remember appreciating something for its beauty? Or its visual interest? Or what we might call its "artistic value"? Please write your answer down.

How old were you? What did you see or experience? How did you perceive it?

I suggest that you set this essay aside for a few minutes and write down all the details you can remember. (We will return to this material later.)

• • •

Before I learned about cupules, I thought that "well over 5,000 years" was an extremely long time. I thought of writing as a very old practice. But if we take the long view, writing is a shiny new technology. As a species, we've been speaking and telling stories for hundreds of thousands of years, perhaps even longer than we have been making visual art. Yet we began reading and writing so recently that our brain anatomy has not evolved to accommodate this activity. To learn how to read (and write), we humans must adapt parts of our brains that evolved to do other things. Steven Pinker, a cognitive psychologist at Harvard University, has written exten-sively about this phenomenon. He explains that human beings instinc-tively speak, but we do not instinctively write:

> Language is a human instinct, but written language is not. Language is found in all societies, present and past. . . . Although languages change, they do not improve: English is no more complex than the languages of Stone Age tribes; Modern English is not an advance over Old English. All healthy children master their language with-out lessons or corrections. When children are thrown together without a usable language, they invent one of their own.
>
> Compare all this with writing. Writing systems have been in-vented a small number of times in history. They originated only in a few complex civilizations, and they started off crude and slowly improved over the millennia. Until recently, most children never learned to read or write. . . . A group of children is no more likely to invent an alphabet than it is to invent the internal combustion engine. Children are wired for sound, but print is an optional acces-sory that must be painstakingly bolted on.

Writing most certainly does not come naturally. Or, as Nancy Frey and Douglas Fisher, both early childhood education specialists, put it, "every brain must be taught to read. . . . Reading is a complex, rule-based system that must be imposed on biological structures that were designed or evolved for other purposes."

No wonder the idea of writing sprang up independently only a handful of times in the entire global history of humanity. We writers are painfully aware that we are building quirkily imperfect contraptions when we write. As it turns out, we do the same thing when we read!

So, how, exactly, do we (metaphorically) bolt on that "optional accessory"? Cognitive neuroscientist Stanislas Dehaene's book *Reading in the Brain* answers that question in great detail. He explains that in the occipital region of the human brain there is an area that recognizes objects, called the fusiform gyrus. Nearby, there is a specialized area for recognizing faces. In the fold between those two areas, called the occipitotemporal fissure, is the area that recognizes written words. In a *fold*—a mere hallway between the rooms of our minds.

As Pinker points out, humans easily and universally tell stories and recite poems. Our literatures existed for tens (or hundreds) of thousands of years as oral traditions—springing from parts of our brains that were evolved specifically for those purposes. I am so grateful to all the ancient griots, bards, troubadours, and al-hakawati who saved our poems and stories for us until we learned, as a species, how to write them down.

• • •

Now, I would like to ask you once again to pause in your reading of this essay and write for a few minutes. Please spend ten minutes—or longer, if you wish—answering the following question: What is your earliest memory of the written word—whether learning to read, wishing that you knew how to read, being read a bedtime story, or reading something that had a strong impact on you?

• • •

I learned about cupules and the ancient history of art from Ellen Dissanayake, a scholar who describes herself as "a theorist of aesthetics and the arts who starts with an ethological point of view." Ethology, a specialization within zoology, is the study of animal behavior—including the human animal. Though I was a biology major in college and therefore took several zoology classes, I never encountered the word *ethology*. I learned it, among many other things, from Dissanayake. Her scholarship has had a profound influence on how I think about my work as a writer and how I think about our collective creative production. In this essay, to thank her for all that she has given to me through her writing and scholarly work, I do her the great disservice of grossly oversimplifying her elegant and complex ideas. (I do this with Ellen Dissanayake's permission and encouragement. In fact, I should take a moment right now to thank her for reading multiple drafts of this essay. I urge you to seek out her books.) One of the hard truths all writers learn is that we must simplify—and even oversimplify—all the time. In fact, according to Dissanayake, it is part of what defines art making, what humans do when they engage in artistic practice. (What a relief!) With that caveat, let's dive into her scholarship.

Ellen Dissanayake says that art making, what she calls "artifying," is a core behavior in all human communities. Art making goes all the way back to the earliest humans, as well as our closest cousins, the Neanderthals, and even some of our more distant cousins, such as *Homo erectus* and *Homo ergaster*. Her idea that making art is a universal, core human behavior leads to an obvious next question: What is an art-making practice? Dissanayake has an answer for that question, too. She says there are five elements, or operations, that are common to art practices worldwide throughout human history, and even earlier. She argues that these five qualities define all artistic practice.

The first element is **formalization**, creating patterns and simplifying. Dissanayake says, "This is what artists do. They simplify . . . They are performing operations on reality, and they are making it more interesting." For the audience experiencing these formalized patterns, she explains, "emotions are heightened or manipulated."

As a nonfiction writer, I find that this idea of art as "simplifying" resonates. Anyone who has ever published any work of nonfiction, no matter its length, has realized that it is a great, hubristic act of oversimplification. We distill shelves and filing cabinets full of material we have read into a book that fits in the palm of your hand. My friend Sasha Su-Ling Welland, a nonfiction writer and gender studies scholar, says, "Writing nonfiction is taking an eyedropper to a waterfall." All writing that attempts to represent the world in some way—whether it's nonfiction or not—is *simplifying* the dizzying complications of reality.

Formalization is not only simplifying, but also filtering. As writers, we look for patterns in the world, filtering our human experience as we represent it on the page. I was very slow to learn this key element of formalization: making something more interesting than reality. My early efforts at writing creative nonfiction were bad for many reasons, but one of the reasons most often cited by my readers was boring dialogue. I took a workshop with author Ted Conover, and he wisely explained to me, "Dialogue is not conversation. It's conversation's greatest hits."

The second element is **repetition**. There is nothing more satisfying than a literary work that masters repetition, and there is nothing more tedious than one that bumbles it. Elizabeth Bishop's poem "One Art," perhaps a perfect villanelle, is an example of sublime repetition—of both line and rhyme. The writer's toolbox for repetition is a large one. We repeat sounds through alliteration, assonance, consonance, and rhyme. Anaphora repeats the first word or phrase of a sentence or poetic line, as in Dr. King's "I Have a Dream" speech. Or we repeat the last word or phrase, in an epistrophe. Those techniques are combined with symploce, in which lines or sentences begin and end in the same way.

Exaggeration, the third element, relates to the silly faces that we all make at babies. Yes, really! We might think this is just play, but it is a key behavior between adults and babies, common to all human communities all over the world. In her book *Art and Intimacy*, Dissanayake explains that such behavior is deeply embedded in our humanity. We convey to babies, in the first weeks and months of their lives, all five of the key elements of artifying. As she explained to me, "The widened eyes, wide mouth, and nodding attracts the attention of even small babies. They are innately receptive to these things. It helps them realize they are part of a mother-child dyad. It helps their brains develop." Even more, she says, when we engage in baby talk with infants, they are teaching us how to engage with them. Through our silly faces, we teach babies how to read social cues, how to engage with other humans, how to prick up their ears for a good story. Dissanayake says that all five of the elements of artifying are transferred to infants by their caregivers during their first weeks and months of life.

Our use of exaggeration extends from baby talk to our literary masterworks. Even if we are writing the most rigorously fact-checked, deeply researched nonfiction, we are exaggerating in some ways. We emphasize some details while downplaying others. A single minute of life might extend over an entire chapter of a novel, after we breeze through a decade in one sentence or leap over it with a mere space break. Through our exaggeration of time and event, we writers try desperately to hold our readers' attentions—which is no small feat.

Ellen Dissanayake uses the term *making special* to explain the fourth element common to all art: **elaboration**. In the MFA workshop that I took with author Bob Shacochis, he often—and rightfully—said to aspiring writers of personal nonfiction, including me, "Just because it happened to you doesn't make it interesting." Just because it happened to *anyone* doesn't make it interesting. The job of the writer—of any creative person—is to *make* it interesting, to "make it special."

The point is not whether the work created is beautiful or whether critics approve of it, but whether it is set apart from the commonplace. Even as the resulting art is part of our daily lives, available to everyone, it is elaborated in some way that sets it apart. When we hear a poem recited, or sit down to read a book, or listen to an audiobook as we walk to the train station, we are entering an intellectual and emotional space apart from our quotidian lives. To be worthy of this setting apart, it must be elaborated—decorated or carefully wrought or well crafted or rich in symbolic meaning. Dissanayake notes that this is one example of how art and ritual are inextricably linked: "Rituals and the arts are *bracketed*, set off from real or ordinary life. A stage of some kind—a circle, a demarcated area, a museum, or platform—sets off the holy from the profane, the performers from audience, the extra-ordinary from the everyday. And both rituals and the arts make conspicuous use of symbols: things have hidden or arcane meanings, reverberations beyond their apparent surface significance."

Ellen Dissanayake saved the best for last: the fifth element of artifying is **manipulation of expectation**. Good writing subverts people's expectations. Surprise is the most delicious literary experience of all. Aristotle includes *thaumaston*—surprise, amazement, marvelous, or invoking awe—in his list of elements of a tragic plot. Interestingly, he notes that *thaumaston* is beneficial, but not essential, to a successful tragic play. He explains in *Poetics* (in Malcolm Heath's translation), "In reversals and in simple actions poets use astonishment to achieve their chosen aims; this is tragic and agreeable. This happens when someone who is clever but bad (like Sisyphus) is deceived, of someone who is courageous but unjust is defeated." Poet Jane Hirshfield explains, "Surprise, then, is epiphany's first flavor. It is the emotion by which we register shifted knowledge, in a poem, in a life." Hirshfield agrees with Dissanayake on the importance of surprise: "How is it that something that lasts half a second can be so essential, not only to art, but to our very survival? Not least is the way startlement transforms the one who is startled. Among other things, surprise magnetizes attention." As Emily Dickinson famously put it: "If I feel physically as if the top of my head were taken off, I know that is poetry."

Dissanayake points out that surprise is the only one of artification's five elements that is the sole province of human beings (as far as we know). I wonder whether the capacity to enjoy the deliciousness of surprise is one of the (very few) attributes that separates humans from other animals.

• • •

When we write a short story, post an essay to a blog, or recite a poem, we are connecting to a tradition that predates our species. I find it very helpful to remember that connection to long tradition; it reduces the writerly pressure I often feel. Dissanayake believes that art grew from ceremony, ritual, and play—other instances in which people make the ordinary into something extraordinary. As people were making art, they were following tradition, not breaking it. For those reasons, originality is (most empathically) not an element of artifying. She explains, "For a long time, art was not original. That was not the point." It was the process, the ritual, that was important. Hirshfield concurs, pointing out that all time-based arts, those that are shared with others, "partake of something that lies at the core of ritual: the reenactment of and entrance into a mystery that can be touched and entered but not possessed."

• • •

No matter *what* you are making special, you are part of a long tradition.

• • •

Remember the questions that I asked you to answer earlier in this essay? Please return to them, either now or at some point in the near future. Please reread your answers to those two exercises and then answer these questions, also in writing:

1. What do these two moments or memories have to do with each other?
2. What do these two moments say about you, as a creative person?
3. How do these specific memories relate to your current writing project?

• • •

The central question is, What makes your writing important to you? As Dissanayake says, "People don't make art about unimportant things." In an essay published two decades ago, she explains, "the desire or need to make special has been throughout human history, until quite recently, primarily in the service of abiding human concerns—ones that engage our feelings in the most profound ways . . . art actually originated and thrived for most of human history as a communal activity. . . . The primary evolutionary context for the origin and development of the arts was in activities

Writing and/as Art / 53

concerned with survival." Now, as we live and write through the Anthropocene, 12,000 years after the end of the Pleistocene, we are facing enormous threats to our species survival—and also to planetary survival.

. . .

Though I am still uncomfortable with the label "artist" as it pertains to my own creative work, I am drawn to the idea of artifying. This concept makes my writing into a practice—which is something more compelling and less intimidating to me. Reading and writing are both difficult for us—they are possible *only* with practice. In order to read and write, our brains have had to repurpose bundles of neurons that evolved to do other things. But through practice, our brains can change. Sets of neurons that are activated over and over again actually change their physiological and biochemical makeup; they develop into faster, more efficient networks. We have known for seventy years that this type of rewiring, called neuroplasticity, is possible. In a 1949 book, Donald O. Hebb presented what has come to be known as Hebb's principle: "Neurons that fire together, wire together." As the neural networks in our brains become more efficient at reading and writing, we can devote more of our mental energy to making meaning. That is to say, practice makes perfect. Or, at least, it encourages excellence.

. . .

The collective human species has been creating visual art for more than three hundred thousand years, but we've probably been talking for longer than that—perhaps much longer. Surprisingly, we don't know when humans, or our prehuman ancestors, developed complex language. It might have been a quarter million years ago, or it might have been five million years ago. Just as cupules, our oldest surviving visual art, likely began as a performance, as a collective effort, so did our oldest literary arts: poetry and story. We humans are, fundamentally, a species that exists in community. Art was in service to community. As Dissanayake explains:

> Until less than a hundred years ago, the primary tasks of artists were not to "create works of art" but to reveal or embody the divine, illustrate holy writ, decorate shrines and private homes and public buildings, fashion fine utensils and elaborate ornaments, accompany ceremonial observances, record historic scenes and personages, and so forth. The artist . . . made these things "special."

Through the vast majority of human history, all over the world, those rituals that artists made possible, that they made special, marked moments of change and stress: the beginnings and endings of lives and of relationships, political upheaval, war, pandemic. Artists still play essential roles in those moments, even if many of us have turned away from ritual. As James Baldwin wrote in his 1962 essay "The Creative Process," "The states of birth, suffering, love, and death are extreme states—extreme, universal, inescapable. We all know this, but we would rather not know it. The artist is present to correct the delusions to which we fall prey in our attempts to avoid this knowledge."

We are here, as writers, to accompany our fellow human beings through extreme states. We don't necessarily need to be original, or beautiful, or entertaining, or educational. We need only make it special.

—2020

Radical Surprise

The Subversive Art of the Uncertain

Barrie Jean Borich

—ᴖ—

Without Change, the Essay Disintegrates

I once had a lover who asked everyone she met a standard question. "Tell me," she said, "about a time you were shocked." This lover and I, we were young and had so many conflicts and differences we were unwilling to negotiate. We didn't last very long. Still, I loved a few things about her. I loved that she painted every weekend in a small drafty room in the attic of her apartment building. She worshipped the painter David Hockney's work and borrowed from his color palette, so her paintings exposed a bright side of her she hardly ever let me see. She also listened to classic Frank Sinatra albums on vinyl—while she painted? I don't remember, but I love the idea of old Frank crooning in the background while she worked. His songs were sexy, she told me. This was the early CD era, before vinyl became cool again, and she was the first person I'd met who collected old records. Her collections seemed then just charmingly weird.

I also loved that she pointed out images to me on posters or in advertisements, the occasional woman holding an odd pose—one hand holding back her messy hair or squinting crookedly when she smiled—that she said reminded her of me. I was happily surprised then to think of my queer self as present in the world beyond my singular body, as an amplified type. But mostly what I loved was her question about shock, and not because of what I said in response. This was more than three decades ago and I don't remember my response, though I do remember how she lingered on the word—SHOCKED—holding the hard *k* in the back of her mouth for an instant, as if she might swallow before she got to the thud of the final *d*. I had not expected the question, and that surprise vibrated in my chest, leading me to think about myself in new ways. What shocks me? What kinds of things did I find shocking?

As writers, and as humans, how do we keep thinking about ourselves and our environments in new ways? When I suggest that the art of essaying requires an embrace of surprise, I am suggesting that the essay is always, in some way, about change. Seeing our work, and our worlds, from new vantage points is the single most important element of intentional progression and of writing the essay. Without change the essay disintegrates, like an old building falling away from its foundation. Change itself is no less precarious, but there is a difference between creative change that comes of action and breaking change that comes of neglect.

• • •

To Leave, to Leap, to Ballet, to Bumble

We see it all the time. Politicians who deliberate on all sides of the big questions are seen as weak—thinkers instead of actors (as if *to think* were not a verb)—and are often accused of waffling. But for essayists the notion that deliberation is a problem is laughable, if by waffling we mean considering one side, then another. The verb *to waffle* does not, in fact, describe the central quest of the writer, nor the critically thinking politician. What *waffle* actually means—aside from breakfast—is "to move in a side-to-side motion," or "to speak vaguely or evasively," or "to go on and on without clear point or aim." Few literary artists worth their salt are vague, but some, particularly the sort who write in parallel or braided forms, do move from side to side.

The best essayists execute those moves with balletic prowess, leaping from one subject to another, leaving behind them a streak of light or fading shimmer of sound, connecting disparate thoughts, breaking indirectly into some kind of new awareness, but then questioning what they find there. The essayer does not so much waffle as baffle. From that confused wonderment emerges surprise.

Surprise itself is not remarkable. Surprise happens. We can't fully plan for surprise, which is what is so . . . surprising. We can, however, expect surprise, desire surprise, make the invitation to ecstatic bewilderment an operative in our process. We train as writers in order to know what to do when surprise barges in.

• • •

Surprise Waits on the Other Side of Discomfort

In one of her many essays about Detroit, Aisha Sabatini Sloan invites surprise by going on a ridealong with her police officer cousin. Sabatini Sloan is a theory-trained artist and her cousin is a career cop. The writer is Black and Italian, and her cousin is from the white side of the family. They both crossed many lines in this endeavor. In doing so, the author has to wrangle with the uncertain:

> There is an implicit understanding among people who love Detroit that you shouldn't talk shit. And I love Detroit more than I do most places in the world. A sense of possibility and kindness emanates from all that chaos in a way that's hard to explain. But censoring trouble doesn't make it go away. James Baldwin and the Buddhists have long argued that healing results only from staring struggle straight in the face. The late philosopher and activist Grace Lee Boggs spoke of Detroit as a kind of ground zero upon which to visualize a new order. So here goes.

I quote this passage from an essay entitled "D Is for the Dance of Hours" from Sabatini Sloan's book *Dreaming of Ramadi in Detroit*, where the author has set the uncertain on the table. I want to write about this beloved place, she tells us, but in doing so I have to show you some things that might not lead you to love the place, too. She wants to protect her dear place from the possibility of our disaffection, or even worse, our fear and hatred. And yet she knows she won't be able to come to anything new without taking us through. Her love is deepened and complicated by the potential of our hate. She is uncertain of the outcomes here. She can't control what will happen if she lets us see her city through all her own complications, but none of us will "visualize a new order" without moving through.

Sabatini Sloan's essay goes on to take account of the city through the view of her cousin's squad car, responding to all manner of surprise, the ride giving her the "not-me" view of her beloved city, versions she could not have conjured without movement in and out of other people's stories. She also braids the city stories with a thread that has to do with music, but not with the famous Motown voices. The music that holds her city together is classical symphony and opera. She uses opera to tell a part of her father's story as well as to resee her family city in terms of something contrary to the canned Detroit narrative, the story she hopes her essay will refute. She uses symphonic music as a disjointed soundtrack. "On a prolonged summer visit to Detroit three years ago," she writes, "I would play classical music in the car while running errands. Each time I turned on the stereo, the world seemed to click—to become suddenly whole."

The description that follows illuminates the common and amplifies the shifting tones of living in this place, this moment:

Colors pair best with their opposites: turquoise and vermillion, blood red and new-growth green. In this way, the east side of Detroit is complemented by music that comes from worlds away: Burned wood and the entrance of the conductor. Overgrown grass and the sweep of a violin bow. A baby carriage tipped over in an abandoned lot and the hush that comes between a song's end and the applause.

When she rescored the space of her exploration, Sabatini Sloan's story changed. In order to write about *her* east side of Detroit, Sabatini Sloan had to actively inhabit the actual character space of her exploration. She had to surprise herself with the tension and discomfort of re-witnessing the sensate terrain she already knew well. She had to act in order to understand, but the consequences of action are always uncertain.

• • •

Surprise Confounds What We See

I'm interested in the disjunction between what *was* and what *is* in those aftershock times, when what we once perceived is no longer perceivable. What we discern after replaces what came before. In the disjunction between what *was* and what *is* we come to new ideas.

What I am thinking about here are hurricanes, the new kind that have become so common since the planet's climate began collapsing.

My mother didn't leave in October 2019 when Hurricane Michael descended on her retirement home in Panama City Beach, Florida. When I called from 1,000 miles away in Chicago to tell her I'd heard evacuation was mandatory, she just laughed. Where would she go, 85 years old and on her own, just six months a widow, with her bad knees and her rambunctious dog and her ailing cat and two turtles who needed lettuce and fresh bathing water every day. Leaving a small city that's a day's drive from any place that could take her (and her entourage) in would have been nearly impossible, even if the roads had not been jammed. I don't blame her for staying. I don't even blame her for thinking it would not be so bad, just another storm, not much worse than all the other storms. Denial is a common form of shelter.

The surprise was, first of all, that the storm was so bad. Though she was okay and did not lose her home, the storm really did wipe out a whole waterfront town just up the beach from her. It really did crack half the trees up from their roots, knock out all the power and phone lines for weeks, break open roofs, turn swimming pool water black, gut the high school, and send countless people who used to have homes to live in tent cities that had to keep moving when the institutional city shut them down. All this in a Panhandle county of Florida where the hurricanes were not supposed to be this bad. They quickly became a county of people who would never again have to pause when they were asked to remember a time they were shocked.

The easiest part of this account for me to write is this: Dear Climate Change Deniers in Florida, look at this photograph of the beachfront town that's been wiped away. Look at that one blue house still standing, the only one built by someone who believed—and could afford—to build his home according to what the scientists have been saying, that yes, the oceans are warming and the waters are rising and the storms are getting much, much worse. Isn't this shock enough to change your mind?

And this is where you think this essay is going, right? Into a straightforward cause-and-effect climate change action argument? Such would be something I support, but this desire of mine to just make a statement is too simple, not radical surprise, and more appropriate to a bullheaded politician beloved for their resolve than for the essayer in the mix, the one who waves away certitude, the one who waffles from side to side to better see the full view. I am swarmed by the uncertain as I push ahead deeper into this hurricane demolition. I am certain there is something here that has to do with the essay, but I am uncertain of how I will translate my instinct into language. My pull toward this event has something to do with an uncovering I fear may be too soft for the open air.

What really surprised me about Hurricane Michael was not the hard evidence of climate change getting worse, but something more difficult for me to understand. The prelude to my surprise was not being able to get a hold of my mother for a week after the storm hit, because all the communications were down, so I had to depend on thirdhand accounts—a sideways stream from my aunt to my cousin through my mother's neighbor's rogue working cell phone, or through a stranger on social media who I saw was a Facebook friend of my mother's. It was news reports of catastrophe writ large, filling my television screen, where squinting I tried to figure out which landscapes were the ones I knew from visiting my parents' and grandmother's retirement town for the past twenty-five years. It was internet mapping tools that hovered over the smashed-up landscape, looking to confirm that my mother's house was okay and still providing a roof over her head. The prelude was that dissolving feeling I finally understood to be fear.

But I didn't see the real story until visiting my mother eight weeks after the storm. The debris. The ongoingness of cleanup. The sodden sofas and broken trees and mounds and mounds of garbage, and everywhere the taut, blue tarps bandaging roof after roof, the repetition that might have looked like a design motif if it weren't for all the broken fences, boarded windows, and one eerie couch, muddy and abandoned, alone in an open field I'd never seen before, because there had always been a privacy fence blocking my view.

· · ·

Surprise Releases Hidden Layers

The real story is the tale that's hardly ever told, the narrative that admits all the ways a writer's presence impacts the telling, especially when we are writing about other people's trauma and broken things.

In her book-length essay-reportage hybrid *The Broken Country*, Paisley Rekdal begins by looking at a wreck of images, a collage that presents itself to her in the form of a sculpture she can't get away from while she is writing in Hanoi, on leave from her university teaching job. The sculpture is a found-object monument to Vietnamese victories in what they call there "the American War." The monument was made of fragments of actual warplanes, material pieces of the war itself, fused into a disconcerting assemblage with the image of a teenage female Vietcong fighter at the top. Rekdal becomes obsessed with this image of war and its aftermath, but she's uncertain as to why. She writes:

> I looked at this sculpture and saw inside its metal parts shapes that, rather like the emotions the work inspired, appeared to morph into strange new images emanating from the sheer enormity of the metal sculpture, menacing its spectators, radiating out through history. I saw some part of my father there, my uncle. I stood before the monument horrified, saddened, enraged.

Rekdal ends up merging her preoccupation with this sculpture into another story, one about an incident of random knife violence in the Utah city where she usually lived and worked. One of the victims was a student in the program where she taught. The man wielding the knife yelled, "Why did you kill my people?" as he stabbed men in a shopping center parking lot; he was a homeless drug addict and a postwar refugee born in Vietnam three years after the fall of Saigon. Rekdal's book is a reverberation between the sculptural welding of war-weapon relics, her memories of her uncle's experiences as a Chinese American soldier on the American side of the same war, and her questions about the inheritance of trauma across generations and emigrations, in this case coming to roost as random violence in an American shopping mall parking lot.

The surprise in this work is not what Rekdal discovers directly by interviewing victims, community members, other postwar refugees, and trauma experts, though every interview adds to her own fused monument. The surprise is in where her reporting takes her, to a point where the questions of her story and her questions to herself become the same questions:

> To narrativize a trauma like war, or domestic violence, or a stabbing, which feels enormous, would be to turn it into something shaped and static: a slab of stone, a poem, a wrapped package. This is the paradox of writing about or even recounting trauma: the conventions you use to express experience may make these same experiences less actually palpable.

Her surprise was how deeply her uncovering led her into the ineffability of trauma and the dangers of retelling that story we want to find, rather than the uncertain layers of what makes up any life, any act, any interpretation.

• • •

Disorder Makes Room for Possibility

The uncertain is an operative concept in the creation of the essay, particularly the long-form essay—the kind of work that becomes the novella-length book that is not a collection of stories or poems, but rather the long-exhaled experience of the uncertain. Catherine Taylor's *You, Me, and the Violence* is this kind of project. Taylor's uncertainty is based in a question: What does one do with an antimilitaristic point of view when a beloved brother is an air force pilot engaged in drone warfare?

She investigates her questions through a braid that includes transcripts of the audio communications of a US drone attack, interviews with her brother, and extended contemplations of the diverse artistic practice and social impact of puppetry—all to try to get at what she calls "murky questions for the ethics of domination." Her brother's arguments that drones are not a particular evil, but merely the manifestation of all warfare and American foreign policy, are sound enough to surprise even the essayist, sending her back to reframe her own pacifist-unless-absolutely-necessary stance. She lands on an ethos that the post-hippie activists of Bread and Puppet Theater call "possibilitarian," a term that when coined by Norman Vincent Peale was a facile framework for positive thinking, but in the realm of theaters such as Bread and Puppet is a profoundly activist, and cheerful, mode of disorderly performance.

Taylor is at first reluctant to get too close to the blatantly agitprop theater of Bread and Puppet. Her critical skepticism made me laugh out loud a few times as she crept in closer. I wrote in the margins "Why is she embarrassed to love the puppets?" and "haha, so she is a hippy, too." Puppets embody a collective and sweetly radical joy. Why do thinking people want to keep an arm's distance away from joy? I, too, struggle to write about loving things I can't defend loving, making the mistake of putting structure before discovery, putting certitude before love—but puppets, as Taylor describes, have a way of breaking through defenses.

Taylor writes this about being drawn to Bread and Puppet:

> So much of my research has turned me toward their work, but I hesitate a long time before driving up to Vermont's Northeast Kingdom to visit them. I'm ambivalent; they are so old school. I find myself resisting their '70s hippie spectacle aesthetic and what I imagine will be a less than complex set of positions, and I find myself wishing they worked with a more contemporary medium and vocabulary. But they are so openly dedicated to anti-capitalism, and this radicalism appeals, so I feel compelled to take a look.

Bread and Puppet's possibilitarian stance is infectious, in part because the puppet-politics version of imagining hope takes what it wants and leaves the rest from traditional folk narratives, so it has the power to be at once familiar and a remaking. Their performance of possibility is a chosen-family affair, the human longing for community the source of their power. Taylor goes on:

> I go back to Bread and Puppet several times. I take my children because I want to encourage their own possibilitarian impulses, because this is what I love about them, because this is what I'm longing for, and because of the high clouds and the sweet fierce people there. One day, watching the puppeteers parade by on stilts waving little wooden fighter jets and paper daffodils in the air, I find myself raising an eyebrow once again at their old-school stylings. I'm a little embarrassed to be here, but also deeply happy and at home. It's a fucked-up feeling, but nice in the way it keeps me close to contradiction, the only truth I think I can know.

In this passage Taylor knows she can't and won't find solutions, but she needs a new idea, a renewed way of seeing the problem. The turning point of the book occurs when she is at once deflated and surprised by the uncertain truth of contradiction:

> Something shifts and my belief that violence is sometimes necessary seems at least arguable. Suddenly, accepting both my brother's position, that there will always be violence and war, while also accepting the utopian vision of pacifism, that this can be changed, feels like a contradiction that is necessary. It seems at least possible to imagine a world where war, like slavery, is not so easily accepted. Yes, I know, slavery persists and erupts, but it is no longer thought to be either necessary or inevitable and, suddenly, I can imagine this for war. Wildly utopian, yes, but I lunge at this thought.

What strikes me about this passage, along with the progression of her thinking, is that she is willing, as Aisha Sabatini Sloan and Paisley Rekdal are willing, to be uncomfortable in the disorderly essayistic space of the uncertain, and she is willing to admit to discomfort. Admitting discomfort flies in the face of professorial-driven knowledge. Admitting discomfort lets in the possibility that others understand better than you. Admitting discomfort makes room for change.

• • •

We Write to Make Out the Bones and Wounded Places

My own radical surprise after Hurricane Michael was in part the helpless experience of watching from afar when you have someone, a mother, caught in a catastrophe zone. But the real transforming surprise was my gut-wrenching realization that a place I knew as one thing could so quickly become another thing entirely.

You might think from what I am saying here that I was shocked by the hurricane because this beach city is beloved to me. Who would not feel devastated by the destruction of the place they loved? But that's the thing: I do not love this place. I love the beach. I always love the beach. But otherwise I have mostly disliked, sometimes hated, and usually resented this place where my mother lived that had never been my home. I resented that my father left his dear Chicago to live in this not-Chicago place. I was repulsed by all the Tea Party right-wingers my Dad—always an old Chicago Democrat—enjoyed arguing with at his gym and jazz festivals, and I felt betrayed by his friendships with these guys, especially after they all became Trumpians, because their political beliefs disrespected both my queer life and my belief in progressive justice movements. I saw no beauty in the golf courses where both my parents played until their knees gave out, and I resented the perfect round corners of the streets all named after fish where my grandmother, the first in our family to leave Chicago for Florida, took her walks, even into her dementia, when she forgot where she was going and had to be escorted home by neighbors she no longer knew.

I resented how the certainty of my southside-Chicago-brownstone-bungalow, lower-middle-class-rooted, blue-state, urban-queer, tattooed-artist, espresso-dependent identity was confused by first my grandmother and then my cousin and parents relocating to this pastel-toned, politically conservative corner of Florida. I particularly resented, on the day I was trying to get to the church for my father's funeral, the man in the over-sized SUV who rolled down his window to give me the finger when I tapped my horn at him. He had cut me off at the traffic circle, the urn with my dad's ashes teetering between my spouse's feet when I slammed on the brakes. In that moment, the man in the flat-faced monster truck became all the biggest-car-wins-shit I resented about this place, and about this country, ever since the 2016 presidential election. My resentment of SUV Man palpitated—whoever he was, whoever either of us were in the sharp July 98-degree heat, a few months before the hurricane would knock all this down. But mostly, I resented my mother for making my father move to Florida when he, I'd long believed, always wanted to stay in Chicago.

When I got down to see Mom after the hurricane, where she was alone and wearied by the mess, she told me something that shocked me. It turns out she was the one who had always hated Florida. She said my father—the father in whose honor, in part, I'd moved back to Chicago after years of making queer family in another city—had been the one who pushed them to move to Florida. He liked the long, hot days, the overdeveloped yet still half-wild waterfront, the long sailboating season, the golf cart in the garage, even his endless arguments with his political foils. Mom said she was the one who would rather have lived in a condo in Chicago like me, like how I live now.

My second shock when arriving in Panama City a few weeks after the storm was the impact of all the wreckage. My response was strange and unfamiliar, as if I had wandered into a conservative, queer-hating crowd of people who believed nothing that I believed, but whose clothing had been unceremoniously ripped off by the storm. I could make out their bones and wounded places. I could see that their clothing was not their bodies. I could see their vulnerability, and in seeing them this way, I had trouble only resenting them. I could even see why my father had been willing, just person-to-person, to be their neighbors, and then I had to love them a little no matter what they thought of me and the way I live, no matter that they would not want my love, no matter that I didn't want their love, no matter what they would say if I asked them what they believed was the reason the wind blew so hard that year.

The uncertain wandering of writing an essay led me to this perplexing feeling of critical compassion. Essaying gave me a new shock to mix into the bitterness I have not been eager to relinquish, am still not sure I can relinquish. But now the possibility of relinquishment, a shift away from resentment, seems more radical than my usual refusal.

• • •

In the Essay's Relinquishment Comes the Shock of Another Life

Certainty is arrogance, and arrogance is unbecoming to the literary page, as well as at parties, meetings, and when cutting off other drivers at the traffic circle. Certainty has its place; of course we want pilots, surgeons, and bridge builders to be certain of their skills. But the uncertain is the only pathway to dismantling infrastructures that prop up oppressive hierarchy and open new routes to change. Dismantling certainty is precisely what it means to essay. It's what the form is for. The essayistic uncertain is subversive because it invites necessary vulnerability, and fear, and through those portals might also come a perplexing and necessary compassion.

Compassion is what led Sloan to ride around in her cousin's police car, and when, in a later essay in the same book, that compassion is coupled with her viewing of Eric Garner's murder by police, her compassion amplifies into the wordless anguish that carries her essaying further still. Rekdal writes of becoming immobilized by compassionate witness of the subjects she interviewed. Taylor works to listen to a brother she is afraid of losing either to their disagreement or to the military violence they attempt to discuss. I am uncertain of what we need to invent next to make a more compassionate place for us all to reside, but my longing for that compassion is part of why I write.

• • •

The Vulnerable Is an Entryway for Wonder

How does one end an essay on the uncertain? We certainly can't end with the certain. So then, what do I leave us with? Perhaps an instruction to turn over a favorite idea and look at it again from the rearview forward, then let that backward thought onto the page? Perhaps I will implore myself—the next time I'm sure I have something important to say in an essay—to back away, to listen, rather than insist? Perhaps, when listening, we can all let the silence lead us back to that memory or image or fragment of information or sodden couch alone in the mud between all the fallen fences that most confounds or frustrates or exposes us, and perhaps we can start trying to relinquish all that keeps the surprise from getting in past our gates, as that's likely to be where the next essay begins.

—2019

On Imagistic Endurance

Jenny Johnson

—ɯ—

Let's begin with a poem that invites us to look closely, by Kamilah Aisha Moon:

The First Time I Saw My Mother without Her Prosthesis

after Hafizah Geter

Like the smooth face of the cliff
she was just thrown from, the left
side of her chest was flat
and blank, save for two tiny
raised scythes. Not a half-carved
turkey, thankless,
but a woman.

It almost seemed as if her breast
could be drawn back on again,
as if the scalpel was merely
erasing cancer, as if the right one
hanging like a luminous brown
tear wasn't the lonely twin.
As if this new lightness
didn't threaten to render her
a widow of his touch,
de-mother her somehow.

Is this a crystal ball moment—
the fanged, wily shadow
never outrun or outwitted?

——

Do you want to see, baby?

I couldn't say no—her love
never flinched, neither would I.

We know from the title that this is a poem about an intimate moment where a speaker sees their mother for the first time after her body has changed. In terms of structure, the poem could have opened with the mother's invitation to gaze: "Do you want to see, baby?" And the speaker's reflective response: "I couldn't say no—" Instead, Moon drops us into description.

As a result, this poem requires imagistic stamina on the part of the writer to sustain and the reader to behold. In the first stanza, we see the left side of the mother's chest, where the breast has been removed. When the space on the chest is figuratively compared to "the smooth face of the cliff / she was just thrown from," we sense the trauma of the surgery. The lens magnifies when we see "the two tiny raised scythes," the scars left from a mastectomy. Next, we see the mother's subjectivity; she is "not a half-carved turkey" but "a woman." You might wonder: What makes a poem's gaze dynamic vs. static or loving vs. voyeuristic? It's moments like this one—when we're made fully aware of the person we are glimpsing, who is so much more than a body with or without a part.

Moon could have let the speaker's gaze shift after the first stanza, but in stanza two, she continues: "It almost seemed as if her breast / could be drawn back on again." Through a series of "as if" statements, we're invited to picture a present that's wished for. We're held in a subjunctive space, where the scalpel could erase cancer, where the right breast isn't a lonely twin, and where the mastectomy does not threaten to complicate touch between the speaker's mother and her father, to "de-mother her," to diminish her mother's sense of self. In this stanza, the speaker manages to hold the gaze on her mother, while also holding the gaze on her mother's fears. Fear finds its way into the third stanza, too, when the shadow on the chest suggests a "crystal ball moment," summoning anxieties about what the future might hold if cancer continues to threaten her mother's life, if the shadow can't be "outrun or outwitted."

In *What I Talk about When I Talk about Running*, Haruki Murakami asks of himself as a marathon runner and as a writer, "How much can I push myself? How much rest is appropriate—and how much is too much?" On the crafting of images, I invite you to ask similar questions of stamina: What is your relationship to looking? What are your strategies for conveying what you see or imagine through language? How long do you hold the gaze in your work? And what might happen if you held it longer, if you kept looking, if you refused to look away?

It's my intention not to suggest that you should never look away when you're afraid, never flinch when confronting and describing complexity, but rather to notice when you do and to ask yourself what might happen if you stayed with your subject. As a part of this inquiry, you will have to consider the kinds of attention your specific subject calls for. In Moon's poem, in which loving the mother and seeing the mother are synonymous acts, imagistic endurance is key.

As a writer and as an occasional runner, I think of endurance as something that is hard to build, but can be strengthened with practice. Often when I feel stuck, I'll lace up my running shoes and I'll jog a familiar loop on a trail near my house. As I climb the often boring, always painful final incline, I tell myself that whatever it's going to take within me to get to the top of this hill is what I'm going to also need to finish my poem. This analogy feels useful because the work we do as writers is both psychically and physically demanding. Here's Murakami again talking about the act of writing:

> The whole process—sitting at your desk, focusing your mind like a laser beam, imagining something on a blank horizon, creating a story, selecting the right words, one by one, keeping the whole flow of story on track—requires far more energy, over a long period, than most people ever imagine. You might not move your body around, but there's grueling, dynamic labor going on inside you.

In fact, there are many elusive processes going on inside us when we sit down to write. For every aspect of craft, a different muscle group works invisibly within us. For example, there is the work of form, of structure, of diction, of sound, of rhythm, of syntax, etc.

Here we will focus primarily on the work of image making, which we can define as the act of attempting to describe a subject to a reader, using our senses. We will consider some methods for perceiving the world and then finding the words—methods to help you sustain your writerly gaze on a subject when you are stuck, lost, or simply unsure if you have the energy to persist.

• • •

Seeing Mosses

In her book *Gathering Moss: A Natural and Cultural History of Mosses*, Robin Wall Kimmerer, plant ecologist and nature writer, offers many useful tips for seeing mosses, which we might apply as writers attempting to see our own subjects more clearly.

Because moss is so small and thus seemingly difficult for humans to observe without magnification, Kimmerer begins with a consideration of human vision. She describes the scale of our seeing as middle scale, which is the eye's ability to see without the aid of any sort of technology—a microscope, satellite, or digital camera. The first tip from Kimmerer that applies to seeing just about anything you're trying to describe is this: "Attentiveness alone can rival the most powerful magnifying lens."

Another tip Kimmerer offers is to "watch out of the corner of your eye, open to possibility." I'll give an example. Because I am an amateur gardener, this summer I noticed that something was eating my broccoli and leaving small holes in the leaves, but I had no clue what it could be. An initial glance in the morning turned up no obvious leaf eaters. Persistent, I returned around lunchtime, newly committed, down on my knees, scanning the veins at the back of each punctured leaf. Finally, I saw the culprit, a very memorable green worm with zebralike stripes crisscrossing down its back—what a Google search affirmed to be a cross-striped cabbageworm. Shockingly, once I spotted one, I spotted another and another. How was it possible that I had overlooked such distinctive larvae? One of the worms was nearly the length of my pinkie finger!

Perhaps you have had a moment of perception like this one, too, where seemingly by accident something invisible to you became visible. Can you train yourself to see better or differently? Yes. Often what we observe is based on our abilities to recognize patterns in our environments. If you take the time to notice a new pattern, you're likely to see one again and again. It turns out that there's a phrase to describe how this happens cognitively. Kimmerer explains, "The sensation of sudden visual awareness is produced in part by the formation of a 'search image' in the brain."

We form search images all the time. Here's another example. A few summers ago, I was painting a room in my house with the help of a friend, who has painted houses professionally. After we finished rolling a few coats on the ceiling, feeling satisfied with our work, I began to celebrate being done; I was ready for dinner.

But then Pino stopped me to say, "Hmm . . . it looks like we've got some holidays."

"Holidays?" I said. "What do you mean?"

Pino explained, "When painters miss a spot because they've drifted off, they call the missed spot a 'holiday.'"

"Where?" I protested, certain we'd done an excellent job.

But then I looked up and saw what I could only wish was an array of shadows cast by the dwindling sun and not an array of faded spots, patches where the roller had obviously skipped. Pino saw these spots that I overlooked immediately, because she had already formed a "search image" for it in her brain, an image that allowed her brain to notice a pattern of spots on the ceiling instantaneously. If one of the ways we read our world is based on pattern recognition, then it's important to consider the patterns that are most legible to us when we describe. But it's also crucial that we consider what skips our attention—that we notice our holidays.

That's not quite right. Since this is a talk about imagery and it's important to admit when my own metaphors fail, lack equivalence, or have their limits, I want to self-correct to say that "holidays" is too gentle of a term to use for all that skips one's attention. The process of categorizing what we see *can* activate valuable habits of attention, just as it *can* activate reductive, clichéd, and uniformed habits, too, of objectification, bias, and stereotyping. Quite often what I miss is the result of my subject position within a given context.

I'll share one more story: Just this week another friend shared something that happened when she went running on a familiar trail in the park. Near a spot where trail traffic bottlenecks at the base of a hill, she heard a mountain biker pedaling behind her. Without seeing the biker, instinctually she stopped and stepped aside to let the biker pass, but as she stepped aside, she heard the biker simultaneously pulling over, too. She wasn't sure why—until a split second later, when a second biker came toward them both on the trail at full speed and then barreled past undeterred, without noticing that two people, a runner and a biker, had come to a full stop to make room.

My friend wanted me to know that she had sensed, before she turned to see the stranger's face, that the biker who'd pulled off behind her was likely a woman. She was right. Meanwhile, she also recognized that the biker who zipped past was a man. This brief interlude made her mad, because as she'll readily admit, trail courtesy is very important to her. But it also made her angry, because of its predictability, because of how familiar she is with this gendered pattern of negotiating space, often with men who are usually straight and cisgendered, who—while their intentions may be good—simply aren't paying attention to how much space they're afforded daily. She said to me, "It was all so fluid; he didn't even have to pause to notice how he was moving." Then we talked about privilege more generally, something we both also know we have in various contexts, and how one of the features of being in a privileged position is that you don't have to spend as much time noticing the choices you're making.

I've shared some moments of pattern recognition, and I'm going to guess that as I've been talking you've been free-associating, too, thinking about your own experiences. Here are some prompts to get you to think further about your own habits of attention—your strengths and maybe also your weaknesses:

- Describe a moment when something that had been invisible to you suddenly became visible.
- If one of the ways our brain processes what we see is based on pattern recognition, what is a pattern that is legible to you? What is something that you are uniquely attuned to when you scan the world around you?

I want to share one more tip I learned from Kimmerer. She writes, "Finding the words is another step in learning to see." As a bryologist (one who studies mosses), Kimmerer values the precision of scientific language. When distinguishing between leaves, for example, she might use words such as *dentate* (for large, coarse teeth) or *serrate* (for a saw-blade edge). But she also acknowledges the power of other kinds of diction, too. She writes:

> When I encounter a new moss species and have yet to associate it with its official name, I give it a name which makes sense to me: green velvet, curly top, or red stem. The word is immaterial. What seems to me to be important is recognizing them, acknowledging their individuality. In indigenous ways of knowing, all beings are recognized as non-human persons, and all have their own names.

When attempting to describe a subject that one is uncertain about, some writers are quick to turn away from such recognition to seek an imagined expert, second-guessing the seemingly obvious language of sensory description, of "green velvet" and "curly top." Inhibitions can kick in that say you're not enough of an authority to accurately name your world with your senses alone. Here I am not suggesting that we shouldn't consult sources as we write. Rather, there are many forms of knowledge, and your five senses are a very valid form of wisdom. One of the things that I value about Robin Wall Kimmerer's writing is that while reading her, I am acutely aware that I am learning about mosses from someone who comes to it from many layers of experience: as a mother, a scientist, a professor, a writer, and an enrolled member of the Citizen Potawatomi Nation. She teaches readers how to better see the natural world through all these frames of knowing, and she affirms in her own storytelling and word choice that many kinds of insights matter.

Ultimately, Kimmerer is an advocate of intimacy, of building relationships with all beings and all subjects through deeper recognition. As writers, you will describe your subjects more dynamically if you attend closely, if you watch out of the corner of your eye, if you grow to recognize that which had been invisible, and if you use your many ways of seeing and knowing to name. "Intimacy," Kimmerer says, "gives us a different way of seeing when visual acuity is not enough."

• • •

Seeing the Canyon

I first came to Jean Garrigue's "The Grand Canyon" via poet Carl Phillips. Phillips briefly discusses this poem in *The Art of Daring*, declaring that it is "one of the most daring poems ever." For Phillips, the poem is daring in large part because of its syntax—it's only four sentences long. The poem is composed of a one-line question, a nine-line sentence, a half-line question, and a 109-line sentence. These choices are memorable, but I am also struck by the poem's imagistic stamina laid bare in the final cinematic sentence, one which attempts to describe the canyon. From this opening excerpt, you should be able to begin to get a sense of the poem's syntax as well as its imagistic scope.

The Grand Canyon

Where is the restaurant cat?
I am lonely under the fluorescent light
as a cook waddles in her smoky region visible through an open arch
and someone is pounding, pounding
whatever it is that is being pounded
and a waitress cracks with the cowboys lined up at the counter
lumberjacked, weathered and bony
intimates, I would guess, of the Canyon,
like the raven that flies, scouting above it,
of the hooked and the almost flat sleek wings.

Where is my cat? I am lonely,
knocked out, stunned-sleepy,
knocked out by the terraced massed faces
of the brute Sublime,

color inflamed,
when I came to the edge and looked over:
violaceous, vermilion
great frontal reefs, buttes
cliffs of rufous and ocher angles,
promontories, projections, jutments, outjuttings
and gnarled mirlitons, so it seemed,
twisting up out of depth beyond depth
gnarled like a juniper tree
rachitic [ruh-kite-ic] with wind I hung on to
as the raven's wing, glassy in the light of its black,
slid over me

there at the edge of this maw, gash
deepest in the world that a river has made
through an upwarp in the earth's crust,
thickets of tens of thousands of gorges eaten out
by freezing and thawing, tempests, waterspouts,
squalls and falls of the river
with its boulders, pebbles, silt and sand sawing down
through the great cake of geologic time,
eight layers laid bare,
the total effect creating what geometrical effect
in a rocky silence so clear
a bird's voice, even a boy's
is sponged out, sucked up by this stillness
stinging, overpowering the ear,
pure condition of the original echoing soundlessness
this voluminous wrung resonance
welling up out of the handiwork
of the demiurge wrestling down there
in an infinity of imperceptible events
some ten million years,

Unexpectedly, this poem begins inside a restaurant. The speaker, if we follow their gaze, is looking for a cat. Remember Kimmerer's word for the
scale of basic human vision? *Middle scale.* The speaker is in a restaurant,
seeing at middle scale. The speaker's present-tense declaration, "I am
lonely," seems unremarkable the first time it's said. But when it's repeated
and the very long sentence starts to unravel, we begin to understand that
a very grand loneliness has been stirred by the Grand Canyon. A kind of

loneliness that isn't easily summarized in a quick sentence. A kind of loneliness that comes from feeling very small and insignificant in the grand scheme of time and space.

Though we see at middle scale as humans, as writers we can craft images that do otherwise; we can accomplish some rather remarkable camera work. Garrigue's establishing shot takes place at the canyon's edge. The speaker comes to the edge to look over and we get their first take, first moment of awe, capturing the canyon's purplish red, "violaceous, vermilion," as well as an initial sense of the canyon's "gnarled" texture and its inexplicability, "twisting up out of depth beyond depth." We also are made aware of the speaker's position within this scene—that its windy, that they're hanging onto a juniper tree, that a raven is flying just above. Keep in mind that this is the last time the "I" in this poem is mentioned.

Next stanza, next shot. We were already looking down, but here we have a more intense high-angle shot. Now we're more fully witnessing the canyon's depth, a depth that Garrigue compares to a "maw," the throat of a hungry animal. She also likens the canyon's open mouth to a "gash deepest in the world that a river has made." Notice that in this stanza we're also seeing so far down within the canyon that, as if in high definition, we can picture such figurative details as the "thickets of tens of thousands of gorges eaten out."

And then, within the same stanza, Garrigue makes us conscious that this poem is not merely an exercise in looking, but also an opportunity to listen. This is an operatic poem, when you consider the exuberance in such alliterative phrases as "violaceous, vermilion." Here the poem's soundscape also manages to amplify the canyon's silence. The *n* or *-ing* sounds that we can hear in a word such as "sting" and then further in a phrase such as "stinging, overpowering"—this kind of consonant work is called *resonance* for its lingering or humming effects. Notice how the *n* sound vibrates, too, through a phrase such as "voluminous wrung resonance." The quality of the silence within the canyon is also captured in the long *o* sound echoing in the word "echo" as well as in many moments of sibilance, whispering through words such as "stillness" and "soundlessness."

In *The Art of Description*, Mark Doty says that "looking and looking causes time to open; sustained attention allows us to tumble right out of progression." Likewise, as this poem further unfolds, we begin to tumble out of the present and into ancient history, as the speaker compares features within the canyon to forms humans built, structures that managed to withstand time—Roman arches, Aztec temples, and Egyptian pyramids. When describing what she longed to do as a poet, Garrigue said that she hoped to make in words "signs for an impalpable imponderable that one seeks to get down before all evaporates."

Can poems withstand time? Some might. Some do. Can poems teach us to see differently and more intimately while we're here together? Absolutely. In the poem's opening stanza, Garrigue describes her fellow restaurant goers as "intimates . . . of the Canyon." By the end of Garrigue's seemingly everlasting sentence, I wonder if we aren't intimates of it now, too. By which I mean that we are closer not so much to the canyon itself as to canyon-like feelings. We are closer to knowing the shimmering and devastating sensations that the speaker describes, when facing the "brute Sublime."

• • •

Seeing the Bug

Often a speaker exposes their uncertainty through their looking, as in this poem by Tommye Blount:

The Bug

lands on my pretty man's forearm. Harmless,
it isn't deadly at all; makes his muscle flutter
— the one that gets his hand to hold mine, or
ball into a fist, or handle a gun. It's a ladybug,
or an Asian lady beetle everyone mistakes
for a ladybug — eating whatever
it lands on. My pretty man is asleep — at ease, or
plotting like the bug. Or maybe the bug
is a blowfly — eating my pretty man's tan
from his pretty arm. My man swats it
without waking, as if he's dreaming of an enemy,
or me. When my pretty man isn't asleep
he's got a temper.

No, he is not

asleep. He's wide awake and wants me to tell you
I'm wrong. Blowflies don't eat skin,
they lay eggs on skin. He knows all about
blowfly larvae. Napoleon used them
to clean war wounds, my cold pretty man

says in that pretty way,
with his cold pretty mouth. He's eaten plenty
of bugs before. On night watch,
over there. Over there, they're everywhere.

Here the gaze is held on not just a bug, but *the* bug, which has landed on the pretty man's forearm. Hence, we're attending to both the bug and the man simultaneously. The man seems to be the speaker's lover, a relationship we might read as queer, given the speaker's play with the phrase "my pretty man." Notice, too, how the speaker uses the word "or," as in the pretty man's forearm is connected to his hand, which he could use to do three different things: hold the lover's hand, or ball into a fist, or handle a gun. "Or" is a conjunction that you can use in your writing to convey a set of possible alternatives. What is striking about the use of these three images, when they are listed consecutively, is that these alternatives are not equivalent—they reveal the pretty man to be tender, but also capable of violence.

The next time we see the word "or" in this poem is when the speaker wonders if the bug is a ladybug or an Asian lady beetle, and then later if it might be a blowfly. These different interpretations of what the bug could be also conflict—some bugs are harmless and others are not. The use of "or" is engaging, too, because as the speaker wonders aloud, we're left suspended between all three possibilities. Likewise, we're suspended between the possibilities or simultaneous truths that the pretty man could be sleeping or plotting and that the pretty man could be dreaming of either an enemy or the speaker. In his essay "The Other Hand," James Longenbach offers that the word *or* can convey "the sound of thinking in poetry—not the sound of finished thought but the sound of a mind alive in the syntactical process of discovering what it might be thinking." Sometimes we don't know what we're looking at when we go to describe a thing. Sometimes a subject shape-shifts during the process. And so, holding the gaze as writers may also require holding the questions and doubts that sustained looking invites. Challenging work, indeed.

One of the most unambiguous moments in the poem is when the speaker concedes that no, the pretty man is not asleep. Then the pretty man corrects the speaker, professing with a tone of authority about blowflies. Importantly, we're catching the pretty man's perspective secondhand, his voice channeled through the speaker's. And so this, too, is a moment of interpretation, of description, made apparent when the speaker says, "my cold pretty man / says in that pretty way, / with his cold pretty mouth." In these lines, Blount again asks readers to hold both, to hold that the man is "cold" and to hold that the man is "pretty." Ultimately, the imagery in this poem resonates because more questions have been raised than resolved. We are moved and haunted by this scene because of all the possibilities and consequences that are suggested—most distressingly, the pretty man's capacity to do harm.

There is much more we could say about this poem. But consider that when you look at something long enough, especially something you are uncertain about, it's bound to change, to morph, to no longer be what it seems. And often there's room on the page to reveal such ambiguities, reservations, and questions.

• • •

Seeing the Face

For three hours, Ruth Ozeki, novelist, filmmaker, and Zen Buddhist priest, stared at her face. Of the exercise she said, "I began to wonder what my fifty-nine-year-old face might reveal if I could bear to look at it for three hours—a painfully long time, indeed."

Ozeki had a few questions, too—koans that she was seeking in earnest to answer, such as, "What is your original face?" and "What did your face look like before your parents were born?" Her experiment led to a book, *The Face: A Time Code*, made up of both time-stamped journal entries from her extended looking session and a collection of mini memoirs further exploring what arose from her experience.

I began this inquiry by asking, What might happen if you kept looking, if you refused to look away? Here's what Ozeki says happened to her:

In the days and weeks and months that have followed, I find myself looking at people's faces more closely. There's a new subjectivity in my gaze when I look at others. Their faces mirror mine, and my face mirrors theirs, and this gives rise to a recursive kindliness and kinship that I haven't felt in quite this way before.

Looking closely can lead to new ways of understanding your subject as well as to a transformative reciprocal exchange. It can lead to the "recursive kindliness and kinship" that Ozeki describes when other people's faces mirrored hers and hers theirs.

It's an odd phenomenon, but it seems that if you look outward and inward long enough at a face, at a bug, at the clouds, at whatever astonishes you, after a while it can become less clear what's what and who is who. If you attend long enough, subjectivities can change, patterns can form and reform, temporalities can open, and new intimacies can arise. And you, the writer—though it may seem as if you're doing so little just by picturing, just by blinking, just by holding still—you are part of the scene, you're shifting, too.

—August 2, 2018

On Enchantment

Lia Purpura

—⟋⟍⟍—

This talk began in the very fertile soil of my doubts. Doubts and lostness in many directions: about how to proceed after my last book, about how and whether to proceed as a more public/advocate-type person and not "just" a writer of poems and essays, and really, about the worth and weight of what it is I do, which is *write*. The most recognizable drives of my writing life have been a belief in hard-to-pin states of being and perceptions and the search for language and form that bodies them forth, as well as faith in the conversational possibilities between objects, creatures, us. Such a belief in *likeness* mostly inclines me toward the lost, disapproved, overlooked, and ruined, though it's been a struggle of late to listen in for more than the ruin we're enduring as a country, difficult to find ways to maintain the practice of alertness in the face of precarity, and especially hard to lean on my near-physiological belief in the capacity of art to "open our contours beyond an exact present," as Lorca said. But I've been trying to keep doubt a breathing thing and to understand the many ways that, as philosopher William Irwin wrote, "doubt enlivens belief by putting it at risk and compelling it to renew itself."

Enchantment finds its roots in the Latin *in* + *cantare* (to sing into, to be endowed with magical properties). I think we're culturally okay with the singing part. It's the "magical properties" part that makes some people itchy. "Magical properties" suggests a willful animism or a worldview that belongs to a so-called primitive past or conjures "enchantment" as a Disneyfied construct—one totally drained of its anarchic and healing capacities. I actually mean to confirm all of these (except the Disney): the animism that once emplaced us and the ability to draw on ways of knowing that won't behave according to conventional sense making or discursive explaining. (As Flannery O'Connor said of the Eucharist: "If it's just a symbol to hell with it.")

But let's just jump in, read some enchanted things, and look at some enchanted gestures that make up enchanted wholes. I'll start with "The City Limits" by A.R. Ammons.

When you consider the radiance, that it does not withhold
itself but pours its abundance without selection into every
nook and cranny not overhung or hidden; when you consider

that birds' bones make no awful noise against the light but
lie low in the light as in a high testimony; when you consider
the radiance, that it will look into the guiltiest

swervings of the weaving heart and bear itself upon them,
not flinching into disguise or darkening; when you consider
the abundance of such resource as illuminates the glow-blue

bodies and gold-skeined wings of flies swarming the dumped
guts of a natural slaughter or the coil of shit and in no
way winces from its storms of generosity; when you consider

that air or vacuum, snow or shale, squid or wolf, rose or lichen,
each is accepted into as much light as it will take, then
the heart moves roomier, the man stands and looks about, the

leaf does not increase itself above the grass, and the dark
work of the deepest cells is of a tune with May bushes
and fear lit by the breadth of such calmly turns to praise.

So here we are at the outskirts, situated along an ecotone, that liminal, threshold space where worlds meet and re-form each other.
The poem is playing with a seemingly rational cause-and-effect construction, a "When/Then" journey. *When* you pay attention to the nature
of radiance and the sheer variety of bodies it touches (without ranking
their worth), *then* this alchemical, fear-to-praise turning happens. The
incantatory phrase "When you consider . . ." kicks off at the left margin
and then takes up residence at the right margin, that threshold spot in
poems where lines break, meanings multiply, surprises bloom, and the
tension between sentence and line is heightened. With the repetition of
that phrase, a density builds up by way of a cascading list of stuff. Think of
the list form here as a spell, with all the surprising ingredients spells require
(bird bones, shit, lichen, guts, and the ever-present dose of radiance,
which leavens the dross) all added in a certain order to effect a change. The
body, your reader's body, by way of the erotics of delay, can feel the accre-
tion as each clause pauses and gathers its power at the gates of those semi-

colons before combining in "as much light as they can take," nearly over-spilling and resolving, finally, in praise.

When you're able to consider (that is, "pay attention to") the radiance—its modes of loving and touching and transforming everything (by not withholding or flinching, by accepting and bestowing)—*then* the enchanted thing happens, "the heart moves roomier," and another state of being—praise, gratitude, maybe a form of ease—is possible, a form of holiness reached by the radical illuminating (democratizing, even) of base materials.

And here at the end is another angle of amazement, too: you can hear the final phrase "turns to praise" in two ways—as the *object* that fear is turned *into* and as the *activity* that fear is *turning toward*. A sort of inner and outer consciousness happen *at once*—get twined together. One of Ammons's great powers (in all his work) is this ability to conjure from a single word or phrase its multiple identities as noun, verb, and adjective, to make a word an object and an action, to have things happen from the inside and outside simultaneously. It's a way to free words from their singular meaning, or fixed root, and allow them, with their multiple faces, to speak a more whole and substantial truth. Syntax *is* the experience. Unlikely objects when partnered up in a shared context become kin. Punctuation, in the form of semicolons, delivers precise dosages of radiance. That there are multiple worlds within words is the revelation.

In a completely different mode, let's look at Lorine Niedecker's "A Monster Owl":

A monster owl
out on the fence
flew away. What
is it a sign
of? The sign of
an owl.

Here's a whittled back, austere flash of mind (and bird) in motion. The speaker moves fast from assertive interpreter (calling the owl a monster) to a more neutral observer (seeing the owl fly away). The line "flew away. What" marks a moment of shock, as in "What the hell just happened?"; it also marks the moment when the owl, though suddenly absent, comes into focus as a mysterious entity and is no longer what the speaker said it was—a monster (in either the very big or the fearsome sense). The next question, embedded in the line "of? The sign of"—presents a final insistent, stubborn, thinky moment, something like a mind saying, "Wait, it's like, it's like …" where, on the tip of the tongue, is what the speaker would like to make this thing *represent*.

Then in a final flash—I'll call it a moment of enchantment, occurring in the open space of the line break—the inquiry halts, or is halted. This creature, "an owl," is neither monster nor sign; it refuses to represent or mean, and in letting go of the drive to frame the owl on her terms, the speaker experiences the owl coming into being as *itself*. In fact, its owly move of flying off opens the speaker to its presence, which is a mystery, being now gone—one of those holy paradoxes of presence inhering in absence, of having to look away to see a thing more clearly.

And how quickly, in a short, bright burst this all happens! The speaker seems to *know*, a priori, that owls are indeed signs, in many belief systems, but *learns* that such a being won't perform its meaning in grabby or denotative circumstances—or rather, it will thwart the frames applied to it. You can feel the learning, too, in the open space at the end—that now-enchanted field where you get to stand with the speaker, reflecting on what the heck just happened. The silence after "an owl" is real and present, too. Wordlessly, that space "reads" as a place to rest, to linger with the effects of the speaker's flash of insight, that sensation of being upended as a human center.

Here's one more way of considering enchantment: I'll call it "language conjuring" in the hybrid poetic/sociological/journalistic experiment, *Let Us Now Praise Famous Men*, by James Agee (with photographer Walker Evans). In this monumental work, Agee wrangles with his ecstatic love of language and the simultaneous queasiness he feels making incursions into others' lives (both physically by his presence and with his language), and throughout, he rages against the indignity of poverty suffered by the two sharecropping families he lived with in rural Alabama in 1936. (Agee, in fact, wrote that he didn't even want to call this a *book*: "If I could do it, I'd do no writing at all here. It would be photographs, the rest would be fragments of cloth, bits of cotton, lumps of earth, records of speech, pieces of wood and iron, phials of odors, plates of food, and of excrement … a piece of the body torn out by the roots might be more to the point …")

It's the full-body contact with language I'm interested in, how a relentless cascade of newly invented language and punctuation constitutes or conjures a way of seeing and naming:

Here then he is, or here is she: here is this tender and helpless human life: subjected to its immediacy and to all the enlarged dread of its future: out of a line, weight, burthen of sorrow, and poison of fatigue whereof its blood is stained and beneath which it lifts up its little trembling body, into standing, wearing upon its shoulders the weight of all the spreaded generations of its dead: surrounded already with further pressures, impingements: the sorrow, weariness, and nescience of its parents in their closures above . . .

Agee's work is powered by a lifetime of *thinking, feeling,* and *wrestling with* issues of injustice, spirit, and art. The wrangling—that is, the full presence of the mind in the act of perceiving and looping back on itself, questing, questioning, doubting, retrying—illustrates the difference between an ethos and a mere message. An ethos is an urgent practice. A message is merely an impatient, concise point. Drawing from the realms of poetry, drama, journalism, art and music criticism, and more, Agee's not so much in control of language as he's practiced in a form of surrender to it—to sound and perception, rhythm and image, music and feeling—and is highly adept at following and sustaining attention to these elements. And that sustained attention—that listening, that language conjuring—utterly remakes the concept and form of what a book might be.

And there are other visionaries to turn to, such as one of my heroes, MacArthur- and Nobel Prize-winning geneticist Barbara McClintock (1902–1992), who studied the DNA of corn plants. Evelyn Fox Keller writes in her biography, *A Feeling for the Organism*: "Over the years a special kind of sympathetic understanding grew in McClintock, heightening her powers of discernment, until finally, the objects of her study have became subjects in their own right; they claim from her a kind of attention that most of us experience only in relation to other persons." In her mind what we call the "scientific method" cannot by itself give us "real understanding." As McClintock said: "It gives us relationships which are useful, valid and technically marvelous; however they are not the truth."

Fox Keller believes it's McClintock's "fidelity to her own experience" that allowed her to be more open than most other scientists about her unconventional beliefs. McClintock felt that "the ultimate descriptive task, for both artists and scientists is to 'ensoul' what one sees, to attribute to it the life one shares with it . . ." It's instructive, I think for us all, to find like-minded folks in vastly different fields who are doing the work of "ensouling." In fact, seeking out a variety of forms of this practice may be more important than we realize right now.

We live in environments characterized by so many soul-hurting events, situations, and images that one is forced to perform constant and often unconscious acts of deflection just to stay in motion and not sink under the weight of a day's accumulation. By "deflection," I mean the active blocking out of so much that's wrong in a world so disenchanted that it's often easier to just comply with the wrongness, to "just get over it," to embody the indifference we, as moderns, are meant to believe is the primary attitude of the universe toward us anyway. Of course, I'm not talking here about the *enormous* issues we confront and deflect—the articulated systemic, institutionalized, and global injustices. These, of course, undergird everything I'm talking about. I'm trying to get at the smaller complexities involved in practicing art day-to-day, the microclimates that shape sensibilities, and the efforts of facing off with all that would wear us to indifference.

• • •

I grew up on Long Island, NY, with much ugliness and ruin (the draining and filling of active salt marshes, estuaries, and other sensitive ecologies for mall development, the rampant privatization of beaches, and Mafia-run dumping of toxic waste)—but also with some very sustaining spots (scraps of green space I fought for, and importantly, the ocean with its inlets and harbors). I got myself to both green space and water as often as I could. Sometimes that meant just putting my face in the grass to jungle-ize things, to alter the scale and feel the green be bigger than me. I liked my neighborhood, especially when I was little—when all the old people from their respective old countries were still living and one had chickens, another had a secret goat, and people cooked for the week starting on Sunday morning and filled the air with the scent of garlic and onions.

Mostly, though, I had to selectively see. Peer around all the wince-inducing things—like Lucite, like the 70s. While the other girls in the rich part of town were ironing knifelike creases in their Calvin Kleins, I was in my overalls and work boots, distilling dandelion wine (after the Ray Bradbury story), baking bread, and trying to make a farm of things.

So, what came of my search for an alternative way? What might be given to one who was bent on collecting herself, as Wallace Stevens said, "out of all the indifferences"? In place of any sustained alignment with the land I was born to (farming it, hiking it), and the blingy culture I opted out of, here are some elements that I can see were strengthened, some ways of perceiving that laid in a kind of bedrock palette I've worked with ever since:

- A belief in the worth of small reprieves.
- The ability to be surprised and cheered on by the beauty that man-

aged to infiltrate, its toughness, its persistence, and the unexpected forms beauty took.

- The understanding that so much of great worth, so much of what's sustaining must be seen, loved, and held before it's gone or "developed" (in other words, I grew an early sense of urgency and impending loss).
- The importance of looking sidelong and slant, under, up, into— that is, from odd angles to suss out the lives in niches and shadows, those "lesser lives," the tide-pool lives, which seemed perfectly content without us.
- The conformity of my stubbornness in pursuit of an elsewhere, a belief in a realm beyond what was given on the surface, a belief that in seeking, in hiddenness, are riches, are voices, are responses; that hiddenness is where the meanings are; that imagination is a real way to make relationships go live; and that such relationships required my assent and my presence.

So, these are some elements I recognize in myself that grew as a result of not really being able to deflect stuff very well.

From here on, my talk is highly idiosyncratic—basically me moving through my world, noticing inhibiting micro-circumstances, and thinking on how to respond. I wouldn't expect you'd have the same reactions—I mean only to suggest that you be alert and practice a "fidelity to your own experiences" as McClintock would say, which might allow you to pay increased attention to inherited concepts and forces intent on squelching your enchantment and how you might lure that enchantment back.

• • •

Exhibit A: A Lawn Bag from Lowe's

So I'm walking my dog, minding my own business and I see this big, stuffed-full lawn bag in front of a neighbor's house. On the front it reads: "What did *YOU* do this weekend?" I'm pretty sure that's the right inflection. And of course, it's not the bagging of leaves—a noble sport—I'm critiquing; it's the tone. Which *is* kind of snarky and funny, on the one hand. And the "posting" of it, via a lawn-and-leaf Facebook-type post, *is* kind of amusing. But then the self-congratulatory smugness starts to rankle me, the writer, out for my walk between drafts. Because what *I* did for a good part of the weekend was work on a ten-line poem. Mend some fragments. Heed some voices. Try to see the shape of something or other that seemed happier to be left in hiding.

My point here is that art time gets no lawn-bag announcement; it's invisible time, it's very, very slow (i.e., "inefficient"), and it can't be judged by usual standards of productivity. Such are the forces that disenchant the kind of time that's most precious to the making of things such as poems and stories: open reverie, mornings that produce nothing of "note," time that's about sensing, fumbling one's way into a rhythm, into a place where the unruly hints toward, but for a long while resists, completion. Such work (enacted in art time and including all the weeding and pruning *that* requires) fills not one little sandwich baggie, much less a big-ass lawn bag.

• • •

Exhibit B: A Kid's T-shirt from Old Navy that Reads "Young Aspiring President" (or Astronaut, etc.—there were many choices)

Similarly, from the "voice of reason" department, from the "art's nice but let's get serious" department—here's a T-shirt for little kids that pretty much says it all: let's not fuss around with art—let's aim high! Nip that impulse in the bud, parents! Old Navy *did* recall this shirt once artists protested and the execs apologized to their customer base ("as a result of customer feedback, blah blah blah")—but they did not apologize to Art—which is still insulted.

• • •

Exhibit C: A Tree with a Name Plaque Nailed In

I hardly know even how to approach this one. What is the drive to nail our name for the tree to the tree? And yes, this sturdy, old pin oak's going to be *fine*. It "compartmentalizes" the wound, says my arborist friend; it's no big deal. Which is exactly the thing . . . it's the smallness of the gesture that arrests me. It's like a gateway gesture, because once you nail a name to a tree, you can do anything to it. Manipulation becomes an option. And right beside it, in this park, is a tree sign popped off and leaning against the tree—a tiny act of urban eco-resistance?

Sometimes the disenchantment comes as a pang, and a primary characteristic is that stymied feeling, that "I have no words for the total wrongness of this" feeling and it's fast-multiplying implications, all of which cause a stiffening in the body, a draining out of language, and a desire to turn away. And of course, as a writer, you're charged at *just this moment* with keeping the faith, knowing that the irritant that starts a poem or story or essay may not be the actual subject, may just be delivering you an image or instance or word to work with, to deepen into. And you stay with it.

• • •

Exhibit D: Aspirational Names for SUVs

So . . . no to the Sequoia. Because, well, SUVs are bad news for sequoias. And the Soul had nothing to do with that ineffable presence (though yeah, cool play on *Seoul*). And well, there's no Escape (even in a monster Denali) because, actually, Climate is persistently everywhere. If the assumption of advertising is that what we are missing can be purchased (or needs be created for the purpose of being fulfilled by a product)—it's interesting to note the *particular* needs these cars seek to fulfill for *Souls* and *Sequoias* and for a place like *Denali* to *Escape* to. And how completely we've altered the means of deepening a relationship with trees and land, by offering a product that merely signals relationship.

• • •

Exhibit E: Survey after a Doctor's Appointment

I got this little survey at the end of a checkup last year. I did not complete and submit my survey because I wanted it for my collection of disenchantments, but here I encountered the protocols for personable behavior developed no doubt by some assessment folks (on break from their university gigs). And now that the corporate manipulations behind simple decent human behavior have been revealed, I'm supposed to assent to this little charade? "Did the doctor make eye contact? Did the doctor connect with you personally by asking questions about your home life?" So, they pretend to be nice and we pretend they mean it? It's the American version of the old Soviet saying "They pretend to pay us and we pretend to work." This survey made me yearn big time for the chain-smoking and dour Dr. Z of my childhood, with freezing hands, full-on sugary lollipops, and two not-at-all-friendly German shepherds eyeing me from behind the front desk.

• • •

Exhibit F: My Childhood Park

Here's what's become of my childhood park: pretty much step-by-step guidelines for a disenchanted afternoon (the twenty-five-point sign reads, in part, "no sliding headfirst, or two by two, or on your stomach, or back, or lying down, or with legs over the edge; no hanging upside down on monkey bars or jumping from the top; while swinging, hold on with both hands, no standing on swings, no pushing, etc.) In other words, Legal came up with a thorough list of every *single* thing I did as a kid—and all high above a special 1970s concrete so sharp I'm pretty sure it was laid in with a stucco knife.

• • •

Exhibit G: A Pamphlet for a Cleaning Service Featuring a Smiling Woman of Color and the Caption "Life is too short to clean your own house"

This one requires lingering on, holding the language accountable for all the ways it normalizes the invisibility of work and asserts the otherness of those who clean houses, who, it seems, must live especially long lives, with extra years to devote to work on behalf of others, and no need for family game time in a fresh house (white family, pictured in pamphlet, around a board game).

• • •

So there's my very partial, day-to-day list. I believe that paying attention to such irritants (pangs, flares, rages) reveals the core of something holy or fragile being offended, embarrassed, rejected, or silenced. I believe paying attention and following them down can help you *enlarge* the contexts in which they occur—*if* you respond to the body that registers these sensations, and *if* you draw from such sensations the energy of resistance or radiance, siphon up that power, and make something with it. I don't so much mean how you might write "about" these "issues"—I mean how being alert to that which you're being asked to deflect might strengthen an aesthetic musculature and build back enchanted gestures and perceptions.

Here are a few ways to respond to disenchanting forces—ways of protecting, courting, and sustaining enchantment—that might clear a path for your own efforts.

• • •

Critiquing the Frame

I'm listening to a segment on the radio about the widespread loss of coral reefs to bleaching. And the interviewer says to our guest scientist, "I'm sure there are listeners out there who perhaps have never seen a coral reef or have other issues in their lives and are wondering why they should care so much about this issue, which after all, is under the ocean and doesn't affect their daily lives." Our scientist takes a very deep, audible breath, and she says (verbatim), "Well, coral reefs are a central part of our marine eco-system, providing nourishment for millions of people. And many global fisheries rely on reefs as nurseries, and they're part of geochemical cycles that keep carbon in check . . ." etc., etc.

And I—who care about such things already—felt myself fuzzing out. Dilating in tiredness. In that breath she took I believe was her understanding that "what there was to care about" had to be defined for listeners by an economic calculus and utility value. And okay. Yes. Funding for research and cleanup comes from somewhere, right, like a concerned citizenry?

But I was listening into the absence: no sense of awe was communicated—at all! No amazement about coral, its lacy multiple lives, its million knit-up minds and cooperative systems, how they suck calcium from water and make their own backbones, how they go fishing with tentacle rods and sometimes snare crabs and feast for days with all the neighbors. All the things that really might have meant something to people yearning for meaning and connection, moments of amazement, access to enchantment—and a way to help. And no mention that, wow, a priori, these lives might deserve to be dignified and protected—just unto them-selves. Without our need for them intervening.

In the hands of a lyrically minded person, someone inclined to sing into, to do the endowing and be unabashed at the magic properties of coral, or salmon, or beavers (see Amy Leach's essays, for instance), the question "Why care?" necessarily considers and conjures awe and sur-prise, the stun of discovery—and, as will happen, the caring comes about by breathing into the language, enchanting it and thereby changing it. The pressure of caring *should* change the language, should change you. What would happen, you might ask yourself, to the language you're comfortable with, which tends to behave for you, when you're fully open to the pres-sure of caring, that is, when the language you've been given by convention is no longer adequate? If this kind of language, the kind that's pressured into being, and that risks at least moments of inarticulateness—if this isn't worked into being, or if it is allowed to go hazy or limp, then the *need* for it vanishes, too. We come to expect the calculus of coral. The utility of oceans.

• • •

Things Come in Slant—Let Them

I'm walking past a group of teenagers, and one says this: "Man, I gotta D, gotta D, gotta DD." Sort of chanting it. *What is it she has to do?* I wondered. What is "D"? Is it like pee? Is it like a text version of "Gotta dance"? Is it DiDi—like DiDi who lived down the street when I was a kid, older, untouchable, harshly beautiful DiDi I was both entranced by and afraid of?

Then I heard the noun of it. Wow, Lia. As in "sucky grade." I GOT A D.

The slippage, though, was really amusing. I sort of thanked my ear for that one, for the rhythm and the surprise, for all the places it sent me, the associative richness. I hadn't thought of DiDi down the street in decades.

Recently, a friend who was meeting me for a walk forgot her glasses and thought, as she walked up the street, that the fully blooming azalea was *me* waiting for her. The only thing that chastened her perception was the fact that I don't wear pink. Then we had a great talk about all the other ways we were or weren't like azaleas. Just last week, there was my (again) mishearing of this event someone invited me to, the Bruise and Bands Festival; I wondered what kind of bruising you had to show, like ID, to get in. Or if they pummeled you first, and then you listened to music.

So, mistakes and chance and very, very free association, the aleatory, yield surprising images and perceptions and memories. Ready-made strangeness: work with those gifts.

• • •

Court the Unlikelies, Assent to Your Astonishment, or One Is Helpless in Love

A few Januaries ago, my family and I were in St. Petersburg at the State Russian Museum, which is the over-the-top, eclectic collection of Emperor Alexander III. So, we're walking through, and our son is holding up just fine under the promise of hot chocolate and cake, and I'm overwhelmed, as is usual after fifteen minutes in any museum, and we get to the end, to the collection of "naïve" art, the folk art, and suddenly I'm in tears. And suffused with something else, not being overwhelmed, but some kind of relief—like a reprieve, a homecoming.

There were the worn and pocked beams from a house etched with leafy tendrils, woven rugs gnawed at by weevils but still fat with design and saturated with color, carved bowls and spoons, and a toy where two wooden men stood on a little plank and would dance like crazy if I could just jiggle it—objects that have been worked on, used, made imperfect by wind and time, water and fire. The words *diurnal* and *tender* applied to them. Everything showed signs of wear and bodies, the oil of hands, and the sheen of breath and spit and blades. Each object felt very much alive in its slow decline. There were nicks and chips and flaws and, I believe, a few bite marks in the spoons.

There at the end of the museum they were gathered, a kind of after-thought. I could breathe with them. These things were not personal expressions of a self (the makers were not even named, the pieces identi-fied as "peasant carving" or "peasant rug"), but they felt more dearly human and intimate than anything I'd seen that day. Then I had this flash of weird guilt: "You come all this way—and seeing Malevich in his own land is cool and you get him more now (and good god that portrait of Tolstoy as a peasant!)—but what seizes you, physically lands, gets in and shifts something in your chest are these little toys?"

My relief, sure, had to do with a kind of sudden collapse of museum concerns—like the clear representation of a school, or inclusion in a lin-eage of owners, or the privileging of skill and "quality" over a different constellation of values and aesthetics—something closer to love and use came forward. These little objects didn't take part in the museum's agenda of greatness. They weren't "addressing the conditions of their exclusion" from the fine-art world, nor were they being judged or even valued by museum criteria. They were not innovative, or cutting edge, not pushing envelopes and shaking up a status quo. It was more than all this.

Just . . . there they *were*, or there they'd *been*, in the pockets and homes and hands of others, winched up, filled with soup, slowly carved at night with a child's pleasure in mind, or that of a child-to-be. Roughened by wind, softened by rain, they were hitched to animals, used for predicting and weighing and healing. There at the end they were: blooming with stains, warping and shrinking, with their cracks and their rust, their tar-nish, their dents—and their souls intact.

—2016

Time and the Imagination

Jennifer Elise Foerster

—◠◠—

Time was not the train passing alongside us as my father and I drove across the prairie. Time was the train's passage into absence, marked by the appearance of its diminishing caboose. Whoever first sees the face of the caboose calls its name. This was a game my father and I played as he drove me to kindergarten in southern Colorado across the floor of the green valley hemmed by a chain of mountains.

The game was a lesson in time and its symbolism. Time is not the object (the train) but the object's action: time passes as the train passes, I learned, and we can see the face of the train's caboose as a symbol of time's imminent passing.

Which one of us would first see the full face of the caboose, how it would turn to us and laugh as it diminished to a speck on the horizon; and who would first see its absolute disappearance and call out its final spark?

Time, I learned, is not the train; it is each of our perceptions of the measure of the train's passing, and each of our perceptions are never exactly the same.

• • •

William Carlos Williams, in *Paterson*, declared the importance of "no ideas but in things." By observing the things and materials of the world, the imagination comes into conversation with reality. Yet the poet shoulders the ultimate failure of words to render a world. The word *tree* does not grow a tree; it only indicates its absence. Likewise, our memory and imagination cannot re-create the real event in the present. Our memory is always a distortion of what happened, so much so that we may never know the real from the imaginary, if both were, in any way, separate states. If there is a binary to be perceived between reality and imagination, it seems only valuable for our understanding of creativity. The interplay of reality and imagination forms the foundational movements of art and poetry's creative action. Consider my memory of the train passing across the field of a moving car's window. The memory of the train, which is shaped by my imagination, has shaped my understanding of the reality of time.

My early lesson in reality (time) was also a lesson in metaphysics. The screen upon which I watched the train move was itself a moving screen. Between the edge of the universe and the universe is—what? A place of paradox, of transformation. It is inner and outer, pushing and pulling. It is the insight that the moment of the caboose disappearing over the horizon may also be the moment of its appearance in someone else's field of vision.

To engage in the paradoxical nature of reality, we must have imagination. As the car window half reflected my face and half framed a changing landscape, I noticed myself as a reflection of time.

• • •

My first education about time may have marked the first absence of whatever freedom I felt as a human. I was maybe five years old. I was beginning to notice the edges of things. I could therefore desire going beyond them. But I was simultaneously learning to stay inside them, to make boundaries of one's imagination as a method of staying in time, which is, ultimately, survival. Being out of time is dangerous to the body, to the structures we survive within.

Poetry became, for me, the only safe place to be outside of time.

• • •

In his poem, *The Prelude*, Wordsworth conceived of "spots of time": isolated moments in time when memories surface and, with the aid of our imagination, have a "renovating" effect on our consciousness:

There are in our existence spots of time,
That with distinct pre-eminence retain
A renovating virtue, whence— . . .
. . .—our minds
Are nourished and invisibly repaired.

These spots of time exist outside of time's linear insistence, just as memory (past moments seemingly removed from the flow of time and applied to the present) interacts with our comprehension of the absolute present. These "spots" are fragmentary, epiphanic. The epiphany is a sudden manifestation of enlightenment or realization. When used by James Joyce as a literary device, the epiphany was expressed as a fragment and pushed against the flow of the narrative's linear time.

Poetry refuses time by engaging with moments of awakening that move in and out of linear time. The poem can unhinge us from time by provoking instantaneous comprehension of paradox, thus enabling a transformation of seeing, a rearrangement of meaning.

While no moment can be removed from the flow of time or from its embeddedness with all/other moments, our creative work—our imagination—makes this removal its very exercise: to hold up, to still, a moment of life. Albert Camus famously wrote, "A man's work is nothing but this slow trek to rediscover through the detours of art those two or three great and simple images in whose presence his heart first opened." We seek to remember those few images as if each could exist in isolation. Upon holding up those images, we hope to re-experience that first opening. Can we ever return to any moment in time? Yes and no. A moment is timeless and transient. It lasts, and yet its lastingness is only in memory.

Each thing that exists in the world is passing, changing. So, when we note, write, create, or record something about that "time," we are writing about something's absence, as it has already passed through that window of time and now exists only in the window of our memory-perception, which rearranges it.

Arrangement is an act of time and uses time as its materials. The poem, too, while ever reaching to achieve a timelessness, is a shaped event; it is a project bound by time, measuring and arranging time. Arrangement is also an act of being artful. While art making and writing rely on time, these imaginative acts equally rely on the absence of time: we create an edge to move beyond it. We experience the presence of the things of the world as existing in relation to their absence. Poetry must contain the void, the infinite, the nothingness to have a "beyond" against which to draw its edge, a blank stone upon which to inscribe its epitaph.

• • •

Through poetry, we can "see the impossibility of seeing," as Giorgio Agamben writes in *Remnants of Auschwitz.* This vision of the invisible is a paradox, bottomless; it is the vision of the Gorgon. "That at the 'bottom' of the human being there is nothing other than an impossibility of seeing—this is the Gorgon, whose vision transforms the human being into non-human . . . the apostrophe from which human beings cannot turn away."

The face of the caboose was my Gorgon. Coming to know time by looking upon the face of its passing opened a void in me. It was like watching the penny of my existence disappear down a bottomless well.

What is a seeing that has no bottom, no boundaries, no window, no screen? What kind of seeing is this but the vision of the invisible?

Poetry is a way of seeing what cannot be seen, a language for what has no language, often evoking the visible (the image) to communicate something more than the thing itself. The caboose was the image my father pointed to out the window to communicate something about the concept of time. The caboose moved across the surface of the field, passing us by. The caboose was time made visible only by its passing.

The invisible world is as much the material of imagination as is the visible world. For me, the work of poetry is to bring both into focus, to create, through image, sound, spaciousness, and illusion, the convergence of the seen and the not seen. And in this convergence is a fathomless point that, like imagination, cannot be pointed to, the *there* that is the *not there.* Mallarmé wrote, "Not the thing, but its effect." It is not the poem itself, but what the poem opens. It is not what the imagination is, but what it does. It is not what the symbol is, but what it symbolizes, which is an evocation, an action, a movement, just like time.

• • •

T. S. Eliot's The *Waste Land* is a language site, a place constructed of fragments of a self and of a culture. It is a form as much as my memory of the green valley is a form: it occupies a space in memory and now on the page. In *The Waste Land* there is music; there are passing images. Rhythms cohere into a meter only for the meter to abruptly discontinue. This poem is alienation trying to fit itself into a form, and yet no certain form results, only a passion which diffuses into fragments of contemporary tag lines, then resurrects itself to assert, again, questions of our place within a fathomless space:

> Your arms full, and your hair wet, I could not
> Speak, and my eyes failed, I was neither
> Living nor dead, and I knew nothing,
> Looking into the heart of light, the silence.

The poet begins with wonder. And yet the poet, ultimately, cannot capture this, or feels that any attempt to capture it would be false, for at some point, "the eyes fail," and one knows nothing, "looking into the heart of light, the silence."

So, what draws Eliot to continue writing beyond such a point? "I cannot connect nothing with nothing." What drives us to attempt to catalogue and string together those fragments that make up our lives? We are driven, perhaps, to seek the "the heart of light, the silence." Yet even Eliot himself, in "Burnt Norton," admitted that this heart, this point, exists nowhere, cannot be isolated or stilled, and can never be reached or attained:

At the still point of the turning world. Neither flesh nor fleshless;
Neither from nor towards; at the still point, there the dance is

A poem exists in time and it uses time—beats, duration, ascending and
descending rhythms—as its materials. Yet it dances around the "still
point" that cannot be fixed, that evades time. Poetry is a form that dances
with formlessness. Form, like poetry, works within time; it transforms.
Form is all about transformation, as is metaphor.

• • •

For Mallarmé and other originators of free verse (including Baudelaire
and the early Modernists), form was a metaphor for content. Baudelaire
stressed the importance of choosing the right form to contain the con-
tents of the imagination. In his prose poems of the 1850s, *Le Spleen de
Paris,* he innovated a new model, or form, for poetry to record the ephem-
erality of the present. Through the prose poem, Baudelaire could capture
the "contemporaneity" that he termed "modernity": "the transient, the
fleeting, the contingent" ("The Painter of Modern Life"). The idea of the
prose poem was, according to Baudelaire, to create a form true to experience: "... supple enough and choppy enough to fit the soul's lyrical movements, the undulations of reverie, the jolts of consciousness."

The desire to find a fusion of form and content was the inciting desire
of free verse in the twentieth century. Free verse evolved out of *vers libre,*
"liberated verse." After Baudelaire's *vers impair* (the damaged line), Rim-
baud and Verlaine were seminal innovators of what came to be called *vers
libre.* Liberation follows from destruction: after the destruction of many
received forms, poets strived to follow a vision truer to contemporaneity,
more accurate to the poet's (and the collective's) conscious and unconscious mind.

Through what forms could we find liberation, if liberation were akin
to flight? The desire among humans for possession of wings is perhaps
related to our desire for imagination—to see the world from an
ungrounded vision, to experience a new relationship with gravity and
dimension, to escape those inescapable forces that determine us in our
bodies for our brief stay here. Imagination allows our hereness to seem
more expansive, to overlap with the sphere of "there." The more liberated
our imagination, perhaps, the more complete the overlap of these two
spheres of knowing: here and there.

The flight of liberation still requires gravity and dimension, a structure through which spaciousness can move and transform. Is language the
vehicle for imagination in poetry? Language is a structure, or architecture,

that engages the imagination and makes meaning. Like language, time is a structural device that can both control and liberate the life of our imagination. Though bound to the sequence of breaths that buoy us in the life stream, aren't we always, in some way, attempting to break free from time? The language of poetry is often in the position of trying to say something beyond itself, and yet, as language, can only do so by exploring itself. Can I ever return to the consciousness I had before I formulated or became formed by the symbolism of the train and its Gorgon-faced caboose? Time, fluid time, turned something in me to stone. Weathered. We erode. We do not last.

• • •

Anne Carson's *Economy of the Unlost* links the concept of a symbol to the Greek object called a *symbolon*, which was that token of mutual obligation between the giver and its receiver. This token, the *symbolon*, was the object that each member of the relationship held a portion of. Gifts can be identified by the fragmentation upon which they rely. For a gift to exist, it must exist in fragments shared by multiple participants in the perpetuation of this gift. We become responsible for the life of the symbol just as we are responsible for others similarly connected through the web of this gift. Carson discusses the concept of *xenia* as cooperative acts undertaken by people who are engaged in each other's well-being: a relationship based on gifts given or received that is in a continuous state of renewal. This kind of economy is perhaps the system that upholds poetries, if poetries are systems of fragments in a perpetual state of realization and renewal.

Fragments are the "things" that endure—surfaced pieces we form into memory, or threads from which we make and remake the stories that determine our reality. The rearrangement of fragments into stories is the enduring act of humanity. Could stories endure without the engagement of the imagination to constantly remake or retell them? It is possible that stories exist in their own will and right as nonhuman entities—that they, too, have an imagination.

• • •

Lyn Hejinian, in her essay "The Rejection of Closure," writes about the "infinite combinatory possibilities of scraps of language." Texts are only ever "scraps," fragments of a communication system, and require imagination for coherence. Each time a poem is read it returns to life, it gathers the fragments of the reader's consciousness and ignites her air of unconsciousness into a heat source that feeds thought and recognition.

One way of organizing, or gathering, these fragments into meaning is the creation of sequences. Poetry that operates as a sequence of poems attempts to cluster fragments into various retellings. The sequence format allows the poet to move around in space and time, untethered from a particular point of view or consequence. We create sequences to embrace the expanse, to create a container for it, to help us organize paradox. Writing a poem of sequence can serve as an annotation of an invisible reality beyond the fractured world of incomplete memories. It can also provide greater freedom to express the irrational sequencing that occurs in memory.

Memory rarely comes to us as a lyrical or logically ordered narrative—it arises in bits and pieces, moments of vague recognition, disordered associations. A poet can either transform these pieces into a lyric poem or use the fragmentation as a poetic device to relate the disjunctive quality of the memory. We can collect or compose these fragments to move toward a synthesis of experience. We can manipulate language to define experience and to design memory—to make, out of our fragments, the shaped event that is a poem.

When composing a poem out of fragments, one is confronted with infinite possibilities for reordering, as Hejinian suggests. The way in which a design—of a poem or otherwise—comes together is mysterious. Every turn, every line in a sequenced creation, is critical, and each arrival is the beginning of another journey. Each fragment may emerge from a buried layer within the previous fragment; it may also follow the lyrical movement of the previous fragment. At any point is a possible bifurcation. And when the points of bifurcation are like Eliot's "still points in the turning world," meaning their location is illusory, how do we orient? Orientation is the world's lyric. To sing of the turning world without becoming disoriented is, perhaps, a fundamental work of the poet. We must become architects, makers of spaces through which the songs echo, screens upon which our memories may surface and pass beyond the vanishing point.

• • •

In *Economy of the Unlost*, Anne Carson writes about the fifth-century BC Greek lyric poet Simonides of Ceos, of whose poetry we only have fragments, and who was known for writing epitaphs commemorating fallen soldiers. Carson writes of Simonides's negation of time and mortality: "The mind that can deny time can say 'No' to mortality, as Simonides did repeatedly and famously throughout his career." Simonides enacted this negation of mortality through the creation of epitaphs to inscribe memory repeatedly into the present. The epitaph is a funerary narration inscribed on stone—these words last as long as the stone's surface takes to weather away.

When an unweathered image surfaces in memory—the train passing across a green valley, for example—is this the undead returning to repeat or retell its memory of itself? Is this the lasting word, the once-buried image unearthed, the epitaph as poem traveling through history, recreating history at every point of its reassertion?

I earlier wrote that staying inside time was survival. Writing, to me, is survival, as it pushes against death. The power of the poet to both confront and deny death drives her to write. But perhaps it is also an inherent character of the poet: to see the absent in the present; to see death in life, simultaneously.

This perception of paradox is fleeting and impossible to hold in vision. Poetry seems to me the most apt chariot to carry something so uncarriable; it the clearest screen through which to turn to the visage of the Gorgon, to face the face of the caboose as it disappears over the vanishing point. And always in this epiphanic, timeless moment, time persists, just as form abides always in formlessness, as light is necessary for the shadow.

The caboose was my epitaph for time, deathless time.

• • •

I return to my memory of the train across the green expanse, the vanishing point of the train's caboose as it disappeared into the creased mountains that appeared, to me, as a singular horizon. My father was teaching me about time, yes—how time did not actually exist, how it is not a thing but a measure. But because he was showing me the existence of the imaginary through an image, through its passage into absence, through its very negation, he was teaching more about imagination than anything else, which was also my introduction to striving, to the inescapable restlessness of life.

I believe my father always saw the caboose before I did. His timeline is different from mine. The moment in time the caboose appeared to me is unique to my reception of this symbol, this fragment; its point of origin never existed, nor did its point of ultimate departure. If neither existed, is the point of origin then the same as that of departure? The canal of birth and death are one. Do we go out the same way we came in? Does the moment of entry and departure converge out of time to be the same moment? A person, a train, comes and goes, but is there a fixed order to this? What if order is vanquished at this vanishing point of entry and departure? Order may only be those steps in between, which are committed to time. If this one point of entry and departure does not exist along a continuum of time, then it is infinite and has no location. It is a point that exists only in negation; it is the nonpoint. It is a void. Do we need this void in order to be alive, to create a structure for our lives that involves time, consequence, and sequence?

As the poet Paul Celan said in his Meridian speech, "To be interested in the earthly, you have to make a system—you also have to disrupt the system." We make maps of language; we make poems and stories as complex systems to create, remember, or navigate memory. We also write to disrupt these maps of language, to create windows of liberation from whatever orders we no longer want to define us.

The mountains that hemmed that southern Colorado valley are an important symbol in my memory, as my conception of time relied on the boundary of that expanse across which I tracked the train's passage into absence. I wanted to go beyond the boundary, as if there were some liberation there, to follow the train past its vanishing point. If we drove faster, we might prolong the present, the laughing face of the caboose; we could avoid, for a little longer, its disappearance. But no amount of magnitude or velocity could get us to and beyond that vanishing point. We are trapped in this loss, the imminent disappearance of things from our line of sight or our particular line of time. We know energy, by the second law of thermodynamics, is only conserved; it cannot be created out of nothing and it cannot be destroyed. But we are time; we are imagination; time is the machine of our mind. Just as we may experience the constant change of the world as loss, we can also experience it as the negation of loss, until we, too, pass from others' screens, the memory of us transforming into forms we cannot yet or ever know. There is no time like the present, in its infinite imaginations.

—*2021*

The Fault Lines of Memory

Embracing Imperfect Memory in Creative Nonfiction

Brenda Miller

—w—

Memory is imagination, and imagination is memory. I don't think we
remember the past, we imagine it. We take a few props with us into the future,
and out of those props we make a model, some stage set, and that's our version
of the past. Of course, models decay, and they change. And so we're constantly
reshaping the past.
—John Banville

San Fernando Quake, 1971

I grew up in Northridge, California, a place prone to big earthquakes. The
San Andreas Fault is a defining feature of California, and we live with the
recognition that the ground can shift at any moment. What was certain
one day can be completely changed in the next.

On February 9, 1971, a few weeks before I turned twelve, a magnitude
6.6 quake shook the ground beneath us while we slept. I woke to my bed
tilting, the blurred figure of my mom in my doorway, the sound of screaming. I remember the smell of vinegar from broken bottles in the cupboards,
the strange feeling of being outside in my pajamas. Did we stand on the
threshold first, the way we were taught (though that information kept
changing too)? Did we rush out into the street, a quiet cul-de-sac, with the
rest of our neighbors as we waited to see if our houses would fall?

My brothers—fifteen and seven years old—would of course have
been with us in a family huddle, but I have no memory of them. Only me
and my mom and dad, as if I were an only child, held between them in a
safe embrace. I remember my father cooking dinners in the aftermath on
the BBQ, since we had no power for days. I remember my junior high
being closed from structural damage, and this unexpected holiday feeling
in the air as the kids ran wild in the cool winter days of Southern California. It was close to my birthday; did we still plan a party? Actually, my

brother's birthday was just a week away; did we do anything for him? How far off would normalcy be?

• • •

Slippage

> Memory's an active, dynamic force, not just a recording one; over the course of a life, as perspective shifts, we keep moving into different relationships to the past, reconsidering, so that *what happened* turns out to be nothing stable, but a scribbled-over field of revisions, rife with questions, half its contents hidden.
> —Mark Doty

Okay, so maybe my memory of that earthquake isn't wholly accurate. How can it be? How can our memories fully encompass all the details from moments in the past, especially those that speed by so quickly we can barely keep up? We continually fill in the gaps. For example, I didn't know the date of the earthquake, so I looked it up, inserted it casually, with no one the wiser. Other details I fill in from the quickest of flashes: my eyes fluttering open before my normal waking time, the blur of myopia, the seasick sensation in my gut, a flash of my mother's nightgown in the hallway.

From the standpoint of decades later, I witness this scene as a dispassionate observer, watching that little girl as she comes to awareness in a world that has slipped sideways. My body remembers the smell of vinegar, but maybe it was ammonia. My body remembers running outside, but I can't really know for certain, unless I ask my parents, one of whom is gone and the other whose memory may be more reliable, but whose perspective was completely different: that of a mother rather than a child.

And to be honest, I don't really care about the *facts* of the situation beyond that the earthquake shook our home and my family and I survived it intact, with a few things missing and broken. What I *do* care about is why I remember it the way that I do, why certain details seem clear while others remain blurred. I want to know where my brothers are in this scene.

And this is a different kind of accuracy. In the etymological roots of the word *accurate*, the key meaning is "taking care." When one is being accurate, one is also being a curator—the two words share the same root, "taking care." As creative nonfiction writers, we curate our memories, assembling them in a way that makes artistic sense. We are taking care of the memories, revising them as we go along and we gain new information, new insights, seeing recurring themes that emerge from the fault lines, the places of slippage and uncertainty.

• • •

Desire for Art

> Life is not a story, a settled version. It's an unsorted heap of images we go through, the familiar snaps taken up and regarded, then tossed back until, unbidden, they rise again, images that float to the surface of the mind, rise, fall, drift—and return only to drift away again in shadow. They never quite die, and they never achieve form. They are the makings of a life, not of a narrative. Not art, but life trailing its poignant desire for art.
> —Patricia Hampl

The first chapter I wrote in the textbook I coauthored with Suzanne Paola, *Tell It Slant,* is called "The Body of Memory." I began with a narrative of my earliest memory, based on having my tonsils out at age four and the "badge of courage" I received as a testament to getting through that particular ordeal. Here is part of it:

> In my earliest memory, I'm a four-year-old girl waking slowly from anesthesia. I lift my head off the pillow and gaze blearily out the bars of my hospital crib. I can see a dim hallway with a golden light burning; somehow, I know in that hallway my mother will appear any minute now, bearing ice cream and 7UP. . . . I'm vaguely aware of another little girl screaming for her mother in the crib next to mine, but otherwise the room remains dark and hushed, buffered by the footfalls of nurses who stop a moment at the doorway and move on.

Do I really remember these things? Why, yes, I do remember them, though I may not be remembering them as if viewing video evidence. But the fact that I remember, yes, that is true.

It goes on:

> I keep my gaze fixed on that hallway, but something glints in my peripheral vision, and I turn to face the bedside table. There, in a mason jar, my tonsils float. They rotate in the liquid: misshapen ovals, pink and nubbly, grotesque.

Later in the memory, my mother appears and spoons me soft ice cream through the bars of the crib. The nurses give me a "badge of courage" certificate that I will display on my bedroom door for years and years to come. My father is nowhere in this memory, nor is my older brother. It's just me and my mother and my excised body parts cohabiting a hospital room as stark and barren as any in a horror film.

When I ask my mother about this odd detail of the preserved tonsils, she has no memory of it, and of course her version is much more likely than mine. I doubt the doctor would have provided this grisly souvenir— and certainly not in a mason jar (!). Still, I have this urge to write it as *I* remember it, because my remembering is, indeed, as factual as the facts themselves. The key is that in order to use it for literary purposes, I need to nudge this memory rather than have it just lie there doing nothing. I have to poke it, examine it, try to understand *why* this jar shows up again and again, a talisman. I have to assemble all the parts like a puzzle: crib bars, ice cream, girl screaming, tonsils in a jar, badge of courage. And if I want to, I can begin to understand this memory as the foundation of a theme that has come up in my writing since the beginning: the body, its fragility, its ability to be transformed at the hands of others, the "courage" I'm supposed to have but rarely find. And my mother—always my mother there, feeding me, trying to soothe the pain.

As N. Scott Momaday writes in his memoir *The Names*: "Memory begins to qualify the imagination, to give it another formation, one that is peculiar to the self. . . . If I were to remember other things, I should be someone else." Our earliest memories, imperfect though they may be, seed the perennial themes that pop up over and over, connecting the disparate events of our lives into a story that makes intuitive sense.

When we re-inhabit these early memories, we do so, as Virginia Woolf says, from the "platform of the present," a landing place that is never stable but keeps shifting as we live from moment to moment, year to year. She calls these early flashes of memory "moments of being," as they are the times the curtain opens, or the ground shifts, and we come to an awareness of ourselves as alive in particular bodies at particular times in particular places. As our moving platform of the present chugs down the conveyer belt of life, we can study the same memory and come away with new understandings or insights.

For example, just now, writing this memory again, from the platform of a daughter who now takes care of her elderly mother, I focus more on that spoonful of ice cream, the urge to protect, the bars between us that will grow in size over the years and then crumble.

• • •

Making Sh*t Up

> And here's where making things up comes in: there is only a de-
> gree to which the narration of history can do the work of achieving
> something as dimensional as reality. . . . 'Making things up' is very
> imprecise. I mean by that phrase a host of things: eliding some mo-
> ments, juxtaposing others because they resonate together or com-
> ment upon one another, stretching time out in certain instances,
> trying to look more deeply into a moment . . .
> —Mark Doty

In his essay "Bride in Beige," Mark Doty describes writing his memoir
Firebird and how much of it is built on a foundation of blurred memories.
In one key scene, he remembers his sister wearing a beige suit to her wedding, and all the questions this memory brings up for him. Why did she
wear beige? Was it mere frugality or a statement of something larger? Did
she choose that matronly suit or was it forced on her, given that she was
already a few months pregnant?

Doty mulls on these questions in his memoir, bringing them forth on
the page, the questions themselves becoming as much a part of the story
as the memory of his sister's wedding. Then, the copyeditor comes in,
wielding the blunt pen of fact and practicality; he writes in the margins:
"Why don't you just ask her?"

Well, of course, one could "just ask," and the mystery would be solved.
Or would it? Certainly, his sister could provide the bare bones of information that would make this scene more "accurate" from a transcription
point of view. But Doty, and many of us, are not after transcription. We
crawl the edges of the fault lines, peering into the earthy dark. We are
courting mystery. We are after the labyrinthian workings of our minds and
consciousness. We are living out the poet Rainer Maria Rilke's mandate to
"love the questions themselves."

"The answer" the essayist seeks is not necessarily the answer of the
facts. It is the answer of connection, of desire, of the metaphors our memories show us.

• • •

The Space in Between

> I don't worry about the 'real' so much as my *perception* of the real, and it's in the working out of the discrepancies between the two realms that a different kind of truth emerges. I can't seem to stay rooted in fact (too boring) or invention (too ungrounded), but instead inhabit that space in between, where anything can happen. I think it does speak to a kind of sincerity on the part of a writer, when you are willing to let the reader in on your thought process and do not rely on presenting something fully formed.
>
> —Brenda Miller in *Metawritings: Toward a Theory of Nonfiction*

I do often "just ask" to fact-check something, though I usually wait until long after the first draft to do so. As Patricia Hampl writes: "For me, writing a first draft is a little like meeting someone for the first time. I come away with a wary acquaintanceship, but the real friendship (if any) is down the road. Intimacy with a piece of writing, as with a person, comes from paying attention to the revelations it is capable of giving."

If I focus too much on the factual accuracy of a piece while in the throes of my "scribbling" (as I call my first drafts), then I know I will shut down my capacity for metaphor making, for the unexpected revelations the writing, itself, might have in store for me. Once I have a first draft down, then I start examining it with a more critical eye, looking not necessarily for inaccuracies that I need to clarify, but for moments of slippage that shake things up, cracking open the crust of the "real" to expose the juicier core of experience.

Sometimes this asking takes place, as many things do these days, on the internet, confirming or correcting certain facts such as dates, names, words, etc. And these facts can also lead to more fodder for contemplation. For example, in the earthquake scene I wrote earlier, the date I discovered in my fact-checking brought up new questions to explore: I hadn't remembered that the earthquake happened so close to my brother's birthday and to my own. The date nudges me to remember more deeply, to speculate on how our lives had been disrupted that day, yes, but also for weeks to come. A child's birthday is one of the most normal and most extraordinary days in their life; how did the earthquake show this child the way we can't really count on anything?

Another example: My friend Dayna and I are sitting together in a coffeehouse we've visited many times together for what we call "Poetry Church." It's a Sunday morning. Usually, a couple more friends join our small congregation, but today it's just the two of us. I can't remember what books we discussed (of course I can't; I've already confessed about my terrible memory!), but we have a bit of time, so we decide to write together, taking out our notebooks. It's around the holidays, and we choose a word at random: *star*. We each quickly write a list of ten images that come to mind. Then we circle one on our list and begin writing for twenty minutes.

The image that leaps to me is the Star of David that my father displayed on our house at holiday time. It suddenly looms large in my memory/imagination, and I begin describing a representative scene from a blurred image of the large wooden Star of David blazing with blue light from the roof of our house. I then muse on my father's motivation for taking the trouble to decorate for Hanukkah, which also leads me to a memory of our electric menorah prominently displayed in our kitchen window.

I'm writing with Dayna in a familiar coffee shop, doing a practice we've done many times before, and my pen has gained momentum. I'm not worried about facts or accuracy; I'm curating this memory now, and time is winding down, so I suspend that moment in time, imagining my father paused on our roof, pleased with his handiwork, gazing out over our neighborhood.

We finish writing and Dayna and I read to each other what we wrote. We're both pleased with our session, having ruffled up some unexpected images that could be viable.

And then I do a little fact-checking, asking my mother about that Hanukkah star. "Oh," she says, "he never climbed onto the roof; he nailed it to the posts of the front porch." I'm a little crestfallen. This won't do at all. The front porch isn't nearly as rich with imagery as that roof, not nearly as good for my purposes. "And," she adds, "he made that star himself." Well, that's a nice detail, and it brings to mind the way my father would spend hours at his workbench in our garage, tinkering, making things that functioned, barely.

I return to my practice writing with this new knowledge in mind. I add the bit about my father making the star, but I can't bear to part with the image of my father on the roof. Here is how it all ended up:

> Every year, my father climbed to the roof in late fall to install his homemade Star of David on the top of our house. It usually happened about the same time the neighbors strung their bright garlands of red and green, their blinking icicles melting in the Southern California heat. He had built the star at his workbench in our garage, measuring and sawing the exact lengths of lumber needed to

create this symbol, then carefully attached strands of blue lights to adorn each of the six points. He must have unfurled an extension cord, run it along the eaves, camouflaged it among the shingles. The light was supposed to look miraculous, the blue star proclaiming our Jewishness among the goys.

It wasn't meant to be an affront, a confrontation, or maybe it was: since Hanukkah could happen as early as Thanksgiving, the star might appear a few weeks before we'd see Christmas trees bundled on top of station wagons, our star the only glow among darkened houses on the cul-de-sac, pulsing its blue message into the night. At the same time, my mother got out the electric menorah, screwed in each bulb on the appropriate night of Hanukkah, until all nine artificial candles glowed in our kitchen window. Sometimes she let us do it, and I remember the tingle in my fingertips as the bulb tightened, the moment before the glow hit my eyes and blinded me.

I understand now that my memory is incorrect; my mother tells me my father affixed the star to the posts on our front porch, which makes more sense. But still, years after he has died, I would like to imagine my father making that treacherous climb upward, gripping his unwieldy creation. I want to picture him staying a few moments longer than necessary, surveying the block, watching Christmas lights appear—gingerbread icing gilding identical rooflines. He liked to do these kinds of things by himself, a man with the proper tools and know-how, a man who could plan out exactly what needed to be done in any situation. I imagine him bathed in blue light, crouched above his family, checking the star one more time, shaking it firmly in place, before touching one foot and then another to the ladder that would lead him down to earth.

Notice how the fact that my father made the star is inserted casually, as if I knew it all along. Though I don't remember watching the construction, the prose acts as if I had. Is this a lie? Perhaps, but a tiny one that's still adjacent to the truth. And then I use an inconspicuous phrase—"he must have"—to signal that I'm in the realm of speculation. I don't know, I didn't witness it, but this image makes sense in the progression of the narrative. It's a small phrase, one that a casual reader might not notice, but it's another phrase that does a lot of labor. It establishes some rules of engagement. We are in the realm of memory/imagination. We create this scene together.

The next paragraph also shows my ignorance in full view of the reader: I really have no idea why my father would go to the trouble to hoist a heavy star onto our house, but I offer a few possibilities from the perspective of an older narrator who might be able to glean the nuances of these types of things, especially in light of the history of Jewish persecution. And while I can't claim to have been aware of it at the time, the blue star echoes the yellow star Jews were forced to wear in Nazi territories, their Jewishness "proclaimed" in a very different way.

The electric bulbs on the star lead me to the electric bulbs in the menorah, and since it's become a reflex for me to add sensory detail when I can, I bring forth the tactile memory of screwing in those miraculous bulbs myself, the moment when they come to life. I'm doing a bit of a close-up there, zooming in. Do I "really" remember that sensation in my fingertips? My mind doesn't, but my body does, so I allow it to stay without fussing about it.

And then comes the crucial moment in this short essay: What am I going to do with my "false" memory as it butts up against what is probably the "real" memory? As I am wont to do, I go ahead and keep it, because I sense that there will be something revealed in that fault line. If I had chosen to go back and simply "correct" my memory to the front porch, the essay would have nowhere to go. There would be that "so what?" moment without an adequate answer. So, I use this line as a transition:

> I understand now that my memory is incorrect; my mother tells me
> my father affixed the star to the posts on our front porch, which
> makes more sense. But still, years after he has died, I would like to
> imagine my father . . .

That transition does a few things: I arrive into the essay as the writer looking back on what she's written; I bring my mother into the memory process with me, affirming her version of events. And then the phrase "But still" brings us to a moment of suspension, of stillness, where something is about to happen. Then "years after he has died . . ." brings in a new context; I'm looking back on this memory in the absence of my father, in the light of long-term mourning.

But what I think is crucial here is that I didn't consciously realize I was writing in that context until I wrote those words "years after he has died." These words emerge from the stillness I've allowed myself at the beginning of that sentence. And now the *writing* is showing me the "why" of this faulty memory; now that my father is no longer a physical presence in my life, I still yearn for him in whatever ways such a presence manifests now. "I would like to imagine my father . . ." and so I do, and I bring you along with me, lifting our gaze to the roof where my father now sits like a gargoyle above us, still a part of the family, still protecting us, still providing his own kind of light.

The real essay is not about the Star of David, or about being Jewish in the suburbs. The essay is about the slippage between spectral memory and the all-too-real world. It is about love and loss and the yearning to keep our beloveds with us. It is about that word "want." It is about "but still." It is about "a few moments longer."

• • •

(Non)fiction

Let's say that fiction and nonfiction aren't categories, but two poles on a spectrum called "narrative" or "story." . . . Everyone seems so determined these days to separate fiction and nonfiction, to define them in opposition to each other, but I'm interested in that place where they overlap, how they hang out and talk to each other.
—Cathy Day

So why not just write fiction if I'm so attached to my made-up versions of the past? As Patricia Hampl says: "Why did I invent, and then, if memory inevitably leads to invention, why do I—why should anybody—write memoir at all?"

It's a good question, and one that I'll keep exploring all my writing life. But for now, I can say that through this exploration of my own tendencies I see that all my work is about desire, and if I were to completely fictionalize or, on the other end of the spectrum, completely nonfictionalize, I wouldn't be telling the truth either way. It's in the disparities that insight lies. Memory is not the "real" story. Fantasy isn't either. It's in the rift between the two that the story simmers. I dive into that crevasse and emerge with a new understanding.

For me it is important, when working this way, to maintain what we call the "pact with the reader": I let them in on my thought process. I'm not doing it behind the scenes. As you've witnessed, sometimes I will simply revise a fact or two after checking, usually when there's no real significance between my faulty memory and the "real" version. But when I sense, intuitively, that an image or metaphor lurks that will make the essay sing, I go for it in full view of my readers. I trust them, and in turn, they trust me to bring them somewhere if not wholly "truthful," at least worth their time.

I've noted several instances of how certain small phrases can act as our packhorses as we venture along the faultiness of memory and imagination. We call this "cueing the reader," but it's also cueing the writer, a signal to go ahead, see where this new path will take you. Here is an incomplete list:

- I don't know, but . . .
- I don't remember, but . . .
- I would like to believe . . .
- Maybe . . .
- Or perhaps . . .
- I imagine . . .
- I now know/understand/have been told . . . but . . .
- But still . . .

You can come up with others that work for you. See what happens when these words appear, what kind of opening they offer to explore the unknown, or the not-yet known.

• • •

"Modulations of Untranslatable Truth"

Sometimes the truth is so elusive that it's just not available, so I usually think of essays as looking to gain clarity on an experience instead of looking for some single tidy answer. And sometimes the fact that you can't know something leads you to another more important discovery.
—Ryan Van Meter

I still live in earthquake country, and during the pandemic I began stocking up on disaster supplies, convinced that the "big one" was bound to happen now, as the world seemed to be falling apart. That hasn't happened yet, and I've already dug into my supplies of Trader Joe's granola bars and Costco cold brew coffee, and I can't remember where I put all those batteries or the combo lantern/transistor/USB charger I bought online. So, when the time comes, I'll still be woefully unprepared, as we all are when the big things happen, no matter how hard we've tried.

Sometimes our imagination is one of our most necessary supplies as we seek truth and new understandings. In his short essay "Capiche?" Bernard Cooper describes meeting a handsome man named Sandro in Venice, Italy, with whom he shares some beautifully intimate moments, all without a common language between them. But then he confesses:

Everything I have told you is a lie. . . . But lies are filled with modulations of untranslatable truth, and early this morning when I awoke, birds were restless in the olive trees. Dogs tramped through the grass and growled. The local rooster crowed fluently . . . and I was so moved by the strange, abstract trajectories of sound that I wanted to take you with me somewhere, somewhere old and beautiful, and I honestly wanted to offer you something, something like the prospect of sudden love . . .

The word *capiche* means "Do you understand?" This little essay is filled with desire: desire for Sandro, yes, but more so desire to understand and to be understood. Desire to offer something of beauty—to himself, and to us. The word *want* repeats like a chant. You can feel the yearning in every sentence, drawing us along into this world, and even the word *honestly* appears, because this fantasy is also a complete truth.

What I'd like to offer you here is the permission to explore those mysterious fault lines where movement happens, where things are revealed that couldn't be known on the surface. It's scary, there's no denying it, maybe even dangerous—shaking things up, questioning our certainties and the certainties of others. But we have the tools we need for these excavations. We are strong enough to go to those deep places and come back changed.

—2021

Lost in the Woods of Brooklyn and Belgrade

The Transformative Possibilities of Disorientation

Scott Nadelson

—⚭—

Turned Around, Upside Down, and Backward

When I was in graduate school in my midtwenties, overwhelmed by the demands of classes and bewildered by teaching for the first time, I would often distract myself by getting lost in the McDonald Forest, a three thousand acre stretch of wooded hills owned by Oregon State University. I don't mean "getting lost" metaphorically; on these walks, I would intentionally try to lose track of where I was, taking trails without looking at any maps ahead of time, turning onto old logging roads, meandering deeper into the trees until the trunks were dense enough to block my view of the horizon.

While walking I paid little attention to where I was going or what I was passing, instead brooding over my writing and teaching, wondering if I'd ever be any good at these things I cared about so deeply. There was little danger in doing so; the woods covered a narrow ridge, and if I stuck with one direction, I knew I'd eventually come out at a road. At worst, I'd have an extra few miles to cover to get back to my car, blissfully exhausting myself so I'd have no energy left to grade composition essays in the evening.

Still, the moment of realizing that I had in fact lost my bearings, when I couldn't tell which direction would lead me back to the parking lot, always jolted me with a charge of adrenaline. No matter that this was exactly what I'd intended; the fear was immediate and instinctive, and it emptied my head of any thoughts other than finding my way out. I could no longer worry about all the work I had to do or my ability to do it well. Instead, I focused intensely on my immediate surroundings, taking note of every tree I passed, every shrub, every fork in the worn-out gravel road. And because I was now alert, I noticed other things, too: the patterns shadows made on the ground, the sound of a woodpecker hammering an old snag, the smell of moss and sap. I'd spot exotic-looking mushrooms, a calypso orchid at the base of an enormous Douglas fir. I was awake, in other words, in a way I hadn't been when I knew where I stood in the landscape, and I stayed that way until returning to familiar ground.

• • •

A decade after those walks in the McDonald Forest, I happened upon an exhibit of artist Paul McCarthy's work in New York's Whitney Museum. McCarthy had been a major figure for decades, and I'd seen some of his video pieces before then, but they hadn't made much of an impact; campy and violent, their primary effect on me was inducing queasiness and discomfort, and though I knew that was likely the intention, I wasn't particularly drawn to see more of them. But this exhibit, titled *Central Symmetrical Rotation Movement*, centered around three large-scale architectural installations, a form in which I hadn't realized McCarthy worked, and I was intrigued even before stepping out of the elevator.

This was in 2008, when the Whitney was still located in its old building on Madison and East 75th Street, with its stacked brutalist squares and few windows. Unlike the new space downtown, which highlights the views outside as much as what's in its galleries, the old museum was all about the art, offering nothing to look at other than the work inside the walls. It had an immersive quality I miss, an ability to make you lose yourself, forget the rest of your life, the moment you walk inside.

On this occasion, the immersion was instantaneous and overwhelming. The three installations were intentionally conceived to overload the senses, to make you abandon any thoughts you carried with you into the space. One piece, called *Bang Bang Room*, featured what looked like part of a house under construction, except that the walls of the house moved as you stood inside of it, and the doors kept opening and slamming shut on their own. In another, *Mad House*, a freestanding room had been placed on a mechanical axis attached to a motor that made it spin maniacally. The third installation, *Spinning Room*, used a rotating live feed of viewers projected onto mirrored walls to create a space that both enclosed the viewer and extended infinitely in reflection upon reflection.

The effect of all three pieces was disorientation—of a sensory kind, even more immediate than getting lost in the woods—and with it an inevitable letting go into the experience of not knowing quite where you stand. You might step away from one of the pieces and try to reorient yourself, but until you've left the gallery altogether, you're in a swirl, unable to find firm footing. I remember struggling to discover the exit, even though the room was a big square with only one way in and out.

I found the three installations mesmerizing, but I still didn't fully grasp what McCarthy was up to until I watched one of the two early film pieces included in the exhibition. In it, McCarthy appropriated the 1965 film version of *The Sound of Music*, except that he ran it backward and upside down, without any sound. Sitting in a dark theater watching the von Trapps walk backward over the Alps, then hang upside down from the ceiling of the abbey's crypt before hurrying backward toward the soldiers pursuing them, was one of the strangest visual experiences I've ever had. The film I'd seen dozens of times as a child—it was one of the few things my parents would let me stay up late to watch, in part, I'm sure, so I could witness Nazis being outwitted—that had seduced me into its drama, made me believe in its characters as real people in the actual world, even when they spontaneously broke into song, suddenly looked as sophisticated as a middle-school play. Every gesture was overdone and absurd. The indoor sets looked as if they were made of foam rubber. By altering our perspective, McCarthy exposed the artifice I may have been aware of but was willing to ignore. Now artifice was all I could see. And when I watched the original version of the film with my daughter a few years later, it was no different; McCarthy's manipulation of the musical had ripped away the lulling narrative façade, and now I was permanently awakened to what I was actually viewing. It didn't ruin *The Sound of Music* for me, just made me see it more clearly, as the stagy construction it had always been.

That's when I really began to understand. The point of McCarthy's disorienting work is to wake us up, break us out of our numb acceptance of what we see and force us to look harder at the world around us. It isn't disorientation on its own that matters; it's the reorienting with a new, heightened sense of perception that makes the work transformative.

• • •

When the Freaks Come Out

Getting purposely lost in the woods is a useful metaphor for the writing process, if perhaps a predictable one: while writing, we want to leave behind the familiar, enter the unknown, awaken ourselves to surprise. Running *The Sound of Music* upside down and backward is also an apt metaphor: we upend what we know well, look at it with fresh eyes, from a new perspective, in order to understand it more complexly.

But here I'm thinking less about process than about results, about the experience we create not just for ourselves but for those who enter the forests we generate. As writers, especially writers of narrative, we often work hard to orient our readers, placing them squarely in the landscape of our stories, keeping them on a clear path, however tortuous and full of obstacles, as they move through conflict, drama, and crisis. And it's true that our readers often need guideposts as they enter the world of a story, need to feel as if they're on firm ground, that they'll eventually come to a clearing and see their way back to the world they know. But on the way there, it's good to remember that it's okay for them to lose their bearings; in fact, those moments of disorientation, of realizing they don't quite know where they are or how exactly they got there, are often the most intense, immersive, and revelatory. When we're lost, our whole body responds: our pulse speeds up, our perceptions are heightened, and our minds are alert. At these moments, the story is no longer a passive experience but one in which we actively participate. We are trying to get around the trees in order to glimpse the horizon.

What I'm advocating, then—for myself as much as for anyone else—is for narrative that at times seems to spin out of the writer's control, when the reader might ask, "Where am I?" or "What the hell is going on here?" It's a hard thing for the writer to do—at least for *this* writer—and it requires a certain amount of trust, not only trusting in one's own ability to eventually reorient readers after disorienting them, but trusting that readers will stick with you even if they don't always know where they stand or what exactly is happening around them.

So let me turn to the question as a reader and start by examining one of those disorienting moments in a recent story I love, "J'ouvert, 1996," by Jamel Brinkley, from his remarkable collection *A Lucky Man*. The story is narrated by Ty, a central-Brooklyn boy struggling between family troubles and the pressures of adolescent desire. Ty's father, a charming but problematic model of masculinity, is incarcerated for drug possession. His disabled brother Omari wears a rubber bird mask all day and talks to an imaginary friend named Angela. His mother and her new boyfriend, Mike, want the kids out of the apartment so they can be alone together. All Ty wants, meanwhile, is to get a real barber haircut. It's West Indian Day, and this is the first time he'll be allowed to go to the parade without his mother; he hopes to look his best to impress other kids, to be more like his father, to begin to cross the threshold away from boyhood. But his mother says they don't have the money for a haircut, gives him a terrible one herself, and sends him and his brother off to roam the streets for the day.

The rest of the story is Ty's journey away from the familiar into the unknown and dangerous territory of burgeoning manhood. At a nearby park, he encounters a classmate, Trip, who makes fun of his haircut, harasses his brother, taunts him about his father's incarceration, and tells him that the West Indian Day Parade is just bullshit for kids, but J'ouvert, the all-night Caribbean carnival celebration is "where *all* the shit happens . . . when the freaks come out." Ty has heard of J'ouvert and suspects that his father used to attend but doesn't know for sure. Rather than invite him, however, Trip only steals his hat and leaves the hair that shames him exposed. Ty finds some comfort with a group of men playing chess in the park, trading banter and a bottle in a paper bag, a substitute for the community he hoped to find at the barbershop. They pass him the bottle and give him a replacement hat, and after he's drunk he leads Omari on an adventure into parts of Brooklyn where they've never been before, until they come to Grand Army Plaza and the start of J'ouvert.

Until now, Brinkley has been careful to orient us at every step. Even when Ty is drunk, we maintain a clear view of where he and Omari are and what's taking place around them. Only when he tells Omari where they are going and describes J'ouvert to him—his imagined version of it— does the solidity of Brinkley's world begin to melt. Ty details:

> . . . a fantastical version of the West Indian Day Parade, with floats that moved like clouds down the street, and music that caused you to dance as soon as you heard it. . . . [T]here was food everywhere, any food you could think of, and that there were people like him, bird-people who had feathers and could fly. The feeling of being there, I said, was the best in the world. Someone would always look out for you and take care of you and let you know you could do anything.

In this first unfettering from the known, we get a glimpse of what Ty hopes to find in it, what he really needs—not the independence of manhood, but what is missing from his childhood, a sense that he and Omari are being looked after, taken care of, given a chance to be who they want to be. But when he lands in the actual event, he quickly finds that his vision is far off. Almost immediately, what he experiences instead of the blissful feeling he described to Omari is sensory overload and confusion:

> . . . then came the sound of a horn, several horns. On the street, raised pitchforks prodded and tickled the air. A cluster of people wielded them, yelling joyfully. They were blue—*blue people.*

At this point, Ty still knows where he is: "ambling down Flatbush Avenue." He tells us, "we walked on the outside edge of the street alongside Prospect Park." But soon enough, he is lost in the forest of J'ouvert, a forest of chaotic sound and color:

They proceeded in a kind of squat dancing, a slow gallop, a low rov-ing strut matched to their risen rhythms of steel drums and cowbells and the flourishes of horns. Groups rolled and surged within the mass, people wearing T-shirts in the same bright color, or gyrating women in mere strips of cloth, or men with bells around their waists and rhinestones patterned on their slacks, faces raised, questioning and answering in song.

What distinguishes this passage is the heightened, almost hallucina-tory, attention to detail. Because Ty is now lost and doesn't know what markers are most important for him to find his way, he pays attention to everything. And we, too, are wide awake now, keeping tabs on the increas-ing strangeness of our surroundings. Because nothing is familiar, every sight and sound and smell gains significance. Rather than speed up and quickly move us through our disorientation, Brinkley slows down, makes us feel Ty's confusion.

Though we know we are still in Brooklyn, surrounded by people cele-brating their heritage, through Ty's eyes we enter a ceremony that's erotic, occult, otherworldly:

> More figures with pitchforks, devils oiled slickly black, rushed at us and began to fling paint or grease or powder or dye . . . they whipped us blue and white and orange and black, and as breathing felt like drowning in color, they seemed to be saying, *There are no observers here.*

Ty soon takes this instruction to heart, getting so caught up in the revelry that he loses control of his own body; he's bumped along with the crowd, gets knocked down and picked back up, until he finally gives in to it all, gives up trying to figure out where he is and what's going on: "I laughed and danced under the sky's slowly paling light, squatting and rubbing and strutting past the impressive eyes of watching policemen . . . I didn't care that my haircut was bad, or that my feet hurt." Here, when fully immersed in the disorientation and unfamiliarity of J'ouvert, he finally lets go of all his surface-level concerns.

And only then does he realize that in the confusion he has lost sight of the thing that really matters. He hears Omari's shouts and catches sight of his mask and struggles through the crowd to find him. Now that he has a clear purpose, a destination, he fights against the confusion of bodies, "the hysterical eyes and cackling mouths," and as he does so, the ecstatic, animalistic, otherworldly appearance of the revelers becomes human again, as does his understanding of them: "They were enjoying themselves.

They didn't mean to be scaring him but they were."

He sees Omari run from the crowd and chases after him, and then finally he's back on familiar ground, over a fence and into Prospect Park. And as he reorients himself, he sees things with fresh eyes: in this case, his memory of his father, coming home the night after J'ouvert, smelling of sweat, but not covered in paint—meaning, Ty realizes, that he hadn't been at J'ouvert at all, but most likely with another woman. His father, he comes to understand, has been the cause of his family's dissolution rather than a victim of it.

And then, with this new, clear vision, which he gains only by getting lost and rediscovering his way, he focuses on the most important thing in his life. He finds his brother in the park, dancing with the imaginary Angela. He lets go of his own desire to be seen and taken care of and recognizes his brother's more pressing need. He watches Omari laughing "without making a sound, still spinning, arms out, hands folded as though grasping onto something," and waits "to see if she would let him go." Once again on solid footing, Ty returns to the world he knows with a new understanding of the role he should play in his brother's life. We, too, return, awakened perhaps to our own responsibilities and the ways in which we have abdicated them in favor of selfish desires.

• • •

The Man in the Black Coat

Other stories take disorientation to greater extremes, getting us lost for longer and more deeply, employing not only heightened attention to sensory detail, which Brinkley uses to such powerful effect, but also syntax, structure, and point of view.

In her surreal story "Gothic Night," for example, the Egyptian writer Mansoura Ez-Eldin uses perspective and narrative distance to disorient us, and in this case she does so in order to blur the lines between the teller of a tale and its audience. She begins with a declarative statement about a male character: "His departure came without explanation." In the second sentence, we hear this character's voice: "His destination was remote, he said, uttering a series of ominous sounds." And only in the second half of the sentence do we learn that he is speaking to a first-person narrator who interprets these ominous sounds as "the name of a city I had never heard of before." Soon the narrator begins receiving letters about this city, which might lead us to expect a classic "frame" tale in which our first-person narrator tells us the story of the "he" telling her a story about his adventures in this unknown city.

And to some extent, we do get such a story within a story, though the source of the tale about the city becomes increasingly complicated. As soon as the narrator's friend leaves, even before she acknowledges receiving a letter, she begins to imagine the place for herself:

In an instant I could see the city he set out for, with its ashen streets. There are no colours save for the grey that cloaks much of the place, alongside surreptitious strokes of black and white. Throngs of people walk slowly in the faded streets, wearing grim expressions and staring at a still point ahead. A leaden silence bears down on everything.

Part of what disorients us here is the tense shift from past to present. Immediately after imagining the city, the narrator inhabits it, in real time. She's there in its streets and watching its citizens, as if walking beside her friend. In the next paragraph, however, she pulls one step back: "I, outside the scene, peer at him worriedly." Where is she exactly? Her imagination brings her to the city but keeps her an observer. She watches her friend in this unfamiliar landscape, unable to interact with him, but she also seems to know more about it than he does, "sensing the arrival of a giant with a black coat, sullen face, and heavy footsteps." She becomes a kind of omniscient narrator, aware of events before her characters, but soon enough the distance again collapses, and she becomes a participant, experiencing what those in the city experience, knowing what they know:

I feel the earth shake under the footfalls of the man in the black coat. I know he appears on the streets from time to time, stepping powerfully with the aid of his ebony cane. His sightless eyes shift over the faces ahead, until they fall on one that will restore his vision. He points his finger at the face, and its owner vanishes from existence.

For the rest of the story, Ez-Eldin keeps us off-balance by modifying the narrative distance. At times, the narrator describes reading her friend's impersonal letters; at times, she's in the city, running from the giant; and elsewhere she even inhabits the giant's point of view, imagining how he lost his sight and how he searches for a way to restore it, experiencing his despondency when his efforts fail.

How much of her understanding comes from her friend's letters and how much from her imagination she never makes entirely clear, but after a time, she tells us, "the city with its Gothic soul takes root in my mind," and she "dreams about the gargoyles on its buildings' façades . . . the giant moves in my mind, his expression transformed once again from sullenness to seduction, as though inviting me to follow him." Eventually, she begins writing letters of her own, about a city perched "on the precipice that sweeps down from the mountains to the raging sea." At first she sends them in response to her friend's letters, but when it becomes clear he hasn't read them, she simply allows them to accumulate, continuing to write, the reader embedded in close psychic distance as she does so:

> . . . ignoring my aching fingers and the pain in my hunched back, blurring the lines between my city and his, between the Gothic architecture with its squares and screaming faces and the perilous precipice with its houses resisting eternal freefall; between his giant with the black coat and blind eyes and the people I see when I open my window, walking cautiously up and down.

By the story's end, the two letter writers have merged completely; the narrator's handwriting has become identical to the friend's, and when she leaves her house, she emerges into the gray city described in the letters. And then she hears, "loud in my ears, the thud of heavy footsteps." In the story's last line, she wonders if those footsteps that cause people to run in all directions are actually coming from her.

All of this disorientation around speaker and perspective makes us pay close attention to where we are getting our information from, how the story is being filtered for us, and finally, which has the most power to sway us in a narrative, the observations of a firsthand witness or the imagination of a compassionate listener who can imagine herself in the shoes of a destroyer and understand his actions. Ez-Eldin leaves us to fight our way through that thicket of questions, not allowing us to take any single perspective for granted.

• • •

Invisible Circus, Invisible History

A final type of narrative disorientation emerges out of the connotations of the word itself. The verb *orient* comes from the Latin word for "rise," which for the Romans also became associated with "sunrise." To orient oneself is to position oneself in the landscape according to where the sun rises. Along the way, of course, the word also came to mean those places beyond the sunrise, the lands that lie to the east, and the people who live there; it became a line between an "us" and a "them" based on geography and culture, with implied hierarchies and prejudices.

So, another way for us to think of disorientation is as a blurring of this imaginary line that separates one group of people from another, an erasure of cultural dominance or perceptions of superiority. This is what the best of Paul Bowles's fiction attempts, when his arrogant Westerners—European and American artists and linguists and journalists—come to Morocco looking for adventure among what they perceive as the uncivilized and primitive natives only to find themselves submerged in a rich and disorienting—and sometimes horrifically violent—culture that has survived centuries of colonization and undermines all attempts to suppress it. His characters lose themselves in unfamiliar surroundings, and even when terrifying things happen to them—more than one of his characters gets kidnapped and tortured—they choose to stay immersed in their new realities rather than return to their previous ways of viewing themselves and others.

But while Bowles's vision does challenge the colonial worldview, it is still a product of it and exoticizes Moroccan culture through an American expatriate's eyes. A more complex version of cultural disorientation appears in the work of the Guatemalan writer Eduardo Halfon, whose novels follow a Guatemalan writer (also named Eduardo Halfon) through a series of journeys and encounters that explore and complicate his sense of identity. Halfon has been compared to both the German writer W. G. Sebald and the Chilean writer Roberto Bolaño, which in itself suggests the melding of different cultural sensibilities: born and raised in Guatemala City, Halfon is the grandson of Lebanese and Polish Jews, one of whom was an Auschwitz survivor; he spent a portion of his adolescence in Florida; he is a Central American who often travels to Europe but also to indigenous villages where his students live; he has been shaped by the oppressive politics of two continents.

What makes Halfon's work so fascinating, aside from its disarmingly casual and mesmerizing prose, is how it confuses the lines between cultural identities, subverts assumptions about what kinds of landscapes are easy to navigate and which difficult—i.e., "first-world" vs. "third-world" countries—and sets the costs of historical horrors—Nazi concentration camps and Guatemalan death squads—side by side so that we consider them in parallel. In the three of his nine books translated into English so far, the fictional Halfon often finds himself disoriented, in Central American villages, in European cities, at Israeli weddings, and even at a Mark Twain conference in Durham, North Carolina, where:

> . . . like some Gulliver, like Alice in an exotic wonderland, or even better, like Snow White in the cottage of the Seven Dwarfs—that's how I felt. Everything was lower down than usual. The bed, the desk, the TV, the nightstand, even the peephole you looked through to

see who was at the door was at waist level. There were rails everywhere and a ramp in the shower. I'm in an invisible circus, I thought.

Everywhere Halfon goes, he's in an invisible circus or a funhouse, where nothing quite makes sense, but where every detail is also connected, a piece of a mosaic the whole of which he can never see. In *The Polish Boxer*, he travels to Belgrade to search for a friend, a talented Roma musician who has disappeared, and even before he arrives he feels as if he "was floating in a dream dreamed by someone else who was surprised to see me but also found it pitiable and let me just carry on floating." Every encounter makes him recall another; he cannot separate what he sees in front of him from what he has seen elsewhere. Here in Belgrade, "the inside of the police station was dirty and crumbling. It stank. Just like a Latin American police station." While dealing with the Serbian bureaucracy, he feels as if he's in a Tarkovsky or a Fellini film, "not the Fellini of tangos and flaming tridents, but the Fellini of every man for himself, gentlemen, galloping off on a sea horse."

In Halfon's work, disorientation arises above all out of the convergence of past and present, or rather, the ever presence of past horrors. There are ghosts of history everywhere as he walks through Belgrade, along with their echoes: "bombed out buildings," "a row of dead animals hung from a clothesline," a "truck groaning . . . like someone in pain, like someone being tortured." He doesn't find his friend, but drawn by their music, he comes upon a Roma community. During the encounter he feels as if he is seeing things in "a faded dream or in a faded dream sequence from an old film." Elsewhere he feels "hypnotized. Comatose, even." And as a teenage girl dances to him, then on him, reaching into his pockets for his money, he feels "dizzy, feverish" and thinks that "sometimes what reigns is confusion, and sometimes confusion holds the reins." He hears a voice that might be calling him "in Romany or maybe in Hebrew" and then believes he hears "far off, as though subliminally, as though tangled up, as though it came from inside me, as though threaded through the rest of that music and all the music of the universe, one of the syncopated melodies" of Thelonious Monk, whom he and his friend had discussed years ago in Guatemala City.

For Halfon, confusion reigns, because his heritage is confusion, because our history is confusion. All our words and all our music are tangled together, a cacophony, though if you close your eyes and listen carefully enough, you can hear strains of beauty playing through it.

—2020

What if I Just Let Go?

Risk and the Creative Process in Zong!

Renee Simms

—⁓—

When I first read *Zong!* I felt as if I'd stumbled into an alternate universe. *Zong!* is a wildly inventive work of poetry and prose, and its author, M. NourbeSe Philip, took great risks: she risked meaning, narrative, grammar, syntax. She created the poems, or "zongs," in the collection by disfiguring and rending apart a legal court decision—first word by word, and then letter by letter—until the alphabet, strewn across its pages, with large areas of white space in between, transformed into a language other than English, revealing new words and visual stories.

Zong! unabashedly mixes genres and discourses, combining legal discourse, poetry, and prose. The prose appears at the end of the book, and it documents Philip's writing process in diary form with dates and places where she composed the poems. In these passages, Philip tells how she struggled with giving up "authorial intention." She knows that the poems challenge the reader's eye as it moves across the page, that the works defy traditional sense. She writes of not wanting to "contaminate" the text from what it wanted to do. And she speaks of letting those who perished on the ship guide the creation of the text.

Zong! defies traditional norms, and it presents me with new ideas about authorial intention and what raw material, beyond my own drafts, I could use as a writer. As poet and scholar Fred Moten put it, *Zong!* is "so prodigious and so profound . . . Everything became different after reading it."

• • •

When Philip began writing *Zong!*, she wanted to make sense of a historical event: the murder of 150 Africans aboard the Dutch slave ship *Zong* in 1781. That year, the ship left off the coast of Gabon en route to Jamaica with 470 Africans on board; however, because of navigational errors by Captain Luke Collingwood, the trip took four months to complete instead of the usual one to two. During this time many become ill and

Zong! #1

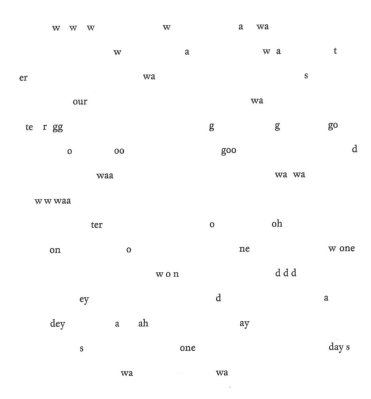

Fig. 12.1. First page of "Zong #1" of *Zong!* by M. NourbeSe Philip

dehydrated, and Collingwood—fearful of the ship owners' responsibility for the cost of Africans who died from natural causes—decided to throw the Africans overboard. It was claimed in court that first they threw themselves into the sea, frenzied with thirst, and later the crew needed to throw overboard many others for the same reason.

Collingwood's rationale was that if the "cargo" was "destroyed" because of unnatural causes, the insurance underwriters would be responsible for the loss. In other words, the slavers could collect insurance monies for the murder of Africans but not for the natural death of these Africans.

The case went to court. Philip writes, "The report of that decision, *Gregson v. Gilbert*, the formal name of the case more colloquially known as the Zong case, is the text I rely on to create the poems of *Zong!* To not tell the story that must be told."

Gregson v. Gilbert

Gregson v. Gilbert. Thursday, 22d May, 1783. Where the captain of a slaveship mistook Hispaniola for Jamaica, whereby the voyage being retarded, and the water falling short, several of the slaves died for want of water, and others were thrown overboard, it was held that these facts did not support a statement in the declaration, that by the perils of the seas, and contrary winds and currents, the ship was retarded in her voyage, and by reason thereof so much of the water on board was spent, that some of the negroes died for want of sustenance, and others were thrown overboard for the preservation of the rest.

This was an action on a policy of insurance, to recover the value of certain slaves thrown overboard for want of water. The declaration stated, that by the perils of the seas, and contrary currents and other misfortunes, the ship was rendered foul and leaky, and was retarded in her voyage; and, by reason thereof, so much of the water on board the said ship, for her said voyage, was spent on board the said ship: that before her arrival at Jamaica, to wit, on, &c. a sufficient quantity of water did not remain on board the said ship for preserving the lives of the master and mariners belonging to the said ship, and of the negro slaves on board, for the residue of the said voyage; by reason whereof, during the said voyage, and before the arrival of the said ship at Jamaica—to wit, on, &c. and on divers days between that day and the arrival of the said ship at Jamaica—sixty negroes died for want of water for sustenance; and forty others, for want of water for sustenance, and through thirst and frenzy thereby occasioned, threw themselves into the sea and were drowned; and the master and mariners, for the preservation of their own lives, and the lives of the rest of the negroes, which for want of water they could not otherwise preserve, were obliged to throw overboard 150 other negroes. The facts, at the trial, appeared to be, that the ship on board of which the negroes who were the subject of this policy were, on her voyage from the coast of Guinea to Jamaica, by mistake got to leeward of that island, by mistaking it for Hispaniola, which induced the captain to bear away to leeward of it, and brought the vessel to one day's water before the mistake was discovered, when they were a month's voyage from the island, against winds and currents, in consequence of which the negroes were thrown [233] overboard. A verdict having been found for the plaintiff, a rule for a new trial was obtained on the grounds that a sufficient necessity did not exist for throwing the negroes overboard, and also that the loss was not within the terms of the policy.

Davenport, Pigott, and Heywood, in support of the rule.— There appeared in evidence no sufficient necessity to justify the captain and crew in throwing the negroes overboard. The last necessity only could authorize such a measure; and it appears, that at the time when the first slaves were thrown overboard, there were three butts of good water, and two and a half of sour water, on board. At this time, therefore, there was only an apprehended necessity, which was not sufficient. Soon afterwards the rains came on, which furnished water for eleven days, notwithstanding which more of the negroes were thrown overboard. At all events the loss arose not from the perils of the seas, hut from the negligence or ignorance of the captain, for which the owners, and not the insurers, are liable. The ship sailed from Africa without sufficient water, for the casks were found to be less than was supposed. She passed Tobago without touching, though she might have made that and other islands. The declaration states, that by perils of the seas, and contrary currents and other misfortunes, the ship was rendered foul and leaky, and was retarded in her voyage; but no evidence was given that the perils of the seas reduced them to this necessity. The truth was, that finding they should have a bad market for their slaves, they took these means of transferring the loss from the owners to the underwriters. Many instances have occurred of slaves dying for want of provisions, but no attempt was ever made to bring such a loss within the policy. There is no instance in which the mortality of slaves falls upon the underwriters, except in the cases of perils of the seas and of enemies.

Lee, S.-G., and Chambre, contra.—It has been decided, whether wisely or unwisely is not now the question, that a portion of our fellow-creatures may become the subject of property. This, therefore, was a throwing overboard of goods, and of part to save the residue. The question is, first, whether any necessity existed for that act. The voyage was eighteen weeks instead of six, and that in consequence of contrary winds and calms. It was impossible to regain the island of Jamaica in less than three weeks; but it is said that [234] other islands might have been reached. This is said from the maps, and is contradicted by the evidence. It is also said that a supply of water might have been obtained at Tobago; but at that place there was sufficient for the voyage to Jamaica if the subsequent mistake had not occurred. With regard to that mistake, it appeared that the currents were stronger than usual. The apprehension of necessity under which the first negroes were thrown overboard was justified by the result. The crew themselves suffered so severely, that seven out of seventeen died after their arrival at Jamaica. There was no evidence, as stated on the other side, of any negroes being thrown overboard after the rains. Nor was it the fact that the slaves were destroyed in order to throw the loss on the underwriters. Forty or fifty of the negroes were suffered to die, and thirty were lying dead when the vessel arrived at Jamaica. But another ground has been taken, and it is said that this is not a loss within the policy. It is stated in the declaration that the ship was retarded by perils of the seas, and contrary winds and currents, and other misfortunes, &c. whereby the negroes died for want of sustenance, &c. Every particular circumstance of this averment need not be proved. In an indictment for murder it is not necessary to prove each particular circumstance. Here it sufficiently appears that the loss was primarily caused by the perils of the seas.

Lord Mansfield.—This is a very uncommon case, and deserves a reconsideration. There is great weight in the objection, that the evidence does not suppose the statement of the loss made in the declaration. There is no evidence of the ship being foul and leaky, and that certainly was not the cause of the delay. There is weight, also, in the circumstance of the throwing overboard of the negroes after the rain (if the fact be so), for which, upon the evidence, there appears to have been no necessity. There should, on the ground of reconsideration only, be a new trial, on the payment of costs.

Willes, Justice, of the same opinion.

Buller, Justice.—The cause of the delay, as proved, is not the same as that stated in the declaration. The argument drawn from the law respecting indictments for murder does not apply. There the substance of the indictment is proved, though the instrument with which the crime was effected be different from that laid. It would be dangerous [235] to suffer the plaintiff to

> recover on a peril not stated in the declaration, because it would
> not appear on the record not to have been within the policy,
> and the defendant would have no remedy. Suppose the law
> clear, that a loss happening by the negligence of the captain does
> not discharge the underwriters, yet upon this declaration the
> defendant could not raise that point.
>   Rule absolute on payment of costs.

Zong! #3

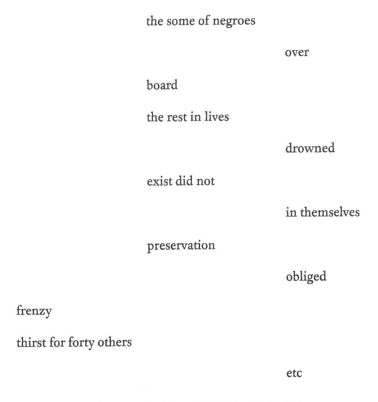

the some of negroes

over

board

the rest in lives

drowned

exist did not

in themselves

preservation

obliged

frenzy

thirst for forty others

etc

Fig. 12.2. First page of "Zong #3" of *Zong!* by M. NourbeSe Philip

• • •

Philip's creative process is an example of what we've been discussing all week in our morning talks. To borrow from Fleda Brown's ideas, Philip wrote beyond language. And she did this in order to arrive at a way to "make out the bones and wounded places," a phrase I borrow from Barrie Jean Borich's talk.

Philip describes her process as excavating what is "locked" in the text. She writes:

> My intent is to use the text of the legal decision as a word store; to lock myself into this particular and peculiar discursive landscape in the belief that the story of these African men, women, and children thrown overboard in an attempt to collect insurance monies, the story that can only be told by not telling, is locked in this text. In the many silences within the Silence of the text. I would lock myself in this text in the same way men, women, and children were locked in the holds of the slave ship Zong."

In other places in the book, she compares her process to sculpting, quoting the sculptor Henry Moore, who describes his process as removing "all extraneous material to allow the figure that was locked in the stone to reveal itself."

Philip must lock herself in the text of *Gregson v Gilbert* because that written decision is pretty much all we have in the historical record. Other evidence, such as the names of those who were thrown overboard, is unknown. When looking for the names of the Africans on the ship, Philip is told by one historian, "Oh no, they didn't keep names." She does find a sales book kept by an agent in Jamaica who did business with the owners of the *Zong*. It contains description like "Negro girl (meagre)."

And the final outcome of the suit isn't known. During the trial, a jury finds the insurers liable; the insurance company appeals, but the evidentiary trail ends there. "I have found no evidence that a new trial was ever held as ordered," Philip writes, "or whether the Messrs. Gregson ever received payment for their murdered slaves, and, long before the first trial had begun, the good Captain Collingwood who had strived so hard to save the ship's owners money had long since died."

• • •

As a writer, I can imagine the disappointment Philip must have felt at the dearth of information in the archives. This is where a writer who doesn't trust the process may fold. Instead, Philip solves her problem by fragmenting the one record of the event, the legal opinion, to see if she can retrieve stories from there. In a 2003 letter to a friend, included at the end of the book, Philip writes:

> The text has exploded into a universe of words. [I] have given in to the impulse to fragment the words of the text—using it as a sort of grand boggle game and set to trying to find words within words. The text—the reported case—is a matrix—a mother-document. I did not come to the decision easily—to break the words open. For a while I feel guilt as if I have broken my own rules, but that is where the impulse leads—to explode the words to see what other words they may contain. I devise a dictionary with each of the mother words followed by the words contained in that particular word—for instance apprehension yields hen, sion, pare and pear, to list a few possibilities. As I put the dictionary together little dramas appear to take place in the margins of the text and so the poem continues to write itself, giving up its stories and resulting in four subsequent movements or books.

Those movements are given Latin names because, as Philip says, it's the language of law: *os*—bone; *sal*—salt; *ventus*—wind; *ratio*—heart of a legal decision.

Although Philip talks about the poem writing itself—and also of letting the text reveal what she must do to unlock the voices within the text—I don't read that as Philip presenting herself as a seer or mystic. Her process is too well-documented for that conclusion. Instead, what Philip resists or gives up is narrativity and traditional uses of language. She also claims to give up on authorial intention. Without the description of her process in the back of the book or the glossary or the legal opinion, understanding her intentions from just the poems would not be clear—but she is okay with this. Not telling is a creative strategy.

I think fragmenting means both giving up and retaining some control. Philip's decision to fragment becomes a mimetic device to approximate the violence done to those on board the ship. Philip writes, "I mutilate the text as the fabric of African life and the lives of these men women and children were mutilated" and "I murder the text, literally cut it into pieces, castrating verbs, suffocating adjectives, murdering nouns, throwing articles, prepositions, conjunctions overboard, jettisoning adverbs . . . etc." The fact that the poems resist coherence and meaning and approach irrationality and confusion is also a way that the author is using the process to

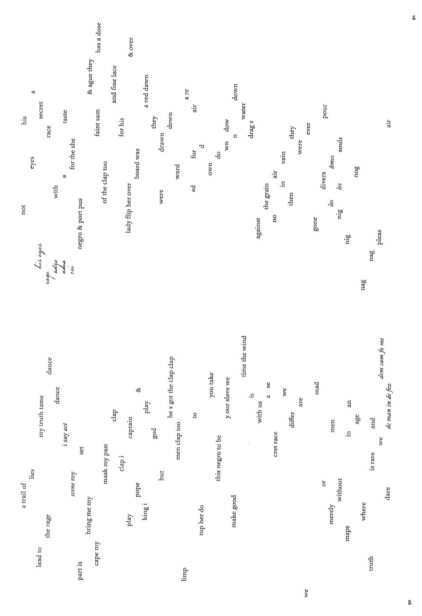

Fig. 12.3. Section of "Ventus" from *Zong!* by M. NourbeSe Philip

Fig. 12.4. Final page of "Ẹ̀bọra" from *Zong!* by M. NourbeSe Philip

mimic the underlying event, the confusion and madness that the Africans
must have felt at the time they were thrust into the sea.

Fragmentation also serves as a way for Philip to critique language in
the tradition of language poets. She writes: "I deeply distrust this tool I
work with—language. It is a distrust rooted in certain historical events
that are all of a piece with the events that took place on the *Zong*. The
language in which those events took place promulgated the non-being of

African peoples, and I distrust its order which hides disorder, its logic hiding the illogic and its rationality, which is simultaneously irrational."

Fragmentation, disrupted narratives, and collage are not new, but these techniques are reinvented with each literary movement. Modernists did it. Postmodernists, too. When I was doing my MFA in 2004–2007, I remember people reading and talking about *House of Leaves* by Mark Danielewski (2000), a novel that had text swirling in weird configurations; it was really two different books, with one appearing in the footnotes. And in the early 2000s, I don't think there was a creative writing workshop for K–12 that didn't cover cross-out or erasure poetry. More recently, Layli Long Soldier's *Whereas* is another example of literature that disrupts and fragments legal documents.

• • •

The visual presentation is as important as the linguistic innovation. Moten has said that when he looks at the pages of this book he sees bodies in the water. So do I. I also see ships, cartography, islands, undercurrents; I see continents. I see form and a lack of form, I see "meagre" girls as they were described in the sales record Philip discovered (I see these girls in the lowercase *i* that floats alone on some of the pages); I see critical mass and abandonment, and at the end, where the font changes from boldly black to gray and ghostly, I see the layering of bodies or perhaps bones as they might appear underwater.

In the end, Philip says (perhaps referring to the words inside words that she discovers when she spaces the letters out) that she learned how "our language—in the wider sense of that word—is often . . . preselected for us, simply by virtue of who we understand ourselves to be, and where we allow ourselves to be placed." And, she writes, "by refusing the risk of allowing ourselves to be absolved of authorial intention, we escape an understanding that we are at least one and the Other. And the Other. And the Other. That in this post post-modern world we are, indeed, multiple and 'many-voiced.'"

What is the revolutionary wonder or ineffable moments in *Zong!*? Not language itself, but the multivoiced, visual stories Philip creates through trusting an antinarrative process. It's her act of recovering silenced voices.

Like most writers, I like to believe I write for people languishing at society's margins, but *Zong!* makes me question how I've given voice to others in my work. What of stories trapped within other material or discourse? What of writing beyond language, of simply letting go?

For me, the lesson of *Zong!* is the creative power of Philip's writerly stance—a stance that is exploratory, open, and without a clear end goal. Philip genuinely trusted her creative process, which is a hard thing to practice or teach. But it is precisely this approach—a meandering pursuit of what one does not know, as James Baldwin says—that is the whole reason for creating art in the first place. When a poetry collection or novel reflects this pursuit, it breaks us open and wounds us with insight so that we might heal. Such writing reveals the capacious spirit that rides shotgun with an artist, and it is evidence of how closely the artist listened and followed the lead.

—2019

Community or Craft?

Unpacking the Genre Debate

Sequoia Nagamatsu

—〜〜—

Isn't This Debate Over?

The issue of genre—how we label authors, where we place books on a shelf, and the kind of language we use in criticism—still seems like a topic worthy of exploring, even though many writers tire of engaging with this debate. The question of whether something is literary or genre or if it should even matter still lingers in workshops and literature classes and the pages of the *New York Times*. Can science fiction be real literature? Or, put another way, can a story of merit with science-fictional elements be written by someone who does not have an MFA—someone who won a Hugo or a Nebula versus an O. Henry or Pushcart—be considered real literature? *Wait a minute . . . this author published in the* Paris Review! *Surely this must be literary*. And readers aren't the only ones who might make these associations—we like to claim people, don't we? We want "that person" for "our team." We like to keep people out of the clubs that we've formed.

We put Ted Chiang, the author of the novella *Story of Your Life*, on which the film *Arrival* was based, in sci-fi and fantasy because this is the general community in which he rose, publishing in journals such as *Fantasy & Science Fiction* and *Asimov's*. But if you've ever read Chiang, you might have been reminded of Italo Calvino, no doubt placed in the hallowed halls of real literature. You might be reminded of J. G. Ballard, who might otherwise have been placed in the science fiction and fantasy section were it not for his other work, such as *Empire of the Sun*. Of course, Ballard was associated with what was called "new wave science fiction"—one of the many early breaks from the "pulp" of the sci-fi and fantasy world toward the literary. Such genres might have been deemed "soft sci-fi," less concerned with the machinations of science and more so with the underpinnings of society and humanity. Authors associated with these types of "soft" genre categories, many of whom have found themselves both in sci-fi and general literature aisles or with the sole moniker of "literature" on book jackets, include Philip K. Dick, Ray Bradbury, and Kurt Vonnegut.

And it's Kurt Vonnegut that I've been thinking a lot about lately in terms of this genre debate and how people might view my own work, how I view it. Later this summer, I'm participating alongside other writers of science fiction in a panel that, in part, celebrates the legacy of Kurt Vonnegut and his influence on the genre. When I first received the invitation, the words "celebrated writers of science fiction" scratched the ego, but the grouping of writers raised the slipperiness of genre. While Matt Bell, Lincoln Michel, and I have published in genre publications, we have largely published in what most would consider to be "literary journals"— particularly journals associated with the MFA ecosystem or particular literary enclaves on the coasts: *The Iowa Review*, *The Southern Review*, *Conjunctions*, *Tin House*, and so on. While many of these kinds of publications publish work that have genre elements, a faithful reader of *Asimov's* or *Lightspeed* might approach these pages with suspicion and caution due partly to reputations of "MFA work" as being the antithesis of genre, the kind of work that is slow, navel gazing, and plotless. These generalizations are, of course, the same way I once resisted publishing in genre journals because I feared how academia might view them on my CV, because I thought so much of the work in those journals covered with rocket ships and aliens was "less serious."

The other panel participant, Charlie Jane Anders, is largely known by genre writers and readers (and increasingly so by the literary world). Anders approaches the rare sphere of the celebrity writer, having also cofounded and edited the popular futurist website io9.com. But when I first read Anders's debut, *All the Birds in the Sky*, I was astounded by how much this book from genre-publisher Tor read like any other literary novel with genre flourishes that might have been published by the likes of Knopf, who helped usher Karen Russell's career—now a staple in "genre-bending" fiction.

And then there is, of course, the question of Kurt Vonnegut, who is often remembered as a giant of science fiction but who never won a major genre award. He befriended modern science fiction and fantasy forefathers such as Theodore Sturgeon, going so far as to base his recurring character Kilgore Trout on him; however, he kept that world at arm's reach, fearing that to be associated with the genre community versus, say, the Iowa Writers' Workshop, where he taught for a time, would mean to be considered niche and less serious (and at the time, he was probably right).

But surely things have changed since Vonnegut's rise. I mean, Neil

Gaiman is kind of taken seriously now, right? Stephen King guest edited the Best American Short Stories, and his book on craft, *On Writing*, is widely lauded. He was even awarded (albeit controversially) the Medal for Distinguished Contribution to American Letters. When students ask me where they can send a "weird" story, I used to have to curate a list; now it would be easier to list the journals who don't accept work playing with genre elements so long as the core of a story rests closer to Kelly Link, Kevin Brockmeier, Kazuo Ishiguro, and David Mitchell on the genre spectrum (in other words, work that privileges some level of interiority and character over the spectacle of science and adventure). Fair enough! This talk isn't meant to convince you that genres are useless for writers thinking about tradition or for publishers needing to sell books. Let me be clear on this point before we move on, because the debate that rages on is about binary thinking (rocket ships = bad, an impending divorce in Montana = good)—the debate persists not so much because it is about craft, but because it's about the entrenched cultures and communities that make up our literary world.

This kind of opinion tends to annoy people since I'm basically calling out their prejudice, privilege, and limited reading history. Instead of conversations between communities of writers and editors and readers, I often view an echo chamber in conference halls and on social media.

My wife's first book was a supernatural YA that had a lot of literary appeal, which also meant that many YA readers were expecting the pace of a commercial thriller versus something more understated and character oriented. An old professor of mine had a similar issue when his publisher used a thriller comp title for something that could be considered not only literary but experimental—I don't blame them for that (and books were sold). With my most recent novel, deliberations about the cover were approached carefully. We wanted to capture genre audiences but also didn't want to alienate my literary base. So, in other words, we would have no spaceship on the cover, but we still wanted to nod at the cosmic, the otherworldly. In online stores such as Amazon and Bookshop.org, I'm listed as both literary and science fiction. But online algorithms do a pretty good job of paying attention to people's habits. On some level, Facebook and Amazon know about your literary prejudices and affinities and offer you choices based on what you've read, what you've looked at, what you've searched, and who is in your social network. Amazon has already listed the books of some of my friends below my own, people I've gone to school with or sat on panels with, people that festivals like to have me in conversation with. But this is just another kind of echo chamber, and even though our reading might be more diverse, our attitudes about the labels themselves might be a bit more static, ascribing one and only one definition to a category as well as viewing features of a particular genre as being representative of the genre itself.

I'll talk more about Ishiguro later in this talk, but I wanted to bring up his novel *The Buried Giant*. First off, I think it might be easy for some to call Ishiguro "literature" with a capital *L*. Academia and scholarly criticism can't deny the Nobel Prize. But Ishiguro, if we're honest, is a writer who is hard to pin down. Nearly every book he has written has played with very different genres, from period pieces about butlers, to detective novels, to science fiction, to fantasy. But in many of these cases, not unlike authors such as Margaret Atwood, critics "allow" these other elements and "understand their inclusion," even though there is still a great deal of suspicion as to the place of genre writing in the halls of serious literature. The debate persists because authors are very well aware of how critics might respond. For decades, Atwood was vocal that she was not a science fiction writer, that novels such as *The Handmaid's Tale* were, to use her own definition, "speculative fiction" (*speculative*, in her words, meaning that the events not only could happen but were based on events that were leading to a precipice of change). When Ishiguro responded to critics and readers about the nature of *The Buried Giant*, he noted that the novel was categorically not fantasy, that he feared people would dismiss his work because of some genre label. He explained that the references to the fantastical—dragons and ogres—were contained in the beliefs of the world of his characters versus being literal. I think that's a fair explanation, but should this disavow the novel from the label entirely? I'm not so sure (and there does seem to be a sense that this response to critics and readers suggested that fantasy was, by default, less serious). Ursula K. Le Guin publicly bristled at the idea that another prominent writer refused to be exiled into the wastelands of genre.

I've thus far been using the blanket term *genre* to refer to kinds of stories such as science fiction, fantasy, horror, romance, etc. that are seen as following particular conventions. We might also use the term *popular fiction* or *category fiction* here. These names are naturally useful if you find yourself wandering the aisles of a bookstore. Anything that is not genre is often labeled "general" or "general literature," and there's an unspoken assumption here that anything that is not genre is "genre-less," or the status quo (whatever the hell that means). I also want to unpack this idea inherent in the borders of genre, that whatever is popular is seen as less worthy and what is not (and even, perhaps, what is less accessible) is the pinnacle of high culture.

. . .

LITERARY (Fiction)

A quick exploration of the term *literary fiction* will lead you to the loose and problematic definition that it is work that has "literary merit." As a teacher of writing, I would get pushback from students if I said that to receive an A, you needed to simply produce work that deserved merit . . . as decided by me. And yet this is largely how the literary and publishing world has operated: this book, as seen by the establishment of often privileged, white men, is worthy as part of our intellectual discourse. Other terms produced when searching for literary fiction on the internet include *highbrow* and *high culture*. The term suggests superiority over other genres regarding artistic technique. And often when we're talking about the literary with regard to the genre debate we are talking about literary realism. But whose reality? A phrase uttered in workshops, "This isn't believable" or "This isn't realistic," may nod at work the author needs to do in order to earn the trajectory of a character, to build their world. But realism in literature is also a cultural and socioeconomic consideration. A piece of realism by one writer might read like a fantasy for a person of color or a member of the LGBTQ+ community.

. . .

Okay, Let's Cross This Genre Bridge Then . . .

There is a bridge, mind you, even though some have attempted to destroy it time and again. Authors such as Jonathan Lethem (who began his career writing a novel with a talking kangaroo detective and later became a literary staple thanks to *Motherless Brooklyn*), David Mitchell of *Cloud Atlas* fame, Neil Gaiman, Helen Oyeyemi, Karen Russell, Marlon James, Colson Whitehead, Brian Evenson, Kelly Link, Benjamin Percy . . . there are generations of writers who came of age not only with comics and pulp and magazines such as *FANGORIA*, but with the internet and new genres of narratives housed in video games and social media. Reality was not what it once was, and I can only imagine how literary realism will be influenced by younger writers emerging out of the COVID pandemic.

Let's quickly take a look at a definition of *science fiction* with these considerations in mind. The Ad Astra Center for Science Fiction & the Speculative Imagination at the University of Kansas says this: "Science fiction is the literature of the human species encountering change, whether it arrives via scientific discoveries, technological innovations, natural events, or societal shifts." That sounds an awful lot like the important fiction that we've taught in high schools and colleges across America for decades.

· · ·

So, Where Does This Genre Category Contention Come From?

We can say that this debate is just a matter of one community not wanting to understand the other, that it's snobbery from both sides, that despite our mainstream pop culture nodding at the speculative regularly, we still hold on to old definitions of reality and believability. To say these things wouldn't necessarily be wrong, but it's helpful to dig a bit deeper.

> It seems necessary to do something—to join a society, or, more desperately, to write a cheque. . . . [The popular novelists] have developed a technique of novel-writing which suits their purpose; they have made tools and established conventions which do their business. But those tools are not our tools, and that business is not our business. For us those conventions are ruin, those tools are death.—Virginia Woolf

This quote speaks to Modernist reactions to popular fiction of the early twentieth century, but I can't help but recontextualize this quote and empathize with it from the standpoint of a literary writer, a writer of genre, and a writer whose work needs to be explained, as it evades easy categorization. The literary folks of today are producing very different books from what the modernists would see as the ideal, but the philosophies of the modernists in moving inward and acknowledging form and difficulty is an attitude that, while writers have moved on to different schools, seems to persist in our criticism of literature and in the halls where literature with a capital *L* is taught, where some (certainly not all) writers are introduced to the canon and take their first writing classes. The language to even talk about popular literature or literary work that contains popular elements has not evolved or kept pace.

Inherent here is a division marked by class and privilege. Did you read the right books? Did you have a certain education? To some degree, I think we still judge people by this kind of knowledge. How many people in this room have lied about a book they didn't read? Or lied about liking something when you actually hated it? How many people have hidden their love for a popular, mainstream franchise?

When I was in junior high, I enrolled at a new school after a move from Hawaii to California. After a tour of campus, the principal asked me about my favorite book during my interview. I proudly and unashamedly pulled out *Jurassic Park* by Michael Crichton from my backpack. The principal said something to the effect of "Well, we're going to have to fix this." I remember feeling insulted and ashamed. This wouldn't be the first time this happened. I would continue to encounter classroom environments where I felt the pressure to stop liking something, to diminish the artistry of a particular work because it fell outside of a particular rubric. Only later in my MFA program would I come to defend books that seemed artless as a form of artistic mastery itself. For doesn't it take skill, skills that often are not taught in MFA programs, to write a page-turner, to understand and move plot, to move beyond the boundaries of a single literary tradition?

Now, I'm not here to challenge Alice Munro or Marilynne Robinson to a lightsaber duel. Look, some people might call me more of a literary writer than a genre writer. But as a professor and writer, I seek to grow and develop from the conversations of different kinds of writing. What kind of teacher would I be if I completely ignored the traditions my students valued? If I introduced only one pathway that seemed at odds with the goals of my students and the modern culture of storytelling? Yes, teach the canon. By all means, deconstruct Chaucer and Beowulf and the plays of Beckett. But aspiring authors need to be aware of how criticism and these genre debates have helped create their generation's conception of literature and how literature continues to evolve through reading cultures or communities and the marketplace.

Often in writing programs there's a focus on the creation of art in early drafts. That's important. But sometimes this comes at the expense of acknowledging how the business of writing and publishing is an inextricable part of craft and genre creation and stewardship. What will people think? What about the social media discourse? How does my book converse with other books on the shelf? Will people buy this? Will a Big Four publisher help turn this into a blockbuster hit, or is this a quieter read that will find a small devoted audience slowly but surely? I don't think writers should start a project with market in mind by and large, but at some point questions of audience, vision, genre influences, and even marketability can be useful to explore. Teachers who ignore what bestselling commercial work is doing, who choose to not teach plot and narrative architecture to students (this is more common than you might think), are only giving a journeyman writer half the tools. And let's be real, some students, some writers dream of seeing their work being widely read . . . but just talking about a limited view of art doesn't seem like the best approach.

• • •

So, How Should We Be Talking about Genre?

Why not let books just be books? Who cares about labels? Well, we care, editors care, agents care, and so do booksellers. And of course, readers care. But just because we use labels doesn't mean we should build walls or see those labels as fixed and not open to interpretation and evolution.

I want to return to Ishiguro again. After *The Buried Giant* was published and debates about whether his novel was literary or fantasy or something in between surfaced, he sat down for an interview about the nature of genre with Neil Gaiman at the *New Statesman*, and both writers nodded at the ambiguous nature of how different people regard genre labels. Gaiman noted, "We need to distinguish between something that's the essence of the genre versus the things that are just characteristic of it. A novel with a cowboy isn't necessarily a cowboy novel. A novel with a rocket ship isn't necessarily science fiction. The superficial subject matter shouldn't determine genre."

Beyond this conversation, there's also a need to simply acknowledge, as suggested by Theodore Sturgeon, that saying 90 percent of science fiction is crap isn't terribly productive when 90 percent of everything is also crap. The destruction of binary thinking that is supposedly enforced to protect literature can, in fact, enrich it and create possibility spaces for new voices, disenfranchised communities, and narratives that are uniquely positioned to comment on twenty-first-century predicaments. Ways of moving the needle in this direction can take many forms, from holding events with writers of different communities to housing those writers in conversation with one another in an anthology. Many presses and literary journals have already loosened their grip on genre elitism and have taken a step further to champion innovations in genre by women, BIPOC writers, and the LGBTQ+ community. Frank conversations in classrooms, in publishing acquisition meetings, at residencies, and at festivals about who a writer is, where their work comes from, and how we've treated certain writers can all make a tangible difference.

In a few weeks at the Vonnegut event, I won't be shy to bring up the fact that Vonnegut's relationship with science fiction was tenuous. And though he became a "name" in American letters, he was always met with some level of suspicion by some of the literati. Case in point: Norman Mailer called him "our Mark Twain" while also putting down elements of his work as schlock, and Gore Vidal praised him at a slant, noting how Vonnegut was always on the fringes because his work was never dull.

In being honest about how we treat writers based on labels that often come from the communities we associate with them, I have to wonder if a book such as Emily St. John Mandel's *Station Eleven* would be treated the same way if it were written by a hard genre writer. *Station Eleven* is an interesting case because it's not so much a genre novel but a novel about genre. Would Justin Cronin's *The Passage*, the first in a vampire trilogy, be called groundbreaking if it were written by someone who always wrote about monsters and didn't have a literary/MFA background? Should we revisit the conversations that led to Raymond Chandler and Philip K. Dick and their ilk becoming more acceptable within the ivory tower? But beyond conversations and market strategies to heal divides, are there other ways of looking at the labels that currently exist? Are there critical ways of circumventing the conflict between categories entirely? Or, quite honestly, are there ways of just being less dramatic about the labels?

Recently, in the essay "Let's Stop with the Realism versus Science Fiction and Fantasy Debate," Lincoln Michel doubled down on the idea that literature (focusing on realism) is not a binary and is, at minimum, a spectrum. Michel adopts a political-ideology axis chart, but instead of right versus left or libertarian versus authoritarian, we have the mimetic on one end of the y-axis and the fantastic on the other (the world scale). On the x-axis we have the naturalistic versus the expressionist (the mode scale). He prompts us to consider visual art in terms of the mode scale, considering how the naturalistic might look closer to our worldview with the expressionistic being twisted or fractured through a lens. And when I think of schools of visual art, I rarely see them as being in a state of civil war so much as expressions that have evolved from each other or that inform each other in some way. After all, isn't all of art a kind of dialogue?

• • •

The Utility of Engaging with the Genre Debate and Acknowledging Other Genres

When I first began writing seriously, I wrote fantasies, and these fantasies were set in a world that looked a lot like our own and were populated by Asian American or Asian characters who didn't behave like myself or anyone I knew in my everyday life. They woke up to the smell of miso soup. I offered Japanese phrases in italics like Zen gifts and translated them in the next sentence or in a footnote. I call these fantasies because I was writing imagined characters based on the expectation or some perceived pressure that this is what was expected of a writer of color. To improve your chances in publishing, you wrote immigrant fiction or fiction that was somewhat exotified. In a workshop, a professor noted of a story I wrote, "this worldly sort of thing" is the kind of fare that prize anthologies like to select. But of course, there are always stories of editors saying, "No, we already have an Asian-off-the-boat story that we're publishing," "We already have a Latin writer in our catalog," or "This just doesn't feel authentic enough."

When I first allowed myself to move beyond these identity fantasies, I rediscovered what we call genre fiction to be inspiring—it was genre in film and television where I first saw people like me who weren't caricatures. The act of imagining has utility in ways that are both mimetic or more realistic and reach further beyond our reality. Imaginative thinking—the kind of world building and system building that we attribute to genre—can help us understand our broken world, the tensions within the moving parts of society. But if we look closely, we see that genre writing also offers up the silences, the deep, introspective journeys into our hearts and minds—but perhaps in a somewhat different way than a "literary" work; that angle or lens can be both thrilling and illuminating. Plot shouldn't just be a utilitarian or a dirty word in an MFA workshop. Plot—maybe the juggling act between a space station and the time-warped past of a character (as in Erika Swyler's *Light from Other Stars*)— can produce emotion in beautifully nuanced ways.

I learned so much about pacing and emotion and character development from authors such as Jhumpa Lahiri and Charles D'Ambrosio and William Trevor; but when it came to unfolding story in the ways I dreamed about (maybe even like a page-turner), it was genre that helped me unpack narrative architecture. Science fiction and fantasy in both books and film taught me how to build walls, where I might place doors and hallways. Literary fiction taught me how to populate those halls with late-night arguments, children eavesdropping, and unspoken histories. And looking more closely after years of writing, I've come to realize that the doors and halls in that mansion of literary tradition don't have to be shut—the light from each tradition can bleed into each other in apparent or invisible ways.

As a teacher, I resist starting with literary realism as the sole foundation as if it functions as "the normal" story. I say open the doors and wander the halls. Please do find your kindred spirits, those people who will always understand you, your cafeteria table. But be kind, be open, and maybe, just maybe, join that weird table in the back of the room and ask what gets them excited.

—*2021*

Radiant Topographies

Borders, Conduits, and Carriers

Oliver de la Paz

—⁓—

Topographies

The large map takes up the entirety of a gallery wall at the ICA in Boston, a beautiful glass building set on the banks of the Boston Harbor. From afar, it is a map of the world, and you can discern individual countries because they are differentiated by color. Countries look to be put together via string or some sort of mesh. Individual countries look as though they are strung up together to catch a fish or to find some way to allow a tangle of vines to ascend up the wall.

But when you step closer, you see each of the strands that compose the countries is electrical wire, and from those wires, sharp protrusions pierce outward. Each country, festooned in thorns. The barbed electrical wires do not merely serve as idle warnings. The entire map is electrified, emitting at intervals sirens of alarm, then inscrutable broadcasts.

Reena Saini Kallat, a Mumbai-based visual artist, describes the map she has constructed as a "wall drawing" and states that her interest in the work is based on the notion of the line. As Kallat posits, the line, which is her subject, is a contentious space. She talks about how the idea of barrier and border situates itself in nature, arguing that borders as artificially constructed by governments are not natural. In other talks about her work, she discusses how animals do not honor such borders and boundaries and that each border and boundary is a site of conflict but also a site of exchange—of potential. And indeed, the hum of electricity through the lines that accumulate and create the thrust of her work is full of potential.

To my mind, her articulation of the function of the line is a useful way of exploring hybridity and cross-genre writing, specifically in recent works that center issues of social justice and history. Her use of electrical wire to demarcate boundaries suggests that the locus of differentiation is also a locus of energy, as she notes how the wires act as barrier, carrier, and con-

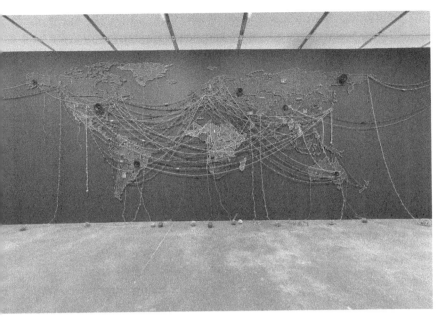

Fig. 14.1. Reena Saini Kallat, *Woven Chronicle*; Installation view, *When Home Won't Let You Stay: Migration through Contemporary Art*, Institute of Contemporary Art/Boston, 2019; photo by Mel Taing

duit. And in similar ways, work that crosses genres—not just in writing but through disciplines—offers a kind of energy and exchange as the work crosses over.

• • •

Hybridity

Kallat's wired demarcations are useful metaphors for notions of hybridity in writing. The crossing over from one type of discourse to another type of discourse is both seamless and differentiated. It is a strange disjuncture where one can understand, intuit, and differentiate where one understanding of genre exists and another genre steps in. This paradox is essential to deriving meaning. There's a purposefulness in the enactment of a performance of disjuncture that can be construed initially as estranging, but then ultimately conducting and bearing weight. Hybridity is a tool, but it can also be an estrangement. Hybridity is a mode but can also be disarticulate. Hybridity is a method, but also a mystery. In thinking about Kallat's work, I'm moved to consider recent books by writers of conscience such as Philip Metres, Tyehimba Jess, and Don Mee Choi. There are many other writers who explore interdisciplinarity, but like Kallat, these three writers consider lines of demarcation in large, resonant, and political ways. In fact, the hybridity of their works is essential to understanding their social justice positions. In many ways, all three of these authors use a similar technique of sensory overload. Kallat's map takes up an entire gallery wall, while the work of Metres, Choi, and Jess dig deep into archives and include as much of the archive as they possibly can, changing and shifting the ways that they call readers' attentions to the subject in question. Each of these authors is deeply invested in multimodal approaches to text as a strategy to overwhelm or accrue.

• • •

Multimodality

To write about something in a multimodal way is to assess that topic in a variety of different mediums and approaches. These approaches can be across genres and across disciplines. Or, if you're inclined to think about things rhetorically, it's taking the topic beyond the words on the page into a type of performative space. Writers such as Tyehimba Jess, Don Mee Choi, and Philip Metres all approach their social justice positions using a variety of approaches as a way to gather, reconcile, negotiate, and contextualize the disparate positions multiple parties, voices, and issues may take as these specific authors traverse histories that are difficult to articulate. For these works, in particular, it is difficult for me to imagine a single mode of discourse in exploring these heavily researched explorations. Foregoing an approach that engages multiple facets to reveal the complexities of their subject matter would seem to do a disservice to the history, especially when engaging with subject matter as fraught as what they are exploring. From Philip Metres's exploration of Palestine and occupation; to Don Mee Choi's archival work exploring narratives of the DMZ in Korea, particularly those orphaned by Syngman Rhee's forces; to the reclamation and reassembly of erased histories, through Tyehimba Jess's rechronicling of Black migration from the South to the North through the use of performance and performativity—like Reena Kallat's installation piece, these three authors examine the line, or the contention of the line. Through their works, they grapple with contentious histories while also insisting on the mysteries of what is known. They explore borders and boundaries—geopolitical, historical, and aesthetic. By using multidisciplinary approaches to text, they offer new intersections of discourse. Ultimately, they ask how one could acknowledge the other without the understanding that sometimes one mode of discourse is insufficient, and that in order to reach understanding or agreement, multimodal approaches may be necessary.

• • •

Border, Conduit, Carrier

To engage in multimodal ways of writing in the service of the works of these political writers is to invite an expansion of the discourse. To recognize that the possibility of what one is saying may resonate in different ways with different communities in one form or another is to also acknowledge both the limits of what is being said and the possibility of new ways of saying what needs to be said. Kallat's meditations in *Woven Chronicle* explore the line as a border, a conduit, and a carrier. It's useful to apply Kallat's notion of the visible line with the ways we consider text. Look to the writers who are combining forms in order to articulate pain, joy, loss, anxiety, fear. Clarity and universality are not necessarily the same as intimacy and complication.

Consider the three ways Kallat posits that a line along geopolitical spaces functions. She talks about the line as a way to signify boundaries between countries, but she also acknowledges that a large amount of commerce occurs between countries, and a large amount of goods and services are carried over and across those boundaries. Taking Kallat's notion of the line, for writing, what kind of work is performed when moving across genres?

• • •

Barrier

When we talk about sites of demarcation, such as the contentious spaces between countries, we are talking about barriers. When it comes to writing, we can turn that idea of a barrier into a space of creative production. To move beyond the barriers, writers often turn inward and create opportunities for their own works of art. When thinking about genre, we often think along the concept of line—how a line constructs a demarcation, whether that demarcation is syntactic, dramatic, or sonic. Many works of contemporary poetry define themselves not just within the space of genre but also across genre. As was previously contended, borders are sites of separation but also sites of exchange, and in works by many recent collections, genre as contentious space gives rise to works that are steeped in a social justice position that questions and contends with genre and the ways genre operate in delivering and extending their information.

Philip Metres, in his latest collection, *Shrapnel Maps*, considers the map but complicates it further, using multimodal approaches to poetry. Metres's poem "One Tree" is part of a triptych that opens his book and serves as the introduction to Metres's meditation on border and barrier spaces. The poem starts simply in a parable-like manner, telling the tale of a dispute between neighbors and a tree at the center of the conflict. The poem then splits into poems that offer different strategies to tell a similar tale. This particular poem, in its way, serves as a primer to the multimodal strategies Metres adopts in writing about Palestine. Metres plays with presence and absence, crossing out lines and images, contesting borders and boundaries of what is written and erased, what is remembered and forgotten.

The sequence begins with "One Tree," with the speaker narrating an incident over a beloved tulip tree. An argument with neighbors over how the tree "throws a shadow over their vegetable patch" creates the chief source of tension. Metres raises the idea of the border and border struggle when the speaker states, "Always the same story: two people, one tree, not enough land or light or love," using the point as a touchstone for the subsequent poems. In "Two Neighbors," the poem that immediately proceeds, Metres's speaker relates a story about walking through the snowy Cleveland streets and being offered a "roide" by a woman who is a stranger with a thick accent. The speaker then contrasts the previous story with a tale about a young Palestinian who climbs a minibus with the speaker but is suddenly detained as they near Jerusalem. And finally, the third poem of the sequence, "Three Books," simultaneously explores three books, suggesting the Old Testament, the Koran, and the New Testament.

Of particular note is that the formal constructions of the poems mirror the content. "One Tree" is written as a single prose poem block. "Two Neighbors" is a pair of prose poem stanzagraphs. And finally, "Three Books (A Simultaneity)" is a triptych, written as three columns of verse that can be read in multiple ways—either from left to right or top to bottom for each section. Metres insists on the rigid forms of the first two poems, each seemingly carved from stone, strongly adhering to the borders defined by their margins. But in the third poem, even the title suggests "a simultaneity" and that the poem should not be seen as defined by its borders. The trouble is that the very fact of its triptych form and the reader's previous relationship to the work raises one's awareness of the notion of a border.

Sometimes the goal of a hybrid work is not necessarily clarity, but complexity. To proclaim that a thing is much more complicated is a way to distinguish the identity of that otherwise component part to a truly individualized perspective. Writing, of course, does this as we write and construct stories and narratives that are personal and we often hope that our audience will understand us. But what is also an acceptable position for the work is to understand its complications and discern how the universal may not apply to this particular subject. Yes, hybrid forms can create barriers. Even though we may all wish to involve ourselves in the discourse, perhaps the writer is complicating a work because the amount of labor readers perform in order to read a passage may not be sufficient to carry its burden of knowledge.

• • •

Conduit

The concept of Kallat's line as conduit certainly applies when thinking about the possibilities afforded when crossing from the written to the visual medium and vice versa. I think the work of Don Mee Choi reveals the spirit of this concept of conductivity. Her work in translation serves as a channel, routing crucial narratives to an otherwise unaware public. In her latest work, *DMZ Colony,* she explores the history of the line that divided Korea into North and South, but in particular, she is interested in narratives of children who were orphaned during the Sancheong-Hamyang massacre of civilians. The sequence juxtaposes handwritten script, Choi's translations of that script, and drawings. Choi's process in constructing these narratives is fascinating—she moves from transcribing oral histories into her own handwritten Korean script, and then she translates that script into English.

The story transforms as it is conducted into its multiple forms: the printed Hangul script of Choi to the typeset English translation by Choi, to later, the sculptural and performative reproduction of the stories. The value that resides within precious metals that are deemed to be conductors is commodified and some may say "negotiated" through trade or through violence. These histories are then taken on by Choi's multidisciplinary approach. It is critical that Choi decides to show the source text in the original Hangul script (Fig. 14.2).

The image allows a visual wait to transfer to the shocking words of the children as they retell their stories. In the translated tale entitled "Orphan Kim Seong-rye (age 15)," Hangul handwriting appears on the left-hand page while the translation on the right reads as follows:

Orphan Kim Seong-rye

(age 15)

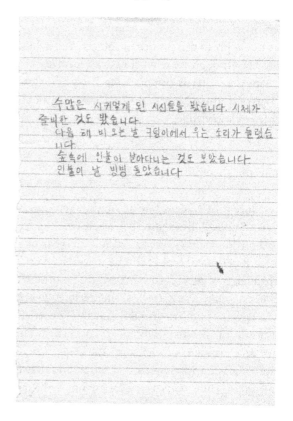

Fig. 14.2. "Orphan
Kim Seong-rye
(age 15)," from
DMZ Colony by
Don Mee Choi

I saw countless charred bodies. I saw rows and rows of corpses.
A year later on a rainy summer day I heard cries from the pit. Oblong
   oblong.
I saw ghosts floating about in the forest. They circled and circled me.

The poem bears witness to the atrocities of the moment.

It's essential that this work is translated by someone who has translated many of these narratives. The translator is an active part of the discourse here, capturing the horror of the moment after having captured other similarly horrible moments. What follows this translation is a translation from an orphan merely listed as "Orphan Nine." The tale of this orphan reveals that they are touring Ilya Kabakov's *School No. 6*, which the narrator describes as "an imaginary school, abandoned in the desert just

Fig. 14.3. "Orphan Nine," from *DMZ Colony* by Don Mee Choi

like an orphan." To the left of the translated prose are drawings seemingly done in a child's hand on photographed notebook paper (Figure 3).

An image of a princess or queen atop what looks to be a flock of geese fly against a backdrop of stars. The impact of these two narratives amidst a handful of other orphan narratives garners the work a conductivity. The accumulation of these narratives and the juxtaposition of the handwritten Hangul and childlike drawings coupled with the deeply troubling narratives offer, for readers, a type of positive and negative current, carrying the reader through the text. The fact that the work operates with so many discourses provides readers with opportunities for multiple types of reading.

Discourse such as this, which is an account of war atrocities, should not require the archive to verify the shock, and yet when the archive is present, the negotiated positions of those in the conversation are reconfigured. To conduct a discourse that bears witness, one must negotiate from a position of vehement interiority.

At the start of these narratives, Choi asserts her position as translator.

She makes it clear that she has not written these texts but is, rather, serving as a conduit for the flow of these testimonies. To be a conductor is to lead a path toward discourse. To conduct or to orchestrate a movement is to bring in synchronous harmony the music of instruments that would otherwise be discordant when played out of lockstep. Think of this as a way of coalition building, a way of creating modes of meaning that are receivable to a larger public.

Choi has also "performed" these works, and this past year she had an exhibit of the orphans' hanboks, or paper dresses, with Choi's transcriptions of their testimonies projected onto the paper dresses.

• • •

Carrier

Kallat talks about how the line is also a carrier, a vessel that holds and contains, and while the two previous authors have written works where the blurring of their genre lines serves as both barriers and conduits for their positions of social consciousness, their works also serve as carriers of history and of an essential archive. In that vein, I'm interested in the work of Tyehimba Jess's *Olio* and how he explores multiple traditional forms, hybridizing them in ways that suit his purposes, while juxtaposing those forms with hand-drawn doodles, photographs, and other formal experimentation. *Olio* is a highly dynamic work, exploring minstrel shows performed by Black musicians but also partially tracing the migration of these Black musicians from the South to the North. The work is vaudevillian, juxtaposing musical and comedic numbers with historic dialogues, monologues, and images. As mentioned, Jess is also interested in traditional forms and in reshaping those forms so that they are carriers of multiple layers of historic context.

Jess's work in *Olio* is heavily referenced with multiple layers of historic context that fold and unfold throughout the work. It is a huge and complicated book, filled with multivalent texts with accounts that are under contention, at times by the very speakers who retell their tales. That these sites of contention are capable of carrying information cannot be forgotten. Whole histories travel along the wires between communities, some of whom are in dispute. What we are talking about is an acknowledgment of one's history. By moving through one's art, one carries that history. Because there is a palimpsest of history, it is difficult to paint over any more layers without first acknowledging that there are layers beneath the layers.

Signals cross. Meanings can collide. Distortion occurs when, for example, one sound impulse runs into another. The collapse of one form can give rise to a new form. As in poetry, the collision of different modes of saying something can revise what is said and how one says it. Jess is fond of the contrapuntal, or syncopated, sonnet form, which has multiple layers of meaning.

In "McKoy Twins Syncopated Star," Jess hybridizes the sonnet form, creating a poem with multiple access points, each carrying the discreet histories and interiorities of their subjects—the McKoy Twins. Millie and Christine McKoy were African American conjoined twins who were forced to participate as sideshow entertainers. Like the Metres poem "Three Books," Jess's poem requires the reader to engage the text on multiple levels. The contrapuntal sonnet is written in such a way that one can read a left side, a right side, and the middle in oppositional dialogue, or the middle lines as a type of chorus for the performance. To further complicate the matter, "McKoy Twins Syncopated Star" is a series of five contrapuntal sonnets arranged in a contrapuntal cross-like pattern, so a reader can read across lines of one poem into the lines of another poem. What's of particular interest is that Jess has chosen the sonnet, a form so steeped in tradition. The contrapuntal series of sonnets in Jess's work carry with them the personal and historical narratives of the McKoy Twins, two figures who had their own interiority.

• • •

Radiant

Reena Saini Kallat's *Woven Chronicle* and her interest in hybrids and hybridizations along the political spectrum were the impetus for this deep dive into writers whose works delve into the documentary and the interdisciplinary. Like Kallat, I am very much interested in work that interrogates lines and limitations. I'm also interested in the application of these ideas toward new works and toward practical applications in the classroom, using these three radiant and socially conscious writers as models. What is inherently useful in the dynamic approaches to their documentary poetic works are the ways that they break down borders of genre, serve as conduits for meaning, and ultimately carry new ideas and ways of thinking about their subjects. The malleability that these artists display is hopefully permission granting. Again, I return to Kallat's notion that these geopolitical borders do not occur in nature. I also think the blurring of genre and mode is natural and can and should be seamless for us as creators. I wholeheartedly believe that the ways we choose to make art and perform art are open and can traverse the boundaries that are sometimes self-imposed, and I believe that the maps of what we as writers are exploring have the opportunity to radiate beyond the margins of any defined stricture.

—2020

Writing Without End

On Suspending the Need for Closure

Kevin Clark

—ɯ—

In the classroom over the last few years, I've been discussing the psychology of closure. That is, not only how to approach a poem's end, but how to calmly resist the premature impulse to create an electric ending. After all, one of the things that can stymie a writing project is the subconscious pressure to get to the ending, to close the work. Too often, we may hasten our writing because the need to finish the work is too much with us. I've asked my students and myself the following questions: How can writers find the path to the ending without worrying about getting there? How can we open the doors to the imagination without concerning ourselves with the finished product?

Poets have heard the following lesson all their lives: "The most important lines of a poem are the first and last." I think fiction writers hear that they should "hook" their readers and then close the story with a bang. I'd like to discuss strategies for deferral and exploration that may help us become simultaneously relaxed and focused while freeing ourselves from the pressure toward closure.

In April of 2007 a friend offered me his empty house in Santa Rosa Beach on the Gulf Coast of Florida for four days, and I began writing what turned out to be an atrocious poem. It was six pages long and not remotely close to finding closure. Even the title was truly awful: "*Luce Ideale*," Italian for "ideal light." For six hours a day for three days I wrote, thinking, *I can wrestle these lines into submission.*

I'd known a long-married guy decades ago who claimed he broke up with his wife because she told him he had no imagination in bed. He couldn't handle the insult. He was incredulous: "'Year after year, same thing in the same order, no matter what,' she'd said." Later, I'd thought to myself, *Hey, that's a subject for a poem—only I'll change the facts and the locale, and I'll make it from his wife's point of view. In fact, she'll tell her friend Dixie how she's going to leave her husband.*

And so there I was on the coast of Florida, writing about a woman who was unhappy about her husband's lovemaking and begins telling her friend everything that's wrong. I knew the poem had to be about more than that, but for three days the poem never found itself. The writing itself was flaccid, and there was inadequate conflict.

I was bending my mind, trying to figure out how to find an ending that revives the poem. And not only was I worried about creating effective closure, but I realized that the poem was too simple: Is she going to break up with her husband simply because he's too rote in bed? Not inattentive, but *rote*? Could that be the only reason? So, I thought, *Okay, say there was some guy from her past who was really loving and imaginative in bed. And say her husband's dull erotics are symptomatic of his all-around lifelessness.* And I start writing about that.

What had I done? I'd broken back into the poem to go find something fruitful. This writing choice involves Kent Meyers's idea of *infinite time*. Kent is a brilliant novelist, the author of *Twisted Tree*. In discussion and lecture, Kent posits that while we are writing we need to act as if we have an infinite amount of time to go exploring. Writers should follow the offshoots, the little streams that take us away from the central narrative or metaphor or impulse. Kent's notion is akin to freewriting, but with a key difference: Freewriting typically takes place when we start writing. Kent's process may take place after we have a good start. We need to let the poem or the novel or the story *happen*, and we do so by following tributaries that may lead nowhere—or they may lead to untold fruition.

One thing I'd like to add to Kent's idea is the notion of *layering*. This is a term you've probably heard before. No matter what genre you work in, the idea is that you write something and then not only do you go down those tributaries to see what may be waiting, but you go back and you add something else. And you do so throughout the entire process. By repeatedly going back and adding something (as well as deleting the unnecessary bits), you provide context, depth, resonance. Layering requires infinite time.

So, with permission to behave as if my poem had infinite time to create itself, I went back and layered in a new idea . . . and then another. I decided the speaker had a lover in college. In fact, back when I was in college a woman I'd known spent junior year in Italy and had a love affair with an Italian guy. So, since I'd lived in Italy myself, I made him an Italian tourist. And, since I wanted to change locales, I opted to have them meet in Mexico during her spring break from college. What happened? Cultural difference led to extra sizzle. This Italian guy was enthusiastic and caring in bed. Plus, he was romantic. And he wasn't just faking it—he was taken with our heroine. He was into Italian poetry, by god, and he read a poem to her that night. In fact, he read several, all by one of my favorite poets, Eugenio Montale, widely considered among the best two or three

Italian poets of the twentieth century. But our heroine had never heard of him and, nearly four decades later, she couldn't remember him at the time of my poem, though she certainly remembered listening to the poetry.

But still, the poem continued as if in a coma. If only the permission we grant ourselves to explore were a guarantee of excellence. But it's not. We know that permission must be linked to commitment. We must commit to come back the next day (or week or month) and explore again. But even then there is no guarantee. Here's just one sad stanza in which the speaker begins to explain to a friend how dull her husband has become:

> *I knew for all untellable reasons, okay,*
> *I'd be with him for life*
> *and then Brita was born and all the while his business took off he never*
> *   left me standing*
> *in the rain, damn well never played around,*
> *never forgets my birthday or shit like that, and I still love him, Dix . . .*

There was no linguistic compression in my poem and there were plenty of clichés. But I had to give myself a chance to see if something would emerge. And even though the woman is telling her story to a friend, there's too much distance between the speaker and the reader. The central character is not very appealing, in part because she's not believable. I had to risk trying to figure out what a middle-aged heterosexual woman would say to a good friend about an unlikely but transcendent sexual experience years ago—and I had to risk sounding stupid in saying it.

And as you can see, I sounded really stupid. But allow me to paraphrase something the poet Brenda Hillman once said to me when we were discussing long poems we'd been working on: "Sometimes it seems that the only writing worth doing is the writing that embarrasses us." Even though it might have turned out to be kind of cheesy, my notion about the Italian tourist reading poetry eventually led to another idea.

Montale often wrote about the quality of light in his hometown of Monterosso al Mare in Cinque Terre along the Ligurian Sea. All along I had to figure that amid the embarrassingly bad passages, maybe some lines were really good. Of course, I couldn't know, because I was in the middle of it. I asked myself: *Could there be a kernel of something savable here?* I thought of Brenda's comment: "We must be willing to embarrass ourselves." Anyway, I returned home from Santa Rosa Beach, and a week later I took out the poem and I thought, *Man, this is awful.* I said to myself, *Kevin, this is embarrassing, even for you.* So, I put it away. I didn't know if I could recue a line. I wrote other poems . . . and then . . .

A few months later I went to Bolinas, a little hippie town on the Pacific coast above San Francisco where the poet Hannah Stein (author of the two brilliant books *Earthlight* and *World in Costume*) and her husband offered me their old cabin where I'd stowed away to write many times before. Something was in the back of my mind. I opened my computer and there it was: "*Luce Ideale*," the poem again . . . and it was still just as bad as it was when I last reread it. Too simple. Not complex enough. The language a joke. But in that cabin in Bolinas, I began musing: What if this woman who lived by the ocean and hung out with surfers was a good Catholic girl? Was there a potential lifelong conflict there? *You know there is,* I said to myself, *because you grew up Catholic. You were an altar boy, for god sakes. You know all about the opposing forces of celebration and prohibition. Committed Catholics always worry about being good. Very few exceptions. There's all these rules that we follow to be good.* And then I thought: *What if the Italian guy she met was raised Catholic himself? After all, he was from Italy, a country over 90 percent Catholic.* Plus: *What if he was a poet who was going to become a professor of Italian literature, an expert in Montale? And what if he was one of these guys who never settles down with one woman?* I thought to myself, *We may have some kind of frisson centered around love, intimacy, and religion. Is there anything more conflict bound than religion?*

Now we were getting somewhere, at least in theory, primarily because I'd given myself permission to re-enter infinite time. I didn't know where it was going to go, but there was a tone bubbling up behind the work. And that's what we want, right? That tone. That magical sensation behind the whole piece. The thing that guides us . . .

Here's John Irving in *The World According to Garp*: "What Garp was savoring was the beginning of a writer's long-sought trance, wherein the world falls under one embracing tone of voice." You've heard of "the music of the spheres"? In a way, I think that's what Irving is talking about. If we worry about the ending, if we want too much to rush to that magical closing moment when the reader is filled with surprise and thrill, we will not fall under the trance that is the music of the writer's sphere. On the other hand, if we are free to explore, we can discover that music. If we have permission to imagine unexpected events or images or metaphors or dialogue, then we give ourselves a greater chance of being overtaken by the writer's music.

So along with the idea of infinite time and layering, we might freely ask ourselves a question I heard the suspense writer <u>Mary Higgins Clark</u> discuss as her own continuing prompt: What if? What if *this* happens? What if *that* happens? Much of what I'm saying concerns narrative considerations. But the question *What if?* applies to many different aspects of writing, including form: Quatrains? Tercets? Irregular stanzas?

Third person? First person? Standard punctuation? No punctuation? Metrics? Syllabics? Free verse?

What if?

As simple as it may seem, it strikes me that this question, even in poetry, is a requisite aspect of infinite time. It involves a form of play that releases anxiety and makes possible creative avenues for exploration. We need to take the time to ask this question, even if we're doing it subconsciously. In fact, over time, that's what we learn to do: we ask it subconsciously. It becomes part of our way of writing. Isn't that the way the best writing occurs? When we're so practiced that we are asking *What if?* without even knowing that's what we're doing? We're not worrying about the ending. Good or bad, we're soaring on and on into the *what comes next . . .* Of course, we'll come back to the desk tomorrow and we'll realize much of it is not working. But often enough, some of it will shine like pearls in mud. And we'll cut away everything else—because we've become good at getting rid of stuff that doesn't work (a topic for another time). But we'll exploit what works, and we'll layer on what else works to whatever worked previously, until we see the piece make a turn for the ending.

Whether we apply the question *What if?* to poetry, fiction, drama, or essays, it can lead us to potentially fertile plotlines, metaphors, lyric tropes, stanzaic arrangements, tonal shifts, etc. *What if* the husband's robotic sexual behavior is due to something else? *What could that be?* I asked myself. *So,* I thought, *maybe he's a vet. Maybe he went to Vietnam and the war screwed him up. Could he have become compulsive? One of those guys who does the same thing in the same way all the time? Might that explain his lovemaking?*

Now I still didn't realize that there needed to be something truly shocking that happened to him, some foundational trauma during the war. Turned out, that event would strike me later in the process. When I told my students various aspects of this process, I reminded them all that this kind of thing *could* happen if you're writing a sonnet. That is, one individual poem or short story might require plenty of infinite time or layering or asking, *What if?* But since I like narrative, I thought to myself, this sounds like a verse novel you've got on your hands here. And so, I came to ask myself: *What if I wrote poems about all three characters?*

In Bolinas, I went outside on the redwood deck without the computer and sat in the sun. I wasn't thinking about the poem, but of course I couldn't stop thinking about it. And suddenly I realized one of the many reasons it was awful from the beginning: the woman's voice was all wrong. I thought, *You've made her a wise-ass Jersey girl without any remorse, even though she's from LA. And you know down deep that she's way more intelligent than she sounds. But how do you make the voice right?* I ask. And I relied on the new tone, the writer's music. And I went back into the cabin and right there in Bolinas I drafted three poems, all in the woman's voice. She now had a name: Marie.

Eventually, long after I'd returned home and was writing the poems pretty much willy-nilly in three voices—Marie's voice and those of the two men—I realized that at one time she was *über-Catholic*, like my mother and so many of my family members! *Who knows?* I thought. *Maybe she still is . . .* And so the verse novel proceeded to center on these questions about the relationship between religious faith and sexual intimacy. While some of it explored the comic aspect of growing up a Catholic girl in Newport Beach, California, with parents who were fervently religious as well as faithful and carnal, some of it grew elegiac. Ultimately, Marie never communicated with her Italian friend again, she had a daughter, and she divorced her husband, not because of his lack of sexual imagination, but because the trauma he suffered during the war made him distant and idiosyncratically compulsive.

Here's a poem from the manuscript, which appeared in *The Cincinnati Review*:

Watching Kira Learn to Surf

A separating parsed out in increments
so fine I hadn't felt the distance
as terminal until it broke hard
like waves on a steep beach.

I must have felt it as respite, a woman
and a man fused only by their love
for a child and the grinding habit
of twice weekly sex. When Kira stood

for those few seconds on her board
as if she'd given herself over, a plummet
become ascent, her arms barely winged
from her sides. The rolling dark surface

seemed an afterthought, her face
a saintly calm I'd last seen nursing.
Then a surge bellowed up
from a dormant, pre-verbal crux

of animal gut, the diaphragm's relief
pushing a volume of stuck air
so fast from my lungs that the cry
exalted in a lowest register—

one burst, two conclusions. Her father
—who'd taught her how to trust
in balance—looked at me with the eyes
of a man gone back in time, then leaned

against me. My heart pressed into a seed
of dust, I leaned back in mercy.
I knew he'd thought I'd returned
from exile, as if I'd come up to breathe.

His face in my hair, he imagined he'd
returned, too. As I held still, Kira
stepped firmly into the undertow,
waving at the apparition on the shore.

I'd originally been using serrated, sometimes terraced five-line stanzas. I hope readers might find that the verse here is more controlled. More importantly, not only is the speaker more charitable in her worldview, but she understands so much more than the speaker of "*Luce Ideale*." She's filled with sadness and her language is, I hope, elegiac. She knows she's about to break up with her husband.

I never wrote the ending to the original poem. Sometimes I manage to push through to an ending, sometimes not. If we are to have liberty to go exploring in any genre, we have to find a way to give ourselves that permission—to read our own signposts, even if it means radically changing the project. Though a necessary step, the first poem written on the coast of Florida was awful, a true failure. Right now I believe the work in this verse novel is better than "*Luce Ideale*," but I understand that much of it may not be working and that perhaps I'll have to rework or abandon some of it. Which means what we all know: in order to write well, every day we must risk utter failure. I think it was Willa Cather who once said, "The end is nothing, the road is all." Thankfully, we can find transport in the daily effort.

—2013

When Life Interrupts the Writing

Rebecca McClanahan

—ఞ—

Given that we are now six months into a global pandemic, I might have named this talk "When Life Interrupts the Life," and any of you could have presented it, listing the countless ways in which the rough draft of your life has been interrupted, upset, revised, and edited, including those portions of your life previously devoted to writing. Yet hasn't life always been good at interrupting our writing? This messy, chaotic, beautiful world simply insists on having its way with us. Even in times that pass as normal, when external forces are not waging battle against our writing life, internal forces intervene to keep us from our work—distraction, doubt, fear, envy, despair, perfectionism, inertia, shame—all those forces living inside us just waiting to interrupt the time and space reserved for writing.

But today I want to focus on those times when we are either engaged with our work or eager to return to it. I will share thoughts on how time, events, and experience affect our work in progress, and I will suggest how we might proceed when real-life circumstances interrupt our writing. I've organized the talk into three main entry points connected to various aspects of the writing process: reentering or revising work in progress, shaping a book of individual pieces written over an extended period, and recognizing when the time is right to begin new work.

• • •

Reentering or Revising a Work in Progress

Is there a draft that you have returned to or wish to return to, something that still calls to you but now feels as if it were written by someone else, maybe an earlier version of yourself? Someone with different knowledge than you have now, perhaps, or who has a different stance on the subject? Maybe the writing began with a sense of urgency, but that sense of urgency is now gone or radically altered. Will you reenter the draft? If so, what might that process look like?

My personal experience with these questions suggests that, to paraphrase the philosopher Heraclitus, you can't step into the same writing twice. I'm not talking here about making minor editorial changes, surface revisions, or those desperate acts that I admit to being tempted, on occasion, to commit—"Wow, what if I change the font from Times New Roman to Calibri? Would that help?" I'm talking about deep revision, the kind that requires reentering a text with new eyes. The kind of revision that the poet William Matthews, my late friend and mentor, warned that one of my poetry manuscripts needed. "Quit going in with tweezers," he said. "Blow the mother up!" Bill was right, of course, and I'm forever grateful for his advice. What he was asking for was what I now think of as violent revision, a process I wholly believe in and practice to this day. He was reminding me that the reviser knows more—or at least something different—than the drafter knew and must now reenter the text with new eyes. In other words, as David Biespiel noted in his talk earlier this week, "Our stories are always in need of a fresh reckoning."

If you have paper and pen in front of you, write the word *knowledge*. Look at it closely. Break it in half. The "know-ledge" represents where you stood when you first drafted the piece. Now, cross out the *k*. Imagine that the knowledge you once had, the ledge of *know* on which you stood—is gone. You are standing (perhaps *teetering* is a better verb) on the "now-ledge," the ledge of *now*. How does the now-ledge affect the work you wish to reenter? It may be difficult, perhaps impossible, to reenter a piece of writing if your previous know-ledge collides with your now-ledge. In my experience, this is especially true when the writing involves actual people, places, or events. Let's look at one example.

Years ago, I began a memoir essay about my nephew. The now-ledge, or what writers sometimes refer to as *the occasion of the telling*, was my present-tense fear that my nephew would not live to adulthood, that the events of his life were transpiring against him. The essay felt urgent (one of those essays that Robert Atwan, editor of the Best American Essays series, once called "inspired rather than required"), and the sense of urgency informed the voice and structure of the draft, leading me to employ the epistolary form, directly addressing my nephew. The draft didn't work. I struggled for a long time, then put it away for a while, hoping it might cool off enough so that I could reenter it, but not so much that I would lose the essence of the original draft. (I've often found that, in cooking as in writing, reheating after cooling is a tricky process.)

In the meantime, life happened. As I said earlier, life is pretty good at doing that. Turns out, life had different plans for my nephew. Some amazingly good plans, in fact, and, for the time being at least, my nephew was all right. More than all right, thank the universe. Of course, the turn of events—*turn* being the operative word here—made me happy beyond measure for my nephew. Alas, it was not such a happy turn of events for my essay. I kept wanting to reenter it; it still felt important to write. But in light of my present knowledge and the fact that the original now-ledge had been removed, it felt wrong to make only editorial level changes. At this point, it appeared that I had several choices:

- Put the essay away, probably forever. This doesn't usually bother me, as I abandon drafts all the time, recognizing them as rehearsals or experiments or scaffolding supporting another structure altogether. In other words, as regards a work in progress, if I feel I can take it or leave it, I leave it. Other drafts, however, keep grabbing onto my sleeve, desperately calling out for help.
- Use parts of it in a fictional story about a character who really is in present-tense trouble.
- Follow Bill Matthews's advice and blow the mother up! Recast it in light of my present knowledge. With this choice, I would be reflecting on a time and set of circumstances, but the urgent quality of the text would change enormously, along with, perhaps, the form and structure.
- Embed it into an essay that suggests my present-tense knowledge as well as my remembered heat-of-the-moment emotion.

Those were some of my choices; you might think of others. But one principle seems clear: if the subject of our writing keeps moving forward—a real-life person, a place that is dynamically changing, an event still in progress—we writers may have tough decisions to make about how to proceed. This is especially true with memoir. The way I imagine this process, the memoir runs panting behind the life but can never quite catch up.

Yet even if our subject itself stands still or seems to (a particular time and place in history, an event long completed, a person who is dead, "trapped in amber" as Justin St. Germain described it in his talk earlier this week), *we* do not. Present-tense life continually reshapes us into a different viewer, participant, or narrator.

But what if our draft does not involve real-life events, places, or persons? What if our subject is, say, an idea or opinion? In Susan Sontag's *Regarding the Pain of Others*, she quarrels with some earlier published arguments she had proposed in *On Photography*: "As much as they create sympathy, I wrote, photographs shrivel sympathy. Is this true? I thought it was when I wrote it. I'm not so sure now." The point is, even if our drafts don't include external elements that change over time, our internal stances and viewpoints toward our subjects are malleable, changeable; when we write something, it may hold true for that moment only.

In the work of some writers, readers can actually witness those moments when the now-ledge interrupts the know-ledge and the writer begins arguing with themself. There it is, on the page: an insurrection of thought, an eruption, a disruption, an interrogation, a reversal. Because it isn't just *life* that interrupts the writing. *Writing* interrupts the writing. We writers often discover what we think, feel, and remember even as the words appear on the page. And even if we haven't set out on a discovery mission, the writing act itself may very well surprise us; this might feel like an ambush. For example, we may realize that a small detail we'd thought so insignificant we almost didn't write it down becomes the real subject. Or the syntax, the rhythms, the quality of the language that emerges, often without our consent, dismantles our original intention. And, in the process, the large idea we'd set out to explore falls away, and we are left questioning where to go next with our ever-changing work in progress.

• • •

Shaping a Book of Individual Pieces Written over an Extended Period

Now we move on to the question of how time, circumstance, and experience affect the writer whose goal is to shape a collection of independent pieces. Let's say that you've accumulated a critical mass of essays, poems, or stories, and you're imagining a book comprising these pieces. Apart from the usual challenges of such collections—finding the book's center, deciding which works to include or exclude and the order in which to place them, choosing a title, aiming for unity while still allowing for variation—you may face additional challenges if these works were written over a long period of time. As I suggested earlier, you might discover various versions of yourself colliding on the page. Or you might find that, like people trapped together during the pandemic, the individual members (your poems, essays, stories) just aren't getting along. Their histories don't align, perhaps, or they aren't speaking the same language, and you wonder if they can ever live harmoniously under the same roof. What then? How might you proceed?

One way is to accept that the individual pieces don't fit seamlessly together and to complete the collection anyway, perhaps including a foreword or afterword letting the reader know how to place the pieces in terms of your now-ledge at the time of the book's publication. One of my favorite pastimes is to read authors' prologues, introductions, or afterwords, especially those in collections that were shaped over several years or even decades. Here are a few of my favorites.

From Edward Hoagland's *The Courage of Turtles*: "The essays on love and pain are . . . not updated to take into better account my recent marriage." (Reading this, I wondered how many books are dedicated to a spouse who, by the time the book finds its way into a reader's hands, is now an ex-spouse.) Other Hoagland comments point to how current events have affected his take on earlier actions. He writes that ". . . two essays have been especially vulnerable to the speed-up of events . . . Already it seems strange that I could lose sleep over tearing up my draft card to protest the Vietnam war . . . A man must take more drastic action to become a hostage now . . . ."

I thought about Hoagland's phrase "the speed-up of events" when I read Wendy Willis's introduction to *These Are Strange Times, My Dear: Field Notes from the Republic*, which collects essays written from 2012 to 2018. She writes, "Recently, going back to some of the earlier essays was like paging through the family photo album: *Ah, look how young we all were then.*" She goes on to speak of how "the insanity of the 2016 election and its aftermath has obliterated what I thought I knew" and thus "some of my earlier grievances now seem a little quaint." In the end, though, she decided to keep the essays as they were to "keep the moments intact," she writes. "I think it is important to see it all of a piece, this era in time, some of it protected by not knowing what is to come."

Willis's notion of work being "protected by not knowing" was an essential element in the shaping of my memoir in essays, *In the Key of New York City*. As in my earlier books of essays and poems, I had no idea while I was writing the individual works that they might ever compose a book. I was simply proceeding as I always had—and still do—by writing what called to me at a particular moment. Each of the New York essays was written as a stand-alone piece, and since they were written over a long span of time (more than the decade in which my husband and I lived in New York), they represent different stages of my relationship to the city. In addition, each essay had what I think of as its own soundtrack, its own mood and mode and structure, and its own emotional landscape. Some were written in present tense, others in past tense. Some were forty pages long; others were five pages. Some contained backstory and reflection; others moved breathlessly forward. Most had been previously published.

But because my goal was to create a memoir in essays rather than a collection of previously published stand-alone pieces, my shaping process became, as it had become for my suite of essays *The Riddle Song and Other*

Rememberings and several books of poems, a violent process. I was, to return to Bill Matthews's phrase, blowing the mother up. In the process, I interrogated every essay, asking why it belonged and how it could be reshaped to serve—to *deserve*—its place in the book. Though the shaping process is different for every writer, for me nothing is set in stone, including previously published works. So, my process included cutting whole sections from previously published essays, writing new sections, and even, at one point, cutting apart a segmented essay and sprinkling the segments (which now appeared as flash pieces) into various parts of the book. One of the flash pieces had originally been published as a poem, but because I felt it was an essential part of the book, I dismantled the line breaks and rewrote it as prose. In some cases, I sacrificed the strongest parts of published essays to serve the whole book, and three of my favorite published essays did not make it into the book at all. They weren't talking to the other essays in interesting ways, or they didn't vibrate on the same musical wave. Letting go of them saddened me for a while. But because I am one of those writers who not only loves revising and reshaping but also believes that abandoned works often find their way into future drafts, I said farewell to them. Not *goodbye*. I said *farewell*, for the time being.

For the time being: another phrase that has served me well. Sometimes all it takes is time for our drafts or individual essays, stories, or poems— even published works—to find their proper home. Or to find several proper homes, each of which might differ from the original based on the contexts in which they appear. Many writers revise, recycle, retitle, or provide new contexts for older published works. I've noticed almost identical sections of Vivian Gornick's work, for instance, appear in published books of hers or in anthologies where the same passage, when excerpted from a longer published work, takes on new life as a stand-alone flash piece. And I recently discovered that one of Stephen Kuusisto's works that appears as a stand-alone essay in an anthology shows up in a very different form in one of his books. One version is in present tense, the other in past. The wording, paragraphing, and transitions differ. The title of Kuusisto's stand-alone essay does not appear in the book; instead, the essay is broken into two parts with new titles, and their placement in the book makes them read more like chapters in a memoir than independent pieces.

Placing previously published work in a new context, either in its original form or as a revision, changes everything about how a reader—at least this reader—experiences the work. It might also affect how the writer themself experiences their work. To prepare my new and selected poems for publication, I drew from four published books, a few poems that had appeared in lectures I'd delivered, and new poems. But once I realized that despite the differences in the books, one predominant thread ran through all of them, I decided to shape the book without regard to chronology and without book divisions, my goal being to create a text that would read as one single utterance.

Perhaps my interest in finding a new context for older work stemmed from the work of Audre Lorde, with whom I had the privilege to study and who encouraged me to submit the manuscript for what became my first book. Lorde often revised earlier published work in various contexts, sometimes combining the work with prose commentary on her revision process. Until the end of her life, even while composing new poems, Lorde continued to revisit and reignite older works in terms of her now-ledge. As she wrote in her introduction to *Chosen Poems-Old and New*, "Here are words of some of the women I have been, am being still, will come to be." *Will come to be*. Let's hold onto the phrase as we move into the final section of my talk.

• • •

Recognizing When the Time Is Right to Begin New Work

For many writers, the urge to begin arises organically. Something calls to them and they answer without hesitation. Other writers hesitate at the door, feeling, as I often feel, that something is holding them back, and it isn't simple inertia, external distractions, or any of the internal forces I mentioned earlier. How do we know when the time is right to begin new work?

Some writers begin when they sense they've reached a level of reflection, enough distance of time, space, and knowledge to imagine shaping their subject into a literary work. Yet what triggers the writing is often a present-tense experience. According to physicists, reflections begin at what is called the point of incidence, the place on a reflective surface where an incident ray encounters the reflective surface. John Dewey, in *Art as Experience*, suggests that the occasion that induces reflection is almost always discord. I think of this point of incidence as the sand in the oyster, the pebble in the shoe, the place where something rubs against something else, the moment of tension. Thus, a helpful question to ask ourselves when we begin a piece is not only, Why am I writing this? but also, Why am I writing this at this time in my life? Why now? Why here? What is the point of incidence?

Some authors reveal this point of incidence in their texts, as Ta-Nehisi Coates does in *Between the World and Me*, his epistolary work addressing his teenage son: "I write you at the precipice of my fortieth year, having come to a point in my life—not of great prominence—but far beyond anything that boy could have even imagined." "That boy" is the child Coates once was, and his choice to describe his earlier self as a third-person character suggests that Coates has reached a reflective distance on his experience. Yet it is a present-tense "incident ray" encountering that reflective surface that makes the text possible: "I write you in your fifteenth year. I am writing you because this was the year you saw Eric Garner choked to death for selling cigarettes . . ." Then, after detailing a list of other police atrocities, Coates continues addressing his son: "And you know now, if you did not before, that the police departments of your country have been endowed with the authority to destroy your body." Both son and father are perched on a "precipice," which seems the perfect metaphor for this author's stance, suggesting as it does a situation of potential peril. A brink.

For other writers, a plateau is a more apt metaphor for how new work begins. In his afterword to *Killings*, a collection of journal pieces he'd published in the *New Yorker* from 1969 to 1986, Calvin Trillin writes, "A reporter tries to catch a story on some sort of plateau—the end of a phase, if not the end of the story . . ." while also acknowledging that "within a couple of weeks or a couple of years there is likely to be another plateau."

How right Trillin was about the swiftness with which a new plateau might appear. By the time I finally completed the revisions to *In the Key of New York City* in the autumn of last year, I thought I'd reached a reflective distance of time and space. In my introduction I recounted the changes that had occurred since the essays were written, including my father's death and my mother's decline into dementia as well as changes in the city itself since we'd moved away, thinking these words would help the reader understand the plateau on which I was standing.

Then, just before the book was scheduled to appear, COVID arrived with a vengeance. Two of my nieces and a one-year-old great-niece were virtual hostages in their New York apartments, terrified to venture out. Ambulance sirens screamed through the nights, hospitals were overwhelmed and understaffed, and Central Park, a major character in my book, was now the site of white-tented field hospitals housing the overflow of patients. My forthcoming book was moving ahead without me while I was stranded on a new plateau, worried about my nieces and friends and colleagues in the city and concerned about the book appearing in this fraught moment. My publisher agreed to delay the publication six months, hoping, as I did, that COVID would be under control by then.

Yet here we are in August 2020, and I find myself wondering how my book would have been different if I were finishing it now, from the new plateau on which I've arrived. Would the pandemic have become the occasion of the telling? The now-ledge that informed how I shaped my book? I think of Joan Didion's daughter dying right before the publication of *The Year of Magical Thinking*, Didion's memoir about her husband's death. Though she later published a book about her daughter's death as well, I can't help but wonder how both books might have been different had Didion begun them later, while perched on a different plateau. And what of how life interrupted—and continues to interrupt—memoirs such as *Brothers and Keepers* by John Edgar Wideman, a collaboration of sorts with his incarcerated brother Robert, who, at the time of the book's release in 1984, was serving a life sentence? In Wideman's postscript to the first edition, he acknowledges the complicated relationship between life and literature: "This book's done, but today and tomorrow the prison remains what it has been. Robby's still inside." Then, more complications ensued: two years after the book's release, Wideman's teenage son Jacob began serving a life sentence for homicide. How would *Brothers and Keepers* have been different if Wideman had written it while both family members were incarcerated? Or even later? A second edition appeared in 2005, with a new preface, but life keeps interrupting. Robby was finally released in 2019, but Jacob's legal situation continues to evolve to this day.

These examples return me to Wendy Willis's introduction to the essay collection I mentioned earlier, where Willis explains her decision to keep the essays intact because, in part, some were "protected by not knowing what is to come." I extend this principle of "not knowing" to writers as well as to their texts; in other words, the state of not knowing the outcome of life events might be a form of protection for the writer during the writing process itself. When I asked Suzanne Berne about the afterword to her memoir, *Missing Lucile: Memories of the Grandmother I Never Knew*, she said that the events she describes in the afterword—her last trips to see her father before his death—happened quite late in the writing of the book, what she called "late in the life of that book." Her father was still alive when she wrote most of *Missing Lucile*, which is, in part, a search to reconstruct her father's mother for him through extensive research, since Berne's grandmother Lucile had died when Berne's father was a young boy. Because I knew that Berne's father died the year before the book was published, I wondered if her father's death had changed her own understanding of what she had written. She emailed me her response:

It seems to me that I thought of it when I was taking a walk in the woods behind my house one day, and called my dog, and then remembered taking a walk there with my father and him telling me that he heard his mother's voice calling the dog in my voice. That idea of "merging" with her somehow, for him, seems to have occurred to me then—the recognition that I had become a bridge between them. Believe it or not, I don't think I'd had that realization (though it seems so obvious!) during all my research and writing. I had thought of myself as trying to provide the mother he didn't know by reconstructing her life, doing an intellectual summoning. I had never conceived of summoning her within myself. But that blurring of identity, I think, must always happen when you spend years trying to understand a person you never met. It seems necessary—and perhaps equally necessary not to realize it in the process.

It appears that what Berne later discovered about her role in the making of the book—that she was not only a researcher but also an emotional bridge between her father and his dead mother—occurred without her conscious searching for that knowledge and without her forcing that role during the writing process itself. *Not to realize it in the process. Protected by not knowing.* These phrases reinforce what I've always believed about writing: that the process is mysterious, that it often proceeds without our consent, and that sometimes we, along with the works we create, are protected by not knowing what is in store for us. Life, it seems, is having its way with us and with our work even when we're not aware of it.

Sometimes life intervenes with such force that we know intuitively not only *what* we need to write but *when*. Sometimes, however, life has other plans. Especially in times of extreme stress, pain, or change, when writing feels impossible, all we can do is just hold on and wait out the difficulty. It will end, one way or another, and when we emerge, we will not be the same as we were before. The novelist Ingrid Bengis, writing as a contributor to the anthology *The Writer on Her Work: Volume I*, describes how this happened for her. She had a clear sense of the book she was about to begin; everything was in place. Then, life intervened and she "went from being a writer who protected my sacred solitude with vehement determination to being a woman so deeply entangled in life's common and uncommon dilemmas that I could scarcely juggle them all, let alone detach myself long enough to extract their meaningful literary essence." During this challenging time, she felt she was holding the "seed of a book" and living inside it.

Finally, though, when the dust of her life had settled and she was able to return to her writing, life surprised her again: "By the time I sat down at the typewriter, I was writing a book quite unlike the one I had planned to write, because I was quite unlike the person who had first considered writing it. I had an altered vision of life, not to mention an altered life." What Bengis came to understand was this: "At the age of thirty-five, I have just begun to become the kind of person who could understand the kind of book I would want to write."

As Bengis's words suggest, our lives are malleable, changeable as the wind. *Tomorrow and tomorrow and tomorrow* has always been time's job to do, not ours. And if the work we create lives and breathes in its own time, dependent in part on what life has in store for us, then perhaps an individual piece of writing—or even an entire book—can never be finished. Crazy as it might sound, this thought excites me, for if we "have just begun to become," that means that life will continue to interrupt our writing, providing us with not only a new story to tell but a new voice with which to tell it.

—2020

Creative Responses to Worlds Unraveling

The Artist in the Twenty-First Century

Ann Pancake

—⚬—

A few years ago, I published a political novel. I'd never intended to write it. Until I was in my late thirties, I'd kept my political concerns segregated from my creative writing. Of course, they crept in anyway, but always indirectly and never deliberately. On the face of it, I was an apolitical fiction writer.

I stayed faithful to that segregation for a couple of reasons. For one, I'd accepted the conventional American literary wisdom that explicit politics can ruin literary art, especially fiction, a conventional wisdom I saw confirmed again and again in many of the 1930s social-realist novels I read for my dissertation research. But a second reason was more decisive: I simply didn't believe fiction could put a scratch in contemporary social and political problems. What good, I asked myself, was imaginative artistic work in the face of "real-world" crises as urgent and overwhelming as the ones we've faced in the last several decades? What was the use of even trying? So I continued scrawling away on my short stories—because I'll lose my mind if I'm not writing fiction—while I shuttled away my political concerns—because I can't live with myself if I'm idle there—into my academic research and writing, into teaching, into direct activism, and, in 2000, into helping my sister make a documentary film about mountaintop removal in our home state of West Virginia.

That's when I got in trouble.

It was July 2000. My sister Catherine Pancake and I were running around the Southern West Virginia coalfields with a new digital camera interviewing people suffering from the fallout from mountaintop-removal mining, a catastrophic form of strip-mining that blasts up to 500 feet off the tops of mountains to get at thin seams of coal. On this day, we were with a local woman named Judy Bonds who was working for a brand-new anti-mountaintop-removal grassroots organization after she'd been fired from her Pizza Hut job for speaking out against the coal companies. She'd protested after she found her grandson standing in the creek in front of her house holding dead fish in his hands and asking her what had happened. Judy was taking us up a hollow called Seng Creek to meet a family who had recently been affected by severe flash floods caused by a mine directly above their house.

This family, whom I'll call the Thomases, had four children. They showed us the flood damage to their trailer and to their yard, and the oldest son, fourteen years old, told us about being knocked out of his bed by a mine blast. They all talked about how frightened they were that on the mountain behind their house was a sediment pond, or a slurry impoundment—a large lake that holds wastewater from processing coal—that was going to crash down on them as a wall of toxic water in the next big rain.

That evening, I found myself in the back of a pickup with three of the Thomas children and a couple of cousins, my sister in front with Mr. Thomas. Then we were bucking up a rough road along a ruined creek toward the mine. As we climbed higher, trees sliding down the sides of the ripped-up hollow, the road blocked by bulldozed mounds in places, pools in the creek glittering a metallic green, these tough little barefoot kids told me how proud they were of their daddy's driving and how scared they were of the floods, how they lay in their beds terrified of what might come down off that mine, how they were bound and determined to someday scale the mountain and see what was really up there. We came to a halt at the foot of a pile of soil and rocks and dead trees as tall as an eight-story building that had been dumped over the side of the mountain as the company blew it up in pieces. The kids piled out to scramble over boulders, their agile bodies a surreal anomaly in all desolation. The ten-year-old, Dustin, turned to say to me what the West Virginia Department of Environmental Protection, the governor's office, and even the White House refused to admit: "This is dangerous." Dustin looked in my eyes as he told me, "This is dangerous."

I left Seng Creek altered. The next morning I tried to scribble down as fast as I could all that had happened because I thought it would make a good journalistic piece. At that point, I still didn't believe that fiction would do proper justice to a subject like this one; I even feared the situation might be trivialized by putting it in a fictional form. Then something new happened.

About two weeks after I went up Seng Creek, I heard in my head the voice of a fictional fourteen-year-old who lived under that mountaintop mine. I wrote down about five pages of what he said. I figured it was a short story, but a few days later, the voice of another kid in that family came, and a little while after that, a third voice. About this time, I realized that what I was writing wasn't a short story, but a novel, which I'd never written before, never thought I'd ever write because I was so bad at plotting, and worse, it was a novel that tackled head-on a complicated and controversial political issue. And both those realizations scared the writer in me nearly to death.

As soon as I let on I was writing a novel about mountaintop removal, my own reservations about political novels were mirrored back. People would ask me why I wasn't writing nonfiction—and by nonfiction, they meant the journalistic variety, not creative nonfiction. Some activists seemed put out that I was writing fiction, as though I were wasting my time. Some writers seemed suspicious, as though I were betraying art. One of the most common questions I get in interviews and Q&A sessions is still "Why didn't you make the book nonfiction?"

I well know there are excellent reasons to be cautious when approaching explicitly political material as a literary artist, and especially as a writer of literary fiction. Nonfiction can directly reflect on ideas, present information, and even advocate for a "side" without violating the promise the genre makes to the reader. Fiction is another story. To treat politics in fiction is hard to carry off without violating the novel or short story's "vivid continuous dream," John Gardner's term for the spell the best novels cast, a spell too often broken by overtly political fiction. Of course, fiction can take some liberties—we have novels of ideas, though less popular today than they were in the past, and there are postmodern experiments that deliberately flaunt that "vivid continuous dream." But generally speaking, in realist fiction, a mere whiff of the didactic or polemic, any glimpse of the work's creator stepping in and directing the reader how to think or feel, can shatter the world the writer has so painstakingly constructed and unravel the reader's suspension of disbelief.

This is also true of much poetry and certain kinds of creative nonfiction. Integrating into any literary genre the facts, information, and context a political subject often requires is very difficult without undermining the art. Making the job even harder is the reality that contemporary American audiences are less familiar with encountering politics in literature than audiences in other countries are. I can also tell you from personal experience that writing political fiction doesn't make you very popular with commercial publishers. It's no mystery why American fiction writers today are actively discouraged from pulling advocacy politics into their work unless those politics are identity politics, which are a natural match for character-driven fiction and many times aren't recognized as politics. Certainly political literature presents myriad challenges to the writer, and in my own novel, I know there are places where I stumbled into exactly the traps I'm pointing out here. But is the fact that it's challenging reason to avoid it altogether?

For me, the question became moot when Appalachia, the place where I grew up and where my family goes back seven generations, the place that gives me my stories and language, was being blown up, physically and culturally. The devastation of my place is bald, unambiguous, impossible to explain away as "natural" or temporary or repairable. It was easy for me to be radicalized by it. But the truth is, this kind of runaway loss, just usually in more subtle and insidious forms, is happening everywhere right now: on the level of the environment, of economics, and of human rights, to name just a few. As artists witness this accelerated unraveling, more and more of them are compelled to treat politics in their art, many for the first time. I know this from my writer and visual artist friends and collaborators, and I know it from my students. As we artists turn more toward these issues, we face hard questions before we even get to how one balances aesthetics and advocacy, the most daunting question perhaps the one I mentioned at the beginning of this essay: Why make art at all? Isn't documentation, the presentation of facts, a more efficient and effective tactic for a writer in crises like these? And isn't direct activism most efficient and effective of all?

After six years now of hearing reader responses to my own political novel, I've finally made peace with my guilt and anxiety about channeling my activist energies into literature. I've at last come to accept that cliché we're told when we're young: you have to trust that your greatest gift is how you are meant to contribute to this life, regardless of what that gift is. As a fiction writer, I will probably reach a smaller audience than a journalist, a scientist, a charismatic public speaker, or a grassroots organizer, but fiction writing is what I do best. I've learned I need to have faith not only in that, but also in that the journalism, science, speaking, and organizing will be carried out by individuals with those gifts. And once I surrendered to the notion that making literature was what I needed to do, something interesting happened: I started to perceive the unique abilities literature, including fiction, has to educate, move, and transform audiences that no other medium, including reportage and documentary, does.

For example, I believe literature is one of the most powerful antidotes we have to "psychic numbing." It's not easy to actually feel, with our hearts, with our guts, overwhelming abstract problems that don't directly affect us, especially now, with so many catastrophes unfolding around us, and it's tough to sustain compassion for the nameless souls struggling with those catastrophes. But we do have great capacity to empathize with the personal stories of individuals. I once heard Wendell Berry point out that "public suffering means nothing if it isn't understood as compounded of an almost infinite private suffering," and he went on to illustrate this with a quote from André Gide's World War II journals: "Thousands of sufferings make a plateau. It's like that bed of nails you can lie down on. But one death, one instance of suffering, one Lear, one Hamlet, is the point of sorrow."

Fiction, creative nonfiction, poetry do exactly that: they immerse the reader in the personal stories of individual people. In our information age, when we can get thousands of facts and sound bites about any subject—and in this way build a bed of nails—literature is one of the few arenas where an individual can actually "live the life" of a person who is a subject of injustice. The reader of a novel or a book-length work of creative nonfiction, for instance, spends hours upon hours vicariously living the lives of other human beings, and such an experience can generate great compassion in the reader.

Of course, journalism and documentary, too, present individual stories. But those genres are restricted to the *exterior* worlds of the people interviewed. A few years ago, I heard Don DeLillo say during an NPR interview that fiction can do something that journalism and nonfiction cannot: show "the impact of history on interior lives." Creative writing, imaginative writing, gives a writer tremendous freedom to explore and portray the *interior* terrain of a range of people. My novel, for example, is narrated from six perspectives, so I was able to submerge my readers in the immediate sensual fears, losses, secrets, desires, and loves of characters, running the gamut from a ten-year-old boy obsessed with machines, to a teenaged girl forced to choose between attachment to land and a viable future, to a disabled miner struggling to reconcile his gut knowledge that the mountains are sacred with the dogmatism of a narrow Christianity. If the writer can evoke these interior lives with complexity and compassion, the reader's understanding of social injustice and environmental disaster is dramatically broadened and deepened. Personal stories in literature can wake up and restimulate readers' sleeping and numbed imaginations, reshaping how readers perceive reality and leading them to understand, in a deep, organic way, why particular power inequities must be changed.

Also significant when we think about the power of literature for advocacy is that fiction, poetry, and the literary essay have a much longer shelf life than information or reportage. Literature radiates far beyond a specific time, place, and issue because art embodies truths that are not literal, that are not time and place bound. Thus, we still read *Grapes of Wrath* when we don't read 1930s newspaper articles about the Dust Bowl, not even those written by Steinbeck. Walter Benjamin, in his essay "The Storyteller," puts it beautifully:

The value of information does not survive the moment in which it was new. It lives only at that moment; it has to surrender to it completely and explain itself to it without losing any time. A story is different. It does not expend itself. It preserves and concentrates its strength and is capable of releasing it even after a long time . . . . It resembles the seeds of grain which have lain for centuries in the chambers of the pyramids shut up air-tight and have retained their germinative power to this day.

Finally, it's essential to remember that the transformative properties of literature are not limited to its content. Literature's form, too—its style, structure, figures of speech, tone, mood, formal originality, experimentation—evokes in readers fresh and profound understandings. Form can be political when it moves an audience to question what seems given. Form can shake up dead paradigms and jolt us into envisioning alternatives. Art's beauty can make an audience yearn for a different kind of reality. Beauty can also simply help heal. As Phil Ochs put it several decades ago, "In such ugly times, the only true protest is beauty."

• • •

As I was writing my novel, I didn't give much thought to all those particulars. I wrote it with the conscious aim of just trying to show the truth about the devastation of a place I loved and with the hope of generating compassion for the living beings suffering because of this devastation. If people understood better, I thought, they would help make change. I didn't hold lofty expectations because I knew how limited the audience for literary fiction is, especially literary fiction about Appalachia, but I was compelled to make my own small contribution.

When I started my novel in 2000, almost no one outside the coalfields whom I told about mountaintop removal had heard of it except hardcore environmentalists. In the thirteen years that have passed since then, the number of people who understand mountaintop removal and are advocating against it has increased beyond anything I'd ever imagined, through the efforts of thousands of residents, activists, scientists, artists, and even a few politicians. Reams of newspaper and magazine articles have been written on the subject, dozens of documentary films have been made, and several laws and regulations intended to limit mountaintop removal have been proposed, although only a couple have ever passed.

This takes me back to that story I started to tell you earlier, the one about Seng Creek, the Thomas kids, Judy Bonds. I live in Seattle now, but I try to get back to Southern West Virginia at least once a year. In 2008, I was having lunch with some elderly friends of mine there when one, Mary Miller, asked, "How long has it been since you've been up Seng Creek?"

Even though my entire novel was set in an imagined landscape based on that hollow where the Thomases lived, I hadn't actually driven back up there since 2000, and I told my friend that.

"Well, we got to get you up there," Mary said.

We got up there. At least as far as we could go. Because in the years since I'd last seen Seng Creek, the upper part of the hollow had been washed out by a flash flood, just like the Thomases had said was coming. After that, the company had swept in and bought and torn down all the homes. The topography was now altered beyond recognition with fill dirt, giant culverts, non-native grass, two drift mouths for underground mines, and a sediment pond where the church used to be. Bulldozers worked the steep slopes above our car. I asked where the people we'd interviewed had gone. My friend said the elderly woman I'd based one character on had moved into Charleston with her daughter. The Thomases? Nobody knew. Finally, Mary said, "We got to get out of here before a rock falls on us."

In 2010, two years after that drive up Seng Creek, I got some news about Judy Bonds, the former Pizza Hut waitress who introduced us to the Thomases. In the time since then, she'd won one of the most prestigious awards in the world for environmental activism, the international Goldman Environmental Prize, and she'd become known as "the godmother of the anti-mountaintop-removal movement." I'd spent a lot of time with Judy in the early part of the last decade, and she was one of several women I drew on for the main character Lace in my novel. But the news I got was that Judy had been diagnosed with brain cancer. By January of 2011, she had died at age 58. Water tests of the creek outside her house—the creek where her grandson held the dead fish—show that it contains polyacrylamide, a cancer-causing agent used for coal processing.

So, I have witnessed the landscape where my work is set and the people who inspired my characters continue to be destroyed by an injustice my creative work tried to address. And these are just representative episodes in the larger context of the expansion of mountaintop removal in the last decade—at least 500 mountains blown up, possibly 2,000 miles of streams filled with toxic rubble, countless people dead from poisoned air and water. This escalation has continued despite drastically expanded public awareness of mountaintop removal and its fallout, despite great public outcry against it. And just as what happened to Seng Creek and to Judy are only two examples of the larger conflagration in central Appalachia, the Appalachian crisis is just one instance in a larger global context crackling with intensifying life-threatening crises, from global warming to mass extinction to the breakdown of economic systems, all of these documented endlessly, ad nauseam, by the press and others.

I, like many of us, have certainly felt despair about all this, especially about my own inefficacy to affect change. I've felt cynicism, at other times apathy; I've felt the impulse to isolate myself, insulate myself. I've wallowed in these states. I've ranted. I've struggled with guilt over my paralysis. Until, finally, an insight broke that paralysis up.

I realized that periods of disintegration most often contain within them profound possibilities for creation. An era like this one, precisely because of the scale and scope of its dissolution, offers tremendous opportunities for sweeping systemic change. I know we still need art that tells truth. But given our circumstances, I believe we artists must open ourselves wider to how art performs politically beyond bearing witness. Because I've concluded that the only solution to our current mess is a radical transformation of how people think and perceive and value. In other words, a revolutionizing of people's interiors. And revolutionizing people's interiors is exactly what art can do better than anything else at our disposal, aside from spirituality and certain kinds of direct experience that are not as easily available as art.

Take, for instance, literature's power to exercise, develop, and revitalize the imagination, the imaginations of both readers and writers. In our culture, imagination is impoverished and misdirected at a time when we desperately need new vision and ideas. The literary arts, especially fiction, make more extensive and sustained demands on a reader's imagination than perhaps any other form of media. Admittedly, the imaginative effort a person must make to read literature means some won't bother to engage with it at all. However, those who are willing to participate can leave the interaction deeply imprinted precisely because they had to engage their imaginations so energetically. And that exercising of the imagination can help readers and writers imagine better in other parts of their lives.

Pushing a little deeper into the relationship between literature and the imagination, I want to point out, too, the way literature—both the reading of it and the writing of it—can reunite an individual's conscious and unconscious. I can't overemphasize how imperative I think this reunion is. I would argue that many of our contemporary ills are caused or exacerbated by our culture's rending the conscious from the unconscious, then elevating the conscious—the intellect, ration—to the complete neglect, if not outright derision, of the unconscious. This is disastrous not only because such psychic amputation cripples people, contributing to feelings of emptiness, insatiability, depression, and anxiety, but also because within that cast-off unconscious, in intuition, in dreams, dwell ideas, solutions, utterly fresh ways of perceiving and understanding that we need urgently in an era of unraveling and transition. I, like all writers, know the power of the unconscious because it's where I've gone for decades for my fiction writing. I know how boundless that realm is, how explosive with energy and light, and I know my unconscious is eons ahead of my intellect, worlds larger in vision than my rational mind. This is exactly where we'll find the materials and the fuel for that transformation of psyche I'm talking about. And our very business as artists is trafficking between the conscious and the unconscious; indeed, we are one of the very last groups in this culture who have a sanctioned day-to-day relationship with our unconscious, with our dreams and intuition.

Now I'll crawl even farther out on my limb and, refining this notion of artists' reintegration of the conscious and the unconscious, I'll propose that artists are also translators between the visible and invisible worlds, intermediaries between the profane and the sacred. How is this pertinent to the case I'm making for art's ability to make change in the world? Only by desacralizing the world over centuries have we given ourselves permission to destroy it. Conversely, to protect and preserve life, we must re-recognize its sacredness, and art helps us do that. Literature resacralizes by illuminating the profound within the apparently mundane, by restoring reverence and wonder for the everyday, by heightening our attentiveness and enlarging our compassion. The magic and transcendence and mystery that characterize true literary art make a piece of literature a microcosm of the wider universe, of the mystery and profundity and transcendence that reside there for those willing to look for it.

If talk of the holy is off-putting, let's just boil it down to love. Jack Turner, in *The Abstract Wild*, insists that only genuine love of our environment will incite us to save it and, further, that aside from direct experience, only art can make us fall in love with the world. "Mere concepts and abstractions," like those in science and public policy, "will not do, because love is beyond concepts and abstractions. And yet the problem is one of love." And for those of us, like myself, who still feel periodically ashamed about not taking more direct action, Turner has this: "We can all drive a spike into a tree, but few can produce visionary fiction or memoirs that transform our beliefs and extend the possibilities of what we might come to love."

Art holds other powers of intervention, but I'll address just one more, the one I believe is literature's most pressing task of all right now: envisioning alternative future realities. My biggest disappointment in my own political novel is not the missteps where I stray into polemics or awkwardly integrate information. My biggest disappointment is that my novel does not provide vision beyond the contemporary situation in central Appalachia. I have learned that it's much easier to represent a political situation in literature than it is to propose alternatives—to dream forward—without falling into Pollyannaism or dystopia. But I've come to believe that my greatest challenge now—and a challenge for many twenty-first-century artists—is to create literature that imagines a way forward that is not idealism or fantasy, is not dystopia or utopia, but still turns current paradigms on their heads. I now feel charged to make stories that invent more than represent, that dream more than reflect. Which is not to say that I have more than glimmers of what such fiction would be. But I do carry a burning urgency that it must be done.

I'm aware that my confidence that literature in 2011 matters in the ways I've discussed seems fantastic and Pollyannaish itself. Literature's audience is too small, readers' attention spans too attenuated, competing media and technologies too distracting and seductive. I drift into this skepticism, too. But I also know that throughout human history, the mythmakers, the culture creators, those who dream forward for their communities, have been the artists. Yes, contemporary culture has trivialized, ghettoized, and marginalized us when it hasn't been able to commercialize us. I fear many of us have internalized this sense of irrelevancy. What I'm suggesting now is that we take ourselves more seriously and make ourselves more relevant. We certainly have nothing to lose.

I ask that we keep the aesthetic bar high and write in a way not duplicated by other media, that performs and affects as only literature can. If we are drawn to treat an overtly political subject, we should do that. To presuppose that literature is not capacious enough to contain politics is to disrespect and underestimate literature. If explicit politics are not our interest, I hope that we remember that art, regardless of its subject, has the power to revolutionize a soul. I ask that we stay motivated, optimistic, and inspired by bearing in mind the gifts we writers can give others: We can return beauty to a world that has lost much of it. We can make meaning in a world that to many appears more and more meaningless. We can help resacralize life in a world that has been long desacralized. And we can assume the honor of dreaming forward.

—2011

Why Write a Novel? Why Read a Novel?
And Why Now?

Suzanne Berne

—⚒—

Since the title of this essay implies that I have the answers to the questions it poses, here are a few disclaimers: My reasons for why novels are worth writing and reading are not an argument for writing and reading novels over other genres. I only want to try to interest those who have never considered writing a novel, and maybe don't often read them, as well as cheer on anyone who is currently writing a novel and feels as if they're floundering in an endless marsh. My aim in part is to try to describe what it's *like* to write a novel—or what it can be like—and why I think that experience and novels themselves matter.

To describe what it can be like to write a novel, I'll offer a bit of my own experience, my first published novel, which began almost thirty years ago with a grudge. You would be amazed by how many novels are inspired by complaint; the advice "start small" has many applications.

I had written another first novel that had been rejected everywhere, usually with polite notes from editors that said something like, "Nice writing, but nothing happens." One summer afternoon I was sitting on my porch, brooding over these rejections, at the same time watching my neighbor mow his lawn with a push mower, wondering why he bothered to wear his toupee while mowing his lawn on such a hot day, and feeling irritated by his push mower, which was making a pointed clattering noise as if in rebuke to my own unmown lawn. And in the same slightly spiteful vein, I thought: *All these editors want something to "happen"? All right, I'll give them something. I'll give them a murder.* That afternoon I wrote what became the first chapter of my novel *A Crime in the Neighborhood*, which is indeed about a murder, but it's also about someone watching her neighbor and speculating uncharitably about him.

The murder itself was more or less written that day on my porch. But it took a long time for me to figure out that the opening crime was not actually the novel's focus—in fact, I decided not to solve it. The *effort* to solve the crime was what I became more interested in, along with what that effort did to the people involved. I wrote draft after draft, trying to locate the right point of view and to figure out the sequence of events. Finally, I gave it to a friend to read, who after several weeks remarked ominously, "I'm almost done with it." More drafts. Then I had a baby, and that of course took up some time, and then, when I finally *did* finish the novel, no one wanted to publish it. After I got fifteen rejections, one editor wrote to me and said that she liked the book until page 168 but following that I missed the mark. However, she said, if I would be open to discussing the book after page 168, she would talk to me about it. So I wrote another draft, had another baby, and that, at last, was that.

I mention all this to explode the still-popular image of the austere novelist in a remote cabin with only a bottle of Jack Daniels and perhaps the Bible for company, who emerges after a few months with a completed manuscript of stern and lyric beauty. The truth is that writing a novel is often a long, crude, insecure business with a dubious outcome. You can spend years and years not sure of what you're doing, writing something that in the end may not be great, and that perhaps no one will read. No one may read it even if it *is* great. I was once shown what was called "the morgue" at the *New York Times Book Review*, a canvas dumpster on wheels filled with review copies of books that weren't going to be reviewed. A sight once seen that can never be unseen.

So for God's sake, why do it? Why spend years writing a novel, especially if you have no idea what will become of it?

One answer is that this lengthy, ambiguous, ungainly period, if you can stand it, allows for something rare these days: the suspension of judgment. Room for indecision. Even for disorientation. Not the kind of disorientation that makes you disbelieve what's right in front of you—a favorite tactic of certain politicians—but the kind that makes you suspect it may take a while to *understand* what is right in front of you. For help with clarifying this vital distinction, I will turn to Margaret Atwood's book *Negotiating with the Dead: A Writer on Writing*.

In her introduction, Atwood reveals that she polled a number of novelists with a question: What did it feel like, she asked, when they "went into a novel?" Not began *writing* a novel, but "went into" one—a question that already hints at the answers, some of which were: "like groping through a tunnel," "like being under water," "like rearranging furniture in the dark," "like sitting in an empty theater before a play or film has started, waiting for the characters to appear." What Atwood concluded from the responses she received was that going into a novel required confusion. Novelists confronted "obstruction, obscurity, emptiness, disorientation, twilight, blackout, often combined with a struggle or path or journey—an inability to see one's way forward, but a feeling that there *was* a way forward, and that the act of going forward would eventually bring about the conditions for vision" (emphasis mine).

Every writer has the experience of heading voluntarily into darkness, hoping for "the conditions for vision." Hoping, as Atwood goes on to say, "to bring something back out to the light." Every poem, essay, short story is an opportunity for illumination. What's particular to novels is that the darkness is so prolonged. For readers, as well as for writers. Two or three hundred pages give you a lot of time to let your eyes adjust. But that is exactly what happens. As you go forward in a novel, your perceptions keep changing about characters and situations that in the beginning you probably thought you understood—because the characters probably began more or less as types, and their situations probably seemed more or less familiar. Yet as the characters become more complicated, their situations are also defamiliarized, and you can no longer predict how you will feel about them.

Usually, this defamiliarizing process requires a lot of stumbling and searching, chiefly by asking a series of questions that lead mostly to other questions. Writing a novel offers an extended experience of not getting to the point. So does reading one.

• • •

"Digressions are the very sunshine of the novel," wrote Laurence Sterne back in the eighteenth century. A reminder that the novel has always been, by virtue of its length alone, *anti-expedient*. A novel meanders, pauses, stares into shop windows. Musings on agrarian reform appear in the midst of a love scene or ponderings about corporate sponsorship during a tennis lesson. And you don't have to be Tolstoy or David Foster Wallace to claim the right to digress. Even the creator of Inspector Maigret, Georges Simenon, who published literally hundreds of novels and wrote most of them in an eleven-day sprint, a novelist in an obliterating hurry, whose novel spines are the width of asparagus stalks—even *he* stops to write passages like this one:

> The train was in the station at Poitiers when the lamps suddenly lit up all along the platforms, though it was not yet dark. It was only later, while they were crossing some pastureland, that they watched night fall and the windows of the isolated farms begin to shine like stars.
>
> Then, abruptly, a few kilometers from La Rochelle, a light fog came up, not from the countryside but from the sea, and mixed with the darkness. A lighthouse appeared for a moment in the distance.

Simenon could have written, "Inspector Maigret took the evening train from Poitiers to La Rochelle." But he wants to capture that liminal moment when lights come on though it's not entirely dark, and then the feeling of traveling from one kind of darkness into another, from that evening train platform into the night countryside with its occasional lit windows, and finally into a marine darkness, where light appears only in flashes. He wants to create atmosphere, which novels need to do as they move you through shades of perception and stages of comprehension, as well as through complications in the plot. He wants to give you time to adjust your eyes.

I'm not encouraging digression for the sake of digression, of course, but I would like to define *digressions* as where the writer changes the lighting. And I'd like to use the term expansively enough to cover everything from what critic James Wood calls the "descriptive pause," to the extended passages in a novel such as *Middlemarch*, where in which George Eliot stops the action to explain that provincial village's attitudes toward politics, science, education, religion, and the appropriate sphere for women. In both cases the digression shades your understanding of the characters and their situations. Thus, while you're waiting to see when idealistic young Dorothea Brooke will realize her mistake in marrying the heart-shriveling Mr. Casaubon, you discover the forces acting on her, why she thought that incarcerating decision was a bid for freedom, which makes it all the more painful to follow the consequences.

Digressions in a novel enlarge its capacity to affect you. They expand your responsiveness. You are being asked to stop, to attend, to hold a more elaborate idea of a setting, situation, or character than you anticipated holding. Digressions are, in fact, *experiences* of capacity.

• • •

In his famous essay "Art as Technique," written in 1917, the Russian critic Viktor Shklovsky argues that human beings are becoming so accustomed to thinking in abbreviated ways that we are in danger of abbreviating ourselves out of conscious existence. We tend to substitute automatic perception—"what a tall mountain," "the sunset is beautiful"—for actually *looking* at whatever is in front of us. We see a general shape, not specific definition.

Shklovsky calls this general way of seeing the "'algebraic' method of thought" in which "things are replaced by symbols." And I do not have to say the word "emoticon" here—though I just did—to indicate how much more "algebraic" our thinking has become since 1917.

The way to counter abbreviated, habitual ways of thinking, says Shklovsky, is art. Because art prolongs perception. "The purpose of art," he writes, "is to impart the sensation of things as they are perceived and not as they are known. The technique of art is to make objects 'unfamiliar,' to make forms difficult, to increase the difficulty and length of perception because the process of perception is an aesthetic end in itself and must be prolonged."

Not surprisingly, I think writing and reading novels are an effective way to practice prolonging one's perceptions. For instance, it can take a while even to say what a novel is *about*. Like a water balloon, grab one part of a novel and another bulges out. Context is everything. Which is what makes novels, in my view, a vital counterbalance to the most prevalent modes of written communication these days, in particular the tweet.

The social philosopher C. Thi Nguyen, who researches the effects of technology on culture, wrote a paper on "How Twitter Gamifies Communication," and in it he notes: "Twitter shapes our goals for discourse by making conversation something like a game. Twitter scores our conversation. And it does so, not in terms of our own particular and rich purposes for communication, but in terms of its own pre-loaded, painfully thin metrics: Likes, Retweets, and Follower counts. And if we take up Twitter's invitation and internalize those evaluations, we will be thinning out and simplifying our own goals for communication."

As an example of how people simplify themselves via Twitter, Nguyen said in a recent interview: "people click 'like' only on things they immediately get."

In Nguyen's view, Twitter has a flattening effect on how we respond to information, just as emoticons flatten emotional expression, everything from joy to grief to existential dread. So it stands to reason that for something to be imaginatively experienced, as opposed to "gotten," it must become multidimensional. Layered, not simplified.

As an illustration of how layered description works to increase "the difficulty and length of perception," here is the first paragraph of Toni Morrison's novel *Sula*:

> In that place, where they tore the nightshade and blackberry patches from their roots to make room for the Medallion City Golf Course, there was once a neighborhood. It stood in the hills above the valley town of Medallion and spread all the way to the river. It is called the suburbs now, but when black people lived there it was called the Bottom. One road, shaded by beeches, oaks, maples and chestnuts, connected it to the valley. The beeches are gone now, and so are the pear trees where children sat and yelled down through the blossoms

to passersby. Generous funds have been allotted to level the stripped and faded buildings that clutter the road up to the golf course. They are going to raze the Time and a Half Pool Hall, where feet in long tan shoes once pointed down from chair rungs. A steel ball will knock to dust Irene's Palace of Cosmetology, where women used to lean their heads back on sink trays and doze while Irene lathered Nu Nile into their hair. Men in khaki work clothes will pry loose the slats of Reba's Grill, where the owner cooked in her hat because she couldn't remember the ingredients without it.

There are many wonderful aspects to this paragraph, but perhaps the most astonishing is Morrison's simultaneous erasure and creation of the Bottom. Again, this is the novel's opening paragraph, so our immediate understanding is that this neighborhood has vanished—it's stated in the first sentence: "there was once a neighborhood." Yet at the same time, Morrison prevents us from "getting" this fact, even as she asserts it. She starts by presenting us with a vivid absence: "the nightshade and black-berry patches" torn from their roots to make way for the Medallion City Golf Course. Then she layers that absence: "The beeches are gone now," and the pear trees, and also the children who used to yell from the branches. Except now we *see* those trees, those children, as if they still exist.

All that's left of the Bottom, Morrison tells us next, are some "stripped and faded buildings that clutter the road up to the golf course." Yet here she intensifies her layering of this world even as she continues to insist that it's gone. She does so by colliding future and past, telling us first that the Time and a Half Pool Hall is going to be razed and *then* giving us those long tan shoes that once pointed down from chair rungs. We see the steel ball that will knock down Irene's Palace of Cosmetology and *then* those heads Irene lathered in sink trays. We are asked to hold contradictory visions, to see something destroyed and complete at the same moment, an extraordinarily dynamic, complex demand on our perceptions. Our emotional response comes from watching the intense particularity of this neighborhood erased seemingly right before our eyes, even though it's already gone. And even though we've only just encountered it.

With apologies to Toni Morrison, imagine, now, an approximately 280-character tweet of this same situation:

The Medallion City Golf Course has replaced native plant species with environmentally unsustainable grass and now plans to wreck last signs of an historic Black neighborhood. Will soon tear down the old pool hall, hair salon, and grill. Protest rapacious suburban blight!

This tweet also tries to elicit an emotional response. It makes its case forcefully. But everything is lost. What is "everything"? Take the final sentence of Morrison's paragraph, in which men in khaki work clothes will pry apart "Reba's Grill, where the owner cooked in her hat because she couldn't remember the ingredients without it." By the time we reach Reba's mnemonic hat, the Bottom has been layered into fabulous dimension, a place of "time and a half" and "palaces." A lost Atlantis. *Now* we know why it matters that its last traces are about to be demolished by the donors of those "generous funds." The Twitter version may momentarily stir me to oppose a golf course, but it will not make me wonder about what lies beneath it.

What's lost in the Twitter version of Morrison's opening paragraph is what Henry James calls "an ado." In his introduction to *The Portrait of a Lady*, he writes, "The novel is of its very nature an 'ado,' an ado about something, and the larger the form it takes, the greater of course the ado."

To *make an ado* means to take something apparently small and magnify it, to demand our attention for something we may not have previously considered worth it. Morrison wants to make an *ado* about a vanished Black neighborhood. In *Portrait of a Lady*, James wants to make an *ado* about Isabel Archer, an ardent, free-spirited young woman, a recent heiress, who hopes for an independent future and briefly seems poised to achieve something like it, until she is cannibalized by cynical sophisticates after her money. One technique for making an ado is to present us with a given—a once-vibrant neighborhood will disappear, a naive young woman will be betrayed—and then find ways to make us hope *against* that given. You can, of course, do this in shorter forms as well; Frank O'Connor does it powerfully in "Guests of the Nation," a story that illustrates what Edward P. Jones calls "monstrous inevitability." But in novels, that experience of *hoping* against reason, of *hoping* against inevitabilities—a complicated and profoundly absorbing act of sympathy—is elongated.

Subplots are another technique for making an ado, and again you certainly find them in shorter forms, such as the braided essay, but they are critical in novels. Subplots layer your impression of a subject by offering up concurrent narratives related to it. In *Sula*, for instance, we follow four or five main characters, mothers and daughters, all residents of the Bottom whose fates are entwined. Subplots not only draw your attention to the multiplicity of experience—the opposite of flatness—they remind you of the many contingencies of your own life. No one has "one" life. In other words, we are all made up of subplots: jobs, families, communities; we feature in the subplots of other people's lives, as other people feature in our own.

• • •

What is worth an ado? I suppose every writer faces that question; but for novelists, with perhaps years of work stretching ahead, it's particularly pressing. Of course, anything on earth is worth an ado, if you can figure out *why*. And that "why," I think, comes back to capacity. What can your subject hold? Not what does it hold, but what *can* it hold? For you and for your readers?

In response to that question, here's another example of a novelistic ado.

When Virginia Woolf began writing *Mrs. Dalloway*, she was revisiting a minor character from an earlier novel, *The Voyage Out*, where "Mrs. Dalloway" was a superficial socialite. This was a type Woolf was fond of deploring, and in her subsequent novel she originally meant to satirize Mrs. Dalloway as a social hostess who plans to give a party and then commits suicide at the end of it. Yet though the novel's structure remains narrowly focused—opening on the morning of Mrs. Dalloway's party and concluding that evening—the story itself expands exuberantly until it becomes all but uncontainable. Starting with the first pages, as Mrs. Dalloway sets out to buy flowers on Bond Street and responds intensely to whatever she encounters:

> in the bellow and the uproar; the carriages and motor cars, omnibuses, vans, sandwich men shuffling and swinging; brass bands; barrel organs; in the triumph and the jingle and the strange high singing of some aeroplane overhead was what she loved; life; London; this moment of June.

Mrs. Dalloway is a human digression—*everything* interests her. And in her enjoyment of that June day, her appreciation of a single moment's many registers, from the "bellow and uproar" of the street to an airplane's "strange high singing," she quickly transcends Woolf's early idea of her as a social butterfly and becomes almost goddess-like in her immersive interest in life around her. Her pleasure in that June moment is itself an ado, one that transforms street noise into opera and an airplane into a soprano. Critic Phyllis Rose calls *Mrs. Dalloway* "perhaps the most buoyant novel ever written."

Not that terrible things don't happen. There *is* still a suicide. There is hurt, harm, mental illness, suffering. The First World War has only just ended. Life in London a century ago was no more fair or forgiving than life in London today. But as Rose points out, what this novel offers in reply "to the decay of the spirit, the deaths it variously records, is an intense response to the moment."

"An intense response to the moment." Here we are in poetic territory. What can the novel add to what is done more penetratingly and certainly more economically in poetry?

Perhaps it's the normalizing of heightened responsiveness, making what would be extraordinary moments of clarity in "real" life seem continual, almost ordinary. The novel's hallmark is an illusion of dailiness, but a dailiness embedded with small revelations, discoveries and visions, all attributed to characters with whom you come to identify. Each chapter contains a slow drip of intense responses that sustain your sympathies with those characters while progressively complicating them. And again, this happens for both writer and reader.

For instance, Woolf's idea of a "hostess" itself became transfigured by Mrs. Dalloway, shifting from dismissal to identification. While she was working on that novel, Woolf noted in her diary: "One writes to bridge over the abyss between the writer and the reader, or between the hostess and the unknown guest."

I love this way of thinking of readers, not as people who must be captured, appealed to, or seduced, but as "unknown guests," a relationship that makes sense to me, perhaps because the questions of responsibility are so clear. How do you greet your readers and invite them in? What will make them feel comfortable enough to stay? Especially if you are hosting them for hundreds of pages, what kind of sustenance and entertainment are you offering? Once a guest is under your roof, the laws of hospitality require you to take care of them. (If you don't believe me, look at what happens in *Macbeth*.) Which doesn't mean that you can't lead your guests on a tour of the dungeons, switch out the lights, and chain them to the wall—if the story requires it—only that you must lead them back out again, and perhaps offer them an aspirin and a glass of water. The reader, the "unknown guest," requires your care. And the experience of being cared for, held by a well-told story, can be transformative, too.

• • •

Along with the rewards of not getting to the point, prolonged darkness, making a fuss over small things, and spending a lot of time with unknown guests, I'd like to offer yet another reason for writing and reading novels: privacy.

Privacy, like the suspension of judgment, is increasingly hard to find in these days of internet tracking, surveillance, and data harvesting. For readers, a novel is a lengthy plunge into invisibility. Alongside your visible life among coworkers, family, friends, you are also living—sometimes for weeks—with people and places *no one else knows*. Even that novel's other readers will not picture its people and places, its scenes, as you do, unless the novel gets made into a movie. While engrossed in reading a novel, you are conducting a dual life, a hidden life, and in that "other" life you are immune from influencers, advertisers, algorithms, clickbait, dark posts, followers. You have no digital exhaust. No one can trace you.

For writers, a novel offers the same privacy, plus something else: a protracted period of deep, necessary concealment while you blunder along in a made-up world, knowing that no one will see what you're doing, or care, quite possibly for years. You can get it wrong again and again.

For example, in my own first published novel I wrote several drafts from the mother of the family's point of view, only to realize after hundreds of pages that I had chosen the wrong character to tell the story, that it was her daughter who should tell it, but in retrospect. It was a realization that made all the difference; and yet, I would not have understood the mother's character nearly as well had I not spent all that time in her head. Choosing the wrong point of view is a valuable mistake. With the novel I just finished, I began with a first-person narrator only to realize after, again, hundreds of pages, that the story should be in third person. And *then*, after many more pages, I realized I needed three perspectives, including that of a character who started out as dead.

Was this all wasted work? Yes, if I were trying to write a novel in eleven days. But if I measure my novel's value partly by its density, by the experience that has gone into it—the thousands of questions I have asked myself, the choices I have weighed, my attempts to do not the obvious thing but the more interesting one—then all that work has been worth it. Every character, description, conversation, action that I spent time writing and then deleted has added to the story. I sometimes think of my novels as built atop a graveyard of ideas, yet that is richly occupied soil.

As Henry James notes, in Yoda-like fashion, "Strangely fertilizing, in the long run, does a wasted effort of attention often prove. It all depends on *how* the attention has been cheated, has been squandered."

• • •

Amid all this useful squandering, however, my goal as a novelist is still to have readers. And so I go along, typing and typing, trying to find the right perspective, creating my characters and figuring out their problems—

occasionally committing a murder just to keep things moving—getting closer and closer to knowing what they want and what they're afraid of. So that by the final drafts when my characters ask *What am I supposed to do here?* I have a coherent response. I've thought about them for so long that I usually know not only what they need to do, but how and why.

A character in a novel is real, E. M. Forster writes in *Aspects of the Novel*, "when the novelist knows everything about it. He may not choose to tell us all he knows—many of the facts, even of the kind we call obvious, may be hidden. But he will give us the feeling that though the character has not been explained, it is explicable, and we get from this a reality of a kind we can never get in real life."

Ironically, to make a character feel "explicable," the novelist has to find ways to keep readers *wondering* about them. Unlike actual human beings, a character is limitable, but novels have room for a lot of emotional crosshatching, for deepening characters' contradictions and seeding new mysteries, for surprising us with gestures we had not thought a character capable of making, and yet looking back we realize those gestures had been promised from the start—all so that we'll agree to spend hours pondering a few invented people and their troubles. Rarely are we as absorbed in wondering about our friends as we are in wondering about characters in a novel, even though, in the end, characters have no secrets, and our friends have so many. In this way, novels again challenge our capacity by offering extended, focused, and sometimes deeply moving experiences of wondering about other people. People you might otherwise never know, or want to know, and yet as Forster suggests, you've been made to feel that you *do* know them.

• • •

But once more back to me, the novelist at her desk, typing and typing, trying to propel my characters forward, worrying about engaging my readers, hoping to reach the end of the story before I die—and all the while something *else* looms closer and closer. A question novelists can avoid longer than most: What am I trying to say?

Such a reasonable question. If you are going to write something hundreds of pages long, shouldn't you be able to say *why* you wrote it? Yet, after decades of novel writing, I have come to believe it's the wrong question. "What am I trying to say?" is the expedient question, the getting-to-the-point question, the tweet question. It's the here's-my-advice question. It is not a *capacious* question. Especially if it strides straight to an answer.

A more capacious question might be "What am I making an ado about?" A question that at least reliably leads to more questions, and away from recommendations and pronouncements. In an 1888 letter to his editor, Anton Chekhov points out, "You are right in demanding that an artist approach his work consciously, but you are confusing two concepts: the solution of the problem and the correct formulation of the problem. Only the second is required of the artist."

An idea taken up by James Baldwin in his essay "The Creative Process": "A society," he writes, "must assume that it is stable, but the artist must know, and he must let us know, that there is nothing stable under heaven. One cannot possibly build a school, teach a child, or drive a car without taking some things for granted. The artist cannot and must not take anything for granted, but must drive to the heart of every answer and expose the question the answer hides."

As an example of Baldwin's prescription to drive to the heart of an answer and expose the question it hides, consider Elena Ferrante's *Neapolitan Quartet*, sixteen hundred pages centered on the friendship between Lila and Lenu. An ado if there ever was one, which begins when they are little girls in Naples in the 1950s and covers forty years. Chapter 1 of Book One, *My Brilliant Friend*, starts like this: "My friendship with Lila began the day we decided to go up the dark stairs that led, step after step, flight after flight, to the door of Don Achille's apartment." A marvelously intriguing first line that seems like the beginning of a good, stable answer: Friendship is important. Hang on to your childhood friends, especially if you're going somewhere dark and mysterious. But as anyone who has read those books will tell you, they chronicle hundreds of temblors in the lives of Lila and Lenu—including long separations, betrayals, periods of great hostility, reunions, more betrayals, rescues, disappearances. And yet there remains a deeply complicated attachment to each other and where they came from. At least on the part of the narrator, Lenu, who never stops wondering about her brilliant, difficult friend.

Therefore a question hidden by the answer "Friendship is important" might be: What binds one person to another? Is it ever possible to know?

Though if Chekhov were to take over here, the question might become: How can we tolerate even a single other human being, when human beings cause each other such suffering and confusion? But we must love each other! But how, but how?

No two readers will frame a novel's questions in the same way.

• • •

Like the novel itself, this essay has digressed. I set out to describe what it can be like to write a novel and why I think it's worth all the work and uncertainty, and the same with reading them. Somehow I wound up wondering how people can stand one another. So I will close by saying that I believe in the *capacity* of the novel, in its formal demonstration of the possibility for greater insight and compassion over time. I believe in the prolonged imaginative privacy a novel affords. I believe in its power to disrupt inevitabilities. I believe in its inconvenience. Especially now, when so much information is continually coming at us, so fast, from all directions, it's hard to know what to pay attention to, what to trust—and anyway, who has time to decide? Something else is always trending.

"When information is cheap," notes science historian James Gleick, "attention becomes expensive."

Writing and reading novels are major investments of time. Novels are long roads full of switchbacks and roundabouts. And they rarely take you where you thought you were going. But the return on that investment is an excursion through a wide landscape of passing joy, hilarity, sorrow, doubt, generosity, cruelty, shocks of beauty, shocks of horror, shocks of love. Above all, the shock of how profoundly things can change. Though novels deal less with shock, I have found, than with a slow, sustaining electrification.

—2022

Epilogue

Playing Backward on the Train

Geffrey Davis

—◆—

I've been thinking:

Maybe you-the-artist are just one of so many passengers with a backward-facing seat on the long line of life's moving train, which we all ride for a while . . .

And maybe, before not too many stops, or after countless stops because the view has been that damn beautiful or that dark with intent, you-the-artist happen to notice that the window at your seat is open—has to have been open since taking your place—something that your body probably learned first after a shift in the weather or a bend in the train's long line of travel pulled at the sound of air moving by . . .

Maybe you-the-artist begin struggling to resist a new urge to reach, to know differently the wind that can be heard and almost seen now against a world that continues falling away beyond the openness . . .

But maybe it takes a few more stops to move your hands because the wind is a little scary, and so you-the-artist mostly wait for the kind of air that enters the train by an accident that your own watching wants to rename . . .

Or maybe your hands move in the moment that follows your recognition because whatever wind you-the-artist can feel thrills a playful reach into the full onrush of where you're heading . . .

Then maybe something brushes up against a bright or misshaped memory that makes you-the-artist question how long to keep yourself connected to the wind like this . . .

But then maybe a myth called *family* or *home* revises the first doubt of what the full wind would do—maybe a remembered joke about time makes you-the-artist more curious about the meaning of your hands— maybe you-the-artist think *bird* or *plane* and that's enough to begin experimenting with turning your reach into a wing . . .

Maybe during the very next beat or once your familiar ideas of flight have been exhausted or become a little boring, you-the-artist long for other images that could say everything or nothing at all about the lift in this wind . . .

Maybe you-the-artist think about the hand shapes that kids from your neighborhood would sometimes use to show the desire and danger of their belonging, or those you've seen elders sometimes use to keep the ground's growing swell beneath them, or . . .

Maybe right away or maybe deep into drafting this litany of images, you-the-artist discover that the wind has begun to sound less like wind: the quiet thought that your hands have something to do with this change adds another note of possibility to your play . . .

Maybe you-the-artist get bold or foolish enough to admit quietly to yourself or with an audible gasp that what you've been making is nearly or definitely something you-the-artist want to call music, which maybe embarrasses but also emboldens you-the-artist to continue . . .

Or maybe this is enough to tuck your humming hands back into your lap with a grin or an internal sigh . . .

But maybe, after getting your breath back, or swept up in wanting to learn this almost music, or without ever taking your hands away from the wind game, you catch a clip of what anyone would have to call a vowel . . .

Maybe it takes a gazillion more little finger strokes—some so odd, you can't help but laugh; some so similar, you silently wonder about your ability to distinguish sounds—but eventually the winded vowel you are making grows into a pattern—no, a word . . .

Maybe while leaning closer to decipher what you've been hearing all along, slowly or suddenly you find the right strokes to hold that word in the margins of clarity: the wind has a voice, and it's saying your name . . .

Maybe you scan the train for a witness and see that someone in a different seat has been watching what you're doing, maybe for a long time, maybe at the very moment you turned the song of your own name. Maybe they have their hands at their window, too. What's clear: the listening you just made is written with astonished pride across the new faith of their nodding face . . .

Dear Reader: The world is your witness. And now you carry that blessing with you. We need to hear the music you swoop into our ongoing traditions. Wherever you go, whatever you risk, however long, keep reaching your hands into the wind of story and poetry—and keep returning to let us hear your names, again and again and again . . .

Amen.

—2022

Acknowledgements

—⚬—

"Creative Responses to Worlds Unraveling: The Artist in the Twenty-First Century" originally appeared in *The Georgia Review*, Fall 2013. Reprinted with permission of the author.

"The Fault Lines of Memory: Embracing Imperfect Memory in Creative Nonfiction" originally appeared in *Fourth Genre Online*, Summer 2022. Reprinted with permission of the author.

"Inside the Conch Shell" appeared in slightly different form in *The Georgia Review* (Winter 2016) and *Mortality, with Friends* (Wayne State University Press, 2021). Reprinted with permission of the author.

Jennifer Richter, "Demeter Accounts for This Year's Indian Summer," from *No Acute Distress*, *Crab Orchard Review* and Southern Illinois University Press, 2016. Reprinted with permission of the author.

Kamilah Aisha Moon, "Imagine," from *Starshine & Clay*. Copyright © 2017 by Kamilah Aisha Moon. Reprinted with the permission of The Permissions Company, LLC on behalf of Four Way Books, fourwaybooks.com

Lia Purpura, "Jump," from *Rough Likeness*, Sarabande Books, 2011. Reprinted with permission of the author.

"Lost in the Woods of Brooklyn and Belgrade: The Transformative Possibilities of Disorientation" originally appeared in *Fiction Writers Review*, October 5, 2020. Reprinted with permission of the author.

Niedecker, Lorine, "A Monster Owl," from *Lorine Niedecker Collected Works*, University of California Press, 2004. Reprinted with permission of University of California Press.

"Orphan Kim Seong-rye (age 15)" and "Orphan Nine," from *DMZ Colony*. Copyright 2020 by Don Mee Choi. Used with permission of the author and Wave Books.

"Radical Surprise" previously appeared in *Assay: A Journal of Nonfiction Studies*, 8.2, Spring 2022. Reprinted with permission of the author.

"The Ram in the Thicket: Midrash and the Contemporary Creative Writer" first appeared in slightly different form in *The Writer's Chronicle*, Volume 51, Number 2, October/November 2018, pp. 29–39. Reprinted with permission of the author.

Reena Saini Kallat, *Woven Chronicle*, 2011–19. Installation view, *When Home Won't Let You Stay: Migration through Contemporary Art*, Institute of Contemporary Art/Boston, 2019. Photo by Mel Taing.

Sean Thomas Dougherty, "Why Bother?" from *The Second O of Sorrow*. Copyright © 2018 by Sean Thomas Dougherty. Reprinted with the permission of The Permissions Company, LLC on behalf of BOA Editions, Ltd., www.boaeditions.org

Tommye Blount, "The Bug," from *Fantasia for the Man in Blue*. Copyright © 2020 by Tommye Blount. Reprinted with the permission of The Permissions Company, LLC on behalf of Four Way Books, fourwaybooks.com

"Watching Kira Learn to Surf" originally appeared in *The Cincinnati Review*, No. 10.2, 2014. Reprinted with permission of the author.

"Why Write a Novel, Why Read a Novel, and Why Now?" originally appeared in slightly different form in *Literary Hub* on January 10, 2023. Reprinted with permission of the author.

"Writing without End: On Suspending the Need for Closure" originally appeared in slightly different form in the *Superstition Review*, 2014. Reprinted with permission of the author.

Works Cited

—⁓—

"BREAKING THE SILENCE," DAVIS

Cave Canem, https://cavecanempoets.org/
Akhmatova, Anna. "Lot's Wife," translated by Stanley Kunitz with Max Hayward, *Poems of Akhmatova,* New York: Mariner/Houghton Mifflin, 1973.
Dougherty, Sean Thomas. "Why Bother?" *The Second O of Sorrow*, BOA Editions, 2018.

"THE RAM IN THE THICKET," SANDOR

"Darash Meaning in Bible—Old Testament Hebrew Lexicon—New American Standard," Biblestudytools.com, https://www.biblestudytools.com/lexicons/hebrew/nas/darash.html
Dubus, Andre. "The Habit of Writing." *On Writing Short Stories*, edited by Tom Bailey, Oxford University Press, New York, 2000.
Leeser, Isaac. *Twenty-Four Books of the Holy Scriptures: Carefully Translated after the Best Jewish Authorities*. Hebrew Publishing, 1905.
Munro, Alice. "Alice Munro, The Art of Fiction No. 137." Interview by Jeanne McCulloch and Mona Simpson, *The Paris Review*, Volume 137, 1994.
Munro, Alice. "Meneseteung." Selected *Stories*, Vintage, 1997.
Purpura, Lia. "Jump." *Rough Likeness: Essays*, Sarabande Books, 2011.
Reeder, Roberta. *Anna Akhmatova: Poet and Prophet*. St. Martin's Press, 1994.
Richter, Jennifer. "Demeter Accounts for This Year's Indian Summer." *No Acute Distress: Poems, Crab Orchard Review* & Southern Illinois University Press, 2016.
Richter, Jennifer. Received by Marjorie Sandor, 29 May 2017.
"Sarah and the Akedah." *My Jewish Learning*, 26 Oct. 2017, http://www.myjewishlearning.com/article/sarah-and-the-akedah/
Zornberg, Avivah Gottlieb. *Murmuring Deep: Reflections on the Biblical Unconscious*. Schocken, 2009.
Zornberg, Avivah Gottlieb. *The Particulars of Rapture: Reflections on Exodus*. Image/Doubleday, 2000.

"DAVINCI'S HELICOPTER, MICHELANGELO'S MARBLE," MEYERS

Csikszentmihalyi, Mihaly. *Creativity: Flow and the Psychology of Discovery and Invention*. HarperCollins, 1996.
Gilbert, Elizabeth. *Big Magic: Creative Living Beyond Fear*. Riverhead, 2015.
Kane, Sean. *Wisdom of the Mythtellers*. Broadview, 1998.
Poincaré, Henri. "Mathematical Creation." *The Creative Process*, edited by Brewster Ghiselin, University of California Press, 1980.

Baldwin, James, and Nikki Giovanni. *A Dialogue*. J.B. Lippincott, 1973.

Graves, Robert. *To Juan at the Winter Solstice*. Trustees of the Robert Graves Copyright Trust, 2007.

Gregerson, Linda. "Pythagorean." *Prodigal: New and Selected Poems, 1976–2014*, Mariner Books, 2015.

Hirshfield, Jane. "The Question of Originality." *Nine Gates: Entering the Mind of Poetry*, HarperCollins, 1997.

Hopkins, Gerard Manley. "Carrion Comfort." *Poems and Prose of Gerard Manley Hopkins: Poems and Prose*, Penguin Books, Baltimore, 1967.

Noyes, Alfred. "The Highwayman." *Collected Poems of Alfred Noyes, Vol I*, Domville-Fife Press, 2013.

Rilke, Rainer Maria. Letter to Baladine Klossowska, 16 Dec. 1920.

Stevens, Wallace. *The Collected Poems of Wallace Stevens*. Vintage Books, 2015.

Wright, James. "Wherever Home Is." *This Journey*, Vintage Books, 1982.

Baldwin, James. "The Creative Process." *Creative America*, Ridge Press, 1962.

Clayton, Ewan. "Where Did Writing Begin?" British Library, 2019, https://www.bl.uk/history-of-writing/articles/where-did-writing-begin

Dehaene, Stanislas. *Reading in the Brain: The New Science of How We Read*. Penguin Books, 2010.

Dickinson, Emily. Letter to T. W. Higginson. 16 Aug. 1870.

Dissanayake, Ellen. "Art as a Human Behavior: Toward an Ethological View of Art." *The Journal of Aesthetics and Art Criticism*, vol. 38, no. 4, 1980.

Dissanayake, Ellen. "The Core of Art: Making Special." *Journal of the Canadian Association for Curriculum Studies*, vol. 1, no. 2, Fall 2003.

Dissanayake, Ellen. Interview by Wendy Call, Video Call, 22 June 2022.

Dissanayake, Ellen. "Prelinguistic and Preliterate Substrates of Poetic Narrative." *Poetics Today*, vol. 32, no. 1, Spring 2011.

Flood, Josephine. "Rock-art and Landscape in Aboriginal Australia." *The Figured Landscapes of Rock-Art: Looking at Pictures in Place*, edited by Christopher Chippindale and George Nash, Cambridge University Press, 2004.

Frey, Nancy, and Douglas Fisher. "Reading and the Brain: What Early Childhood Educators Need to Know." *Early Childhood Education Journal*, vol. 38, no. 2, 2010.

Gutman, Rachel. "A 'Mic Drop' on a Theory of Language Evolution." *The Atlantic*, 12 Dec. 2019.

Handwerk, Brian. "An Evolutionary Timeline of Homo Sapiens." *Smithsonian Magazine*, 2 Feb. 2021.

Heath, Malcolm. Introduction to Aristotle's *Poetics*, translated by Malcolm Heath, Penguin Books, 1997.

Hirshfield, Jane. *Ten Windows: How Great Poems Transform the World*. Alfred A. Knopf, 2017.

Lorblanchet, Michel, and Paul Bahn. *The First Artists: In Search of the World's Oldest Art*. Thames & Hudson, 2017.

Malotki, Ekkehart, and Ellen Dissanayake. *Early Rock Art of the American West: The Geometric Enigma*. University of Washington Press, 2018.

McGuinness, Diane, and Stephen Pinker. "Foreword." *Why Our Children Can't Read, and What We Can Do about It: A Scientific Revolution in Reading,* Simon & Schuster, 1999.

"RADICAL SURPRISE," BORICH

Rekdal, Paisley. *The Broken Country: On Trauma, a Crime, and the Continuing Legacy of Vietnam.* University of Georgia Press, 2017.
Sloan, Aisha Sabatini. *Dreaming of Ramadi in Detroit: Essays.* 1913 Press, 2017.
Taylor, Catherine. *You, Me, and the Violence.* Mad Creek Books/Ohio State University Press, 2017.

"ON IMAGISTIC ENDURANCE," JOHNSON

Blount, Tommye. *Fantasia for the Man in Blue.* Four Way Books, 2020.
Doty, Mark. *The Art of Description.* Graywolf Press, 2010.
Garrigue, Jean. *Selected Poems.* University of Illinois Press, 1992.
Kimmerer, Robin Wall. *Gathering Moss.* Oregon State University Press, 2003.
Longenbach, James. *The Resistance to Poetry.* University of Chicago Press, 2004.
Moon, Kamilah Aisha. *Starshine & Clay.* Four Way Books, 2017.
Murakami, Haruki. *What I Talk About When I Talk About Running.* Vintage Books, 2008.
Ozeki, Ruth. *The Face: A Time Code.* Restless Books, 2015.
Phillips, Carl. *The Art of Daring.* Graywolf Press, 2014.
Upton, Lee. *Jean Garrigue: A Poetics of Plenitude.* Associated University Presses, 1991.

"ON ENCHANTMENT," PURPURA

Agee, James, and Walker Evans. *Let Us Now Praise Famous Men.* Houghton Mifflin, 2001.
Ammons, Archie R. "The City Limits." *The Selected Poems of A.R. Ammons, Expanded Edition,* Norton, 1986.
Irwin, William. "God Is a Question, Not an Answer." *New York Times Opinion,* 26 Mar. 2016.
Keller, Evelyn Fox. *A Feeling for the Organism: The Life and Work of Barbara McClintock.* Henry Holt and Co, 1983.
Lorca, Federico Garcia. "Play and Theory of the Duende." *Deep Song and Other Prose,* translated by Christopher Maurer, New Directions, 1975.
Niedecker, Lorine. "A Monster Owl." *Poetry,* September 2013.
Stevens, Wallace. "Final Soliloquy of the Interior Paramour." *The Palm at the End of the Mind,* Vintage Books, 1972.

"TIME AND THE IMAGINATION," FOERSTER

Agamben, Giorgio. *Remnants of Auschwitz: The Witness and the Archive,* translated by Daniel Heller-Roazen, Zoan, 1999.

Baudelaire, Charles. "The Painter of Modern Life." *Selected Writings on Art and Artists of Baudelaire*, Cambridge University Press, 1981.

Baudelaire, Charles. *Le Spleen de Paris: Petits Poémes en prose,* translated by Edward K. Kaplan, University of Georgia Press, 1989.

Carson, Anne. *Economy of the Unlost.* Princeton University Press, 1999.

Celan, Paul. "The Meridian." *Selected Poems and Prose of Paul Celan,* translated by John Felstiner, Norton, 2001.

Eliot, T. S. *The Waste Land and Other Poems.* Signet Classic, 1998.

Hejinian, Lyn. "The Rejection of Closure." *The Language of Inquiry,* University of California Press, 2000.

Williams, William Carlos. *Paterson,* edited by Christopher MacGowan, New Directions, 1995.

Wordsworth, William. *The Prelude, 1798–1799,* edited by Stephen Parrish, Cornell University Press, 1977.

"THE FAULT LINES OF MEMORY," MILLER

Cooper, Bernard. "Capiche?" *Maps to Anywhere*, University of Georgia Press, 1997.

Day, Cathy. "Genesis; or the Day Adam Killed the Snakes." *Metawritings: Toward a Theory of Nonfiction*, edited by Jill Lynn Talbot, University of Iowa Press, 2012.

Doty, Mark. "Bride in Beige." *Truth in Nonfiction*, edited by David Lazar, University of Iowa Press, 2008.

Hampl, Patricia. *The Art of the Wasted Day*. Penguin, 2018.

Hampl, Patricia. "Memory and Imagination." *I Could Tell You Stories: Sojourns in the Land of Memory*, Norton, 2000.

Knopp, Lisa. "'Perhapsing': The Use of Speculation in Creative Nonfiction." *Brevity*, January 8, 2009.

Miller, Brenda. "The Dog at the Edge of the World." *Metawritings: Toward a Theory of Nonfiction*, edited by Jill Lynn Talbot, University of Iowa Press, 2012.

Miller, Brenda. "Star of David." *Psaltery & Lyre*, 2022.

Miller, Brenda, and Suzanne Paola. "The Body of Memory." *Tell It Slant: Creating, Refining, and Publishing Creative Nonfiction*, McGraw Hill, 2019.

Momaday, N. Scott. *The Names.* University of Arizona Press, 1996.

Rilke, Rainer Maria. *Letters to a Young Poet.* Norton, 1993.

Van Meter, Ryan. "I Was There." *Metawritings: Toward a Theory of Nonfiction*, edited by Jill Lynn Talbot, University of Iowa Press, 2012.

Woolf, Virginia. *Moments of Being,* edited by Jeanne Schulkind, Harvest, 1985.

"LOST IN THE WOODS OF BROOKLYN AND BELGRADE," NADELSON

Brinkley, Jamel. "J'ouvert, 1996." *A Lucky Man,* Graywolf Press, 2018.

Ez-Eldin, Mansoura. "Gothic Night." *The Uncanny Reader*, edited by Marjorie Sandor, St. Martin's Press, 2015.

Halfon, Eduardo. *The Polish Boxer.* Bellevue Literary Press, 2012.

Moten, Fred. "Blackness and Poetry." *YouTube*, 19 Mar. 2015, https://www.youtube.com/watch?v=Su7iCumqLvo

Philip, M. NourbeSe. *Zong! As Told to the Author by Setaey Adamu Boateng*. Wesleyan University Press, 2008.

"COMMUNITY OR CRAFT?," NAGAMATSU

Gaiman, Neil. "'Let's Talk about Genre': Neil Gaiman and Kazuo Ishiguro in Conversation." *New Statesman*, June 4, 2015.

Michel, Lincoln. "Let's Stop with the Realism Versus Science Fiction and Fantasy Debate." *Literary Hub*, Sept. 17, 2020.

Woolf, Virginia. *Mr. Bennett and Mrs. Brown*. Hogarth, 1924.

"RADIANT TOPOGRAPHIES," DE LA PAZ

Choi, Don Mee. *DMZ Colony*. Wave Books, 2020.

Jess, Tyehimba. "McKoy Twins Syncopated Star." *Olio*, Wave Books, 2016.

Kallat, Reena Saina. *Woven Chronicle. When Home Won't Let You Stay: Migration through Contemporary Art*. 23 Oct. 2019–26 Jan. 2020, Institute of Contemporary Art, Boston.

Metres, Philip. *Shrapnel Maps*. Copper Canyon Press, 2020.

"Reena Saina Kallat." *YouTube,* uploaded by KunstmuseumWolfsburg, May 23, 2018, https://www.youtube.com/watch?v=P_izd7d2wGU&t=3s

"WRITING WITHOUT END," CLARK

Clark, Kevin. "Watching Kira Learn to Surf." *The Cincinnati Review*, No. 10.2, 2014.

Clark, Kevin. "Writing Without End: On Suspending the Need for Closure." *Superstition Review*, Jan. 25, 2014.

Irving, John. *The World According to Garp*. Dutton, 2021.

"WHEN LIFE INTERRUPTS THE WRITING," MCCLANAHAN

Bengis, Ingrid. "The Middle Period." *The Writer on Her Work: Seventeen Essays by Twentieth-Century American Writers*, edited by Janet Sternburg, Norton, 2000.

Berne, Suzanne. *Missing Lucile: Memories of the Grandmother I Never Knew*. Algonquin Books, 2010.

Coates, Ta-Nehisi. *Between the World and Me*. Spiegel & Grau, 2015.

Dewey, John. *Art as Experience*. Putnam, 1980.

Hoagland, Edward. *The Courage of Turtles*. North Point Press, 1985.

Lorde, Audre. "Introduction." *Chosen Poems: Old and New*, Norton, 1982.

Sontag, Susan. *Regarding the Pain of Others*. Penguin Books, 2019.

Wideman, John Edgar. *Brothers and Keepers*. Holt, Rinehart and Winston, 1984.

Willis, Wendy. "Introduction." *These Are Strange Times, My Dear: Field Notes from the Republic*, Counterpoint Press, 2019.

Block, Melissa, and Don DeLillo. "*Falling Man* Maps Emotional Aftermath Of Sept. 11." *All Things Considered*, NPR, 20 June 2007.

Benjamin, Walter. "The Storyteller." *Illuminations*, edited by Hannah Arendt, translated by Harry Zohn, Mariner Books, 2019.

Turner, Jack. *The Abstract Wild*. University of Arizona Press, 1999.

Atwood, Margaret. *Negotiating with the Dead: A Writer on Writing*. Virago, 2005.

Baldwin, James. "The Creative Process." *Creative America*, National Cultural Center, 1962.

Chekhov, Anton. Letter to A. S. Suvorin, 1888.

Ferrante, Elena. *My Brilliant Friend,* translated by Ann Goldstein, Text Publishing Company, 2018.

Forster, E. M. *Aspects of the Novel*. Penguin Books, 1966.

Gleick, James. *The Information: A History, a Theory, a Flood*. Vintage Books, 2012.

James, Henry. "Preface to *The Portrait of a Lady*." *The Art of the Novel*, University of Chicago Press, 1934.

Jones, Edward P. "Frank O'Connor's 'Guests of the Nation.'" *The Norton Anthology of Short Fiction*, edited by Richard Bausch and R. V. Cassill, Norton, 2015.

Nguyen, C. Thi. "How Twitter Gamifies Communication." *Applied Epistemology*, edited by Jennifer Lackey, Oxford University Press, 2021.

Nguyen, C. Thi. Interview by Ezra Klein. *The Ezra Klein Show, The New York Times*, Feb. 25, 2022.

Rose, Phyllis. *Woman of Letters: A Life of Virginia Woolf*. Harcourt Brace Jovanovich, 1987.

Shklovsky, Viktor. "Art as Technique." 1917.

Simenon, Georges. *Maigret Goes to School,* translated by Linda Coverdale, Penguin Books, 2017.

Wood, James. *Serious Noticing: Selected Essays 1997–2019*. Picador, 2021.

Woolf, Virginia. *Mrs. Dalloway*. Penguin Books, 2021.

Author Bios

Rick Barot

Rick Barot's most recent book of poems, *The Galleons*, was published by Milkweed Editions in 2020 and was long-listed for the National Book Award. His work has appeared in numerous publications, including *Poetry, The New Republic, Tin House, The Kenyon Review*, and *The New Yorker*. He has received fellowships from the Guggenheim Foundation, the National Endowment for the Arts, and Stanford University. He lives in Tacoma, Washington, and directs the Rainier Writing Workshop, the low-residency MFA program in creative writing at Pacific Lutheran University.

Suzanne Berne

Suzanne Berne is the author of five novels, most recently *The Blue Window*, and a book of nonfiction. Her first novel, *A Crime in the Neighborhood*, was awarded Great Britain's Orange Prize, now the Women's Prize for Fiction. She has written frequently for *The New York Times* and published essays and reviews in numerous magazines and journals. Over the past thirty years she has taught creative writing first at Harvard University and then at Boston College, and she was on the faculty of the Rainier Writing Workshop from 2009 to 2022.

Barrie Jean Borich

Barrie Jean Borich is author of *Apocalypse, Darling*, which was short-listed for the Lambda Literary Award. Her memoir *Body Geographic* won a Lambda Literary Award, and her book-length essay, *My Lesbian Husband*, won the Stonewall Book Award. Borich's essays have been anthologized in *Isherwood in Transit, Critical Creative Writing, Waveform: Twenty-First Century Essays by Women*, and *After Montaigne: Contemporary Essayists Cover the Essays* and have been cited as notable in *Best American*

Essays and *Best American Nonrequired Reading.* Borich is a professor at DePaul University in Chicago, where she directs the interdisciplinary LGBTQ Studies minor and edits *Slag Glass City,* a journal of the urban essay arts.

Fleda Brown

Fleda Brown's *Flying Through a Hole in the Storm* (2021) won the Hollis Summers Poetry Prize and is an INDIES finalist. Her poetry has appeared in *The Best American Poetry*; has won the Pushcart Prize, Felix Pollak Prize, Philip Levine Prize, and Great Lakes Colleges Association New Writers Award; and has twice been a finalist for the National Poetry Series. Her memoir *Mortality, with Friends* is an MIPA finalist and won the Midwest Book Award. She is professor emerita at the University of Delaware and was poet laureate of Delaware (2001–2007). She was on the Rainier Writing Workshop faculty for fifteen years.

Wendy Call

Wendy Call co-edited *Telling True Stories: A Nonfiction Writers' Guide* (Plume/Penguin 2007), wrote the award-winning *No Word for Welcome: The Mexican Village Faces the Global Economy* (Nebraska 2011), and translated two collections by Mexican Zapotec poet Irma Pineda: *In the Belly of Night and Other Poems* (Pluralia 2022) and *Nostalgia Doesn't Flow Away Like Riverwater* (Deep Vellum 2024). Her literary projects have been supported by Artist Trust, the Fulbright Commission, and the National Endowment for the Arts. She is a faculty member of the Rainier Writing Workshop and lives in Southeast Seattle, on unceded Duwamish land.

Kevin Clark

Kevin Clark's third volume of poems, *The Consecrations*, is published by Stephen F. Austin University Press. His second book, *Self-Portrait with Expletives*, won the Pleiades Press prize. His first collection, *In the Evening of No Warning*, earned a grant from the Academy of American Poets. His poetry appears in *The Georgia Review, The Southern Review, Ploughshares, Prairie Schooner, Iowa Review, Poetry Northwest, Gulf Coast*, and *Crazy-*

horse. A regular critic for *The Georgia Review,* he's published essays in *The Southern Review, Papers on Language and Literature,* and *Contemporary Literary Criticism.* He teaches at the Rainier Writing Workshop. His website is www.kevinclarkpoetry.com.

Geffrey Davis

Geffrey Davis is the author of three books, most recently One Wild Word Away (BOA Editions 2024). His second collection, *Night Angler* (BOA Editions 2019), won the James Laughlin Award from the Academy of American Poets, and his debut, *Revising the Storm* (BOA Editions 2014), won the A. Poulin, Jr. Poetry Prize. He has received fellowships from Bread Loaf, Cave Canem, the National Endowment for the Arts, the Vermont Studio Center, and the Whiting Foundation for his involvement with the Prison Story Project. Raised by the Pacific Northwest, Davis teaches for the University of Arkansas's Program in Creative Writing & Translation and serves as Poetry Editor for *Iron Horse Literary Review.*

Oliver de la Paz

Oliver de la Paz is the author of *Names above Houses, Furious Lullaby, Requiem for the Orchard, Post Subject: A Fable,* and *The Boy in the Labyrinth,* a Massachusetts Book Award finalist. His newest work is *The Diaspora Sonnets* (Liveright 2023). He co-edited *A Face to Meet the Faces: An Anthology of Contemporary Persona Poetry.* Oliver is a founding member and co-chair of the Kundiman advisory board. He has received grants from the NEA, NYFA, Artist's Trust, and Massachusetts Cultural Council and has been awarded multiple Pushcart Prizes. He teaches at the College of the Holy Cross and the Rainier Writing Workshop.

Jennifer Elise Foerster

Jennifer Elise Foerster is the author of three books of poetry, *The Maybe Bird, Bright Raft in the Afterweather,* and *Leaving Tulsa,* and is Associate Editor of *When the Light of the World Was Subdued, Our Songs Came Through: A Norton Anthology of Native Nations Poetry.* The recipient of an NEA Creative Writing Fellowship, she was a Wallace Stegner Fellow in Poetry at Stanford, holds a PhD in literary arts from the University of

Denver, and teaches poetry at the Rainier Writing Workshop. Foerster grew up living internationally, is of German/Dutch and Mvskoke descent, and is a member of the Muscogee (Creek) Nation of Oklahoma.

Jenny Johnson

Jenny Johnson is the author of *In Full Velvet* (Sarabande Books 2017). Her honors include a Whiting Award, a Hodder Fellowship, and an NEA Fellowship. Her poems have appeared in *The New York Times*, *New England Review*, *Waxwing*, and elsewhere. She is an Assistant Professor of Creative Writing at West Virginia University, and she is on the faculty of the Rainier Writing Workshop, Pacific Lutheran University's low-residency MFA program. She lives in Pittsburgh.

Rebecca McClanahan

Rebecca McClanahan's eleventh book, *In the Key of New York City: A Memoir in Essays*, was published in 2020. Her work has appeared in *Best American Essays*, *Best American Poetry*, *The Georgia Review*, *Gettysburg Review*, *Kenyon Review*, *Boulevard*, and *The Sun* and in anthologies published by Simon & Schuster, Beacon, Norton, and Bedford/St. Martin's, among others. A recipient of two Pushcart Prizes, the Glasgow Award in Nonfiction, the Wood Prize from *Poetry* Magazine, and the NC Governor's Award for Excellence in Education, McClanahan teaches in the MFA programs of the Rainier Writing Workshop and Queens University, Charlotte.

Kent Meyers

Kent Meyers has written a memoir, a book of short fiction, and three novels, two of which have been listed as *New York Times* Notable Books. His work has won numerous awards, including a Society of Midland Authors award and a High Plains Book Award. Meyers has published fiction and essays in various literary journals and magazines, including *Harper's* and several times in *The Georgia Review*. He lives in Spearfish, South Dakota.

Brenda Miller

Brenda Miller's most recent books are *A Braided Heart: Essays on Writing and Form* and *Telephone: Essays in Two Voices,* a collection of collaborative essays with Julie Marie Wade. She is the author of five more essay collections, including *An Earlier Life*, which received the Washington State Book Award for Memoir. She coauthored, with Suzanne Paola, the textbook *Tell It Slant: Creating, Refining, and Publishing Creative Nonfiction,* now in its third edition from McGraw-Hill Higher Education.

Scott Nadelson

Scott Nadelson is the author of a novel, a memoir, and six collections of short fiction, most recently *While It Lasts*, winner of the Donald L. Jordan Prize for Literary Excellence. His work has appeared in *Ploughshares*, *Crazyhorse*, *New England Review*, *Harvard Review*, and *The Best American Short Stories*, and it has been honored with an Oregon Book Award, the Reform Judaism Fiction Prize, and the Great Lakes Colleges Association New Writers Award. In addition to the Rainier Writing Workshop, he teaches at Willamette University, where he holds the Hallie Brown Ford Chair in Writing.

Sequoia Nagamatsu

Sequoia Nagamatsu is the author of the nationally best-selling novel *How High We Go in the Dark*, a New York Times Editors' Choice, as well as the story collection *Where We Go When All We Were Is Gone*. His work has appeared in journals such as *Conjunctions*, *Iowa Review*, *Southern Review*, and *Tin House*. His honors include notable nods from *The Best American Nonrequired Reading* and *The Best Horror of the Year*, short-listing for the Waterstones Debut Fiction Prize and Ursula K. Le Guin Prize, and fellowship support from Bread Loaf. He is an associate professor of creative writing at St. Olaf College and on the Rainier Writing Workshop faculty.

Ann Pancake

Ann Pancake is a native of West Virginia. She's published two short-story collections, *Given Ground* and *Me and My Daddy Listen to Bob Marley*. Her novel, *Strange as This Weather Has Been*, was a *Kirkus* top-ten fiction book of the year, the Appalachian Book of the Year, and a finalist for the Orion Book Award and Washington State Book Award. She's received the Whiting Award, NEA grant, Pushcart Prize, Bakeless Prize, and Barry Lopez Visiting Writer in Ethics and Community Fellowship. Her work has appeared in venues such as *Orion*, *The Georgia Review*, *Manoa*, *Poets & Writers*, *Journal of Appalachian Studies*, and *New Stories from the South: The Year's Best*.

Lia Purpura

Lia Purpura is the author of nine collections of essays, poems, and translations. Her essay collection *On Looking* was a finalist for the National Book Critics Circle Award. Her awards include Guggenheim, NEA, and Fulbright Fellowships, as well as five Pushcart Prizes and the AWP Award in Nonfiction. Her work has appeared in the *New Yorker, New Republic, Orion, Paris Review, Emergence,* and elsewhere. She lives in Baltimore, MD, where she is Writer in Residence at The University of Maryland, Baltimore County. Her latest collections are *It Shouldn't Have Been Beautiful* (poems) and *All the Fierce Tethers* (essays).

Marjorie Sandor

Marjorie Sandor is the author of five fiction and nonfiction books. Her novel *The Secret Music at Tordesillas* was the Foreword INDIES 2020 Gold Winner for Historical Fiction, and her story collection *Portrait of My Mother, Who Posed Nude in Wartime* won the 2004 National Jewish Book Award for Fiction. Marjorie's work has appeared in *Ploughshares, The Georgia Review, AGNI,* and *Harvard Review,* among others, and been anthologized in such annuals as *The Best American Short Stories* and *The Pushcart Prize*. She is the editor of the short-fiction anthology *The Uncanny Reader: Stories from the Shadows*. She is professor emerita at Oregon State University and has taught at the Rainier Writing Workshop since 2004.

Renee Simms

Renee Simms is a recipient of a National Endowment for the Arts Creative Writing Fellowship, a John Gardner Fiction Fellowship at Bread Loaf, and fellowships from Ragdale and the Vermont Studio Center. She's an associate professor of African American Studies and English at University of Puget Sound and teaches with the Rainier Writing Workshop. Her debut story collection *Meet Behind Mars* was a Foreword INDIES Finalist for Short Stories and listed by *The Root* as one of twenty-eight brilliant books by Black authors in 2018. Renee is currently at work on a book about the Black suburban space.

.